The Decline and Fall of the Ptolemies

Ptolemaic Egypt 146–30 BC

John D. Grainger

First published in Great Britain in 2024 by
Pen & Sword History
An imprint of Pen & Sword Books Limited
Yorkshire – Philadelphia

Copyright © John D. Grainger, 2024

ISBN 978 1 39909 012 4

The right of John D. Grainger to be identified as
Author of this Work has been asserted by him in accordance
with the Copyright, Designs and Patents Act 1988.

A CIP catalogue record for this book is
available from the British Library

All rights reserved. No part of this book may be reproduced or
transmitted in any form or by any means, electronic or mechanical
including photocopying, recording or by any information storage and
retrieval system, without permission from the Publisher in writing.

Typeset by Mac Style
Printed in the UK by CPI Group (UK) Ltd, Croydon, CR0 4YY.

Pen & Sword Books Limited incorporates the imprints of After
the Battle, Atlas, Archaeology, Aviation, Discovery, Family History,
Fiction, History, Maritime, Military, Military Classics, Politics,
Select, Transport, True Crime, Air World, Frontline Publishing, Leo
Cooper, Remember When, Seaforth Publishing, The Praetorian Press,
Wharncliffe Local History, Wharncliffe Transport, Wharncliffe True
Crime and White Owl.

For a complete list of Pen & Sword titles please contact:

PEN & SWORD BOOKS LIMITED
47 Church Street, Barnsley, South Yorkshire, S70 2AS, England
E-mail: enquiries@pen-and-sword.co.uk
Website: www.pen-and-sword.co.uk
or
PEN AND SWORD BOOKS
1950 Lawrence Road, Havertown, PA 19083, USA
E-mail: uspen-and-sword@casematepublishers.com
Website: www.penandswordbooks.com

Contents

List of Maps		vi
List of Illustrations		vii
Maps		viii
Introduction		xi
Chapter 1	The Arrival of Ptolemy VIII	1
Chapter 2	The Shadow of Rome	16
Chapter 3	Civil War and Rebellions	28
Chapter 4	The Red Sea and the Way to India	42
Chapter 5	A Confusion of Rulers	58
Chapter 6	The 'War of Sceptres': A Final Syrian War	73
Chapter 7	Royal Brothers: Dissension and Rebellion	89
Chapter 8	Ptolemy XII and his Competitors	105
Chapter 9	The Tribulations of Ptolemy XII	118
Chapter 10	The Menace and Greed of Rome	132
Chapter 11	The Emergence of Kleopatra VII	147
Chapter 12	The Reign of Kleopatra VII	161
Chapter 13	Kleopatra and Antony	172
Chapter 14	Actium, and After	184
Chapter 15	The End of the Ptolemaic Kingdom	197
Conclusion: The End of the Dynasty		203
Abbreviations		208
Notes		209
Bibliography		224
Index		228

List of Maps

1. The Indian Sea Routes — viii
2. Kleopatra's Kingdom — ix
3. The Campaign of Actium — x

List of Illustrations

1. Drachma coin from *c.*138 BC showing portrait of Ptolemy VIII. (*American Numismatic Society via Wikimedia Commons*)
2. Probable bust of Ptolemy IX. (*J. Paul Getty Museum via Wikimedia Commons*)
3. Bust of Ptolemy X Alexander. (*Wikimedia Commons*)
4. Tetradrachm coin of Ptolemy X Alexander, *c.*101 BC.
5. Bust of Ptolemy XIII, father of Kleopatra and king of three decades. (*Wikimedia Commons*)
6. Wall relief of Ptolemy XIII at the Temple of Sobek receiving the Breath of Life. (*Adobe Stock*)
7. Kleopatra VII, the classical view – the portrait that is usually accepted as a good likeness of the queen. (*Wikimedia Commons*)
8. A possible coin portrait of Kleopatra VII. (*PHGCOM via Wikimedia Commons/CC BY-SA 3.0*)
9. Kleopatra, the Egyptian view. (*Kevin Dinno via Wikimedia Commons/CC BY-SA 3.0*)
10. Julius Caesar, careworn and old.
11. Mark Antony.
12. Kleopatra and Antony coins. (*CNG Coins*)
13. Octavian, soon to be Augustus. (*Carole Raddato via Wikimedia Commons/CC BY-SA 2.0*)
14. M. Vipsanius Agrippa, the great commander. (*Marie-Lan Nguyen via Wikimedia Commons/CC BY 2.5*)
15. The field of victory – the remains of Nikopolis, the city founded as a monument to the victory at Actium. (*Mark Landon via Wikimedia Commons/CC BY 4.0*)
16. 'Egypt taken'. A coin issued in Octavian's name to publicise and celebrate his victory. (*CNG Coins*)

Maps

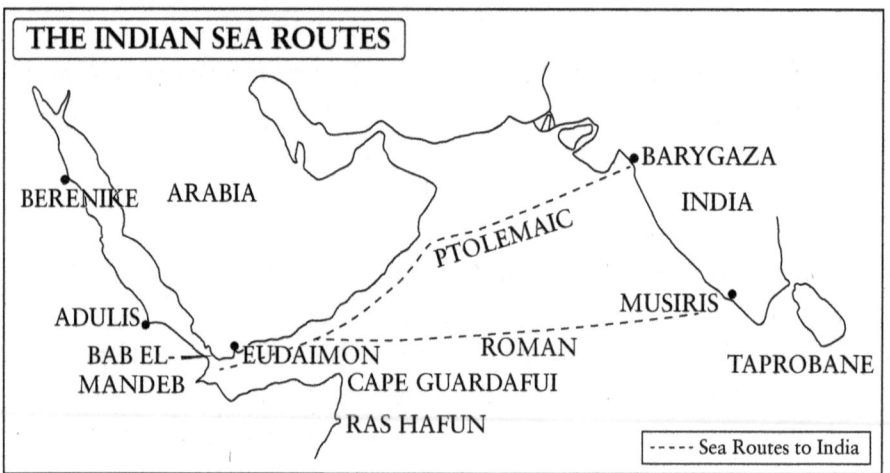

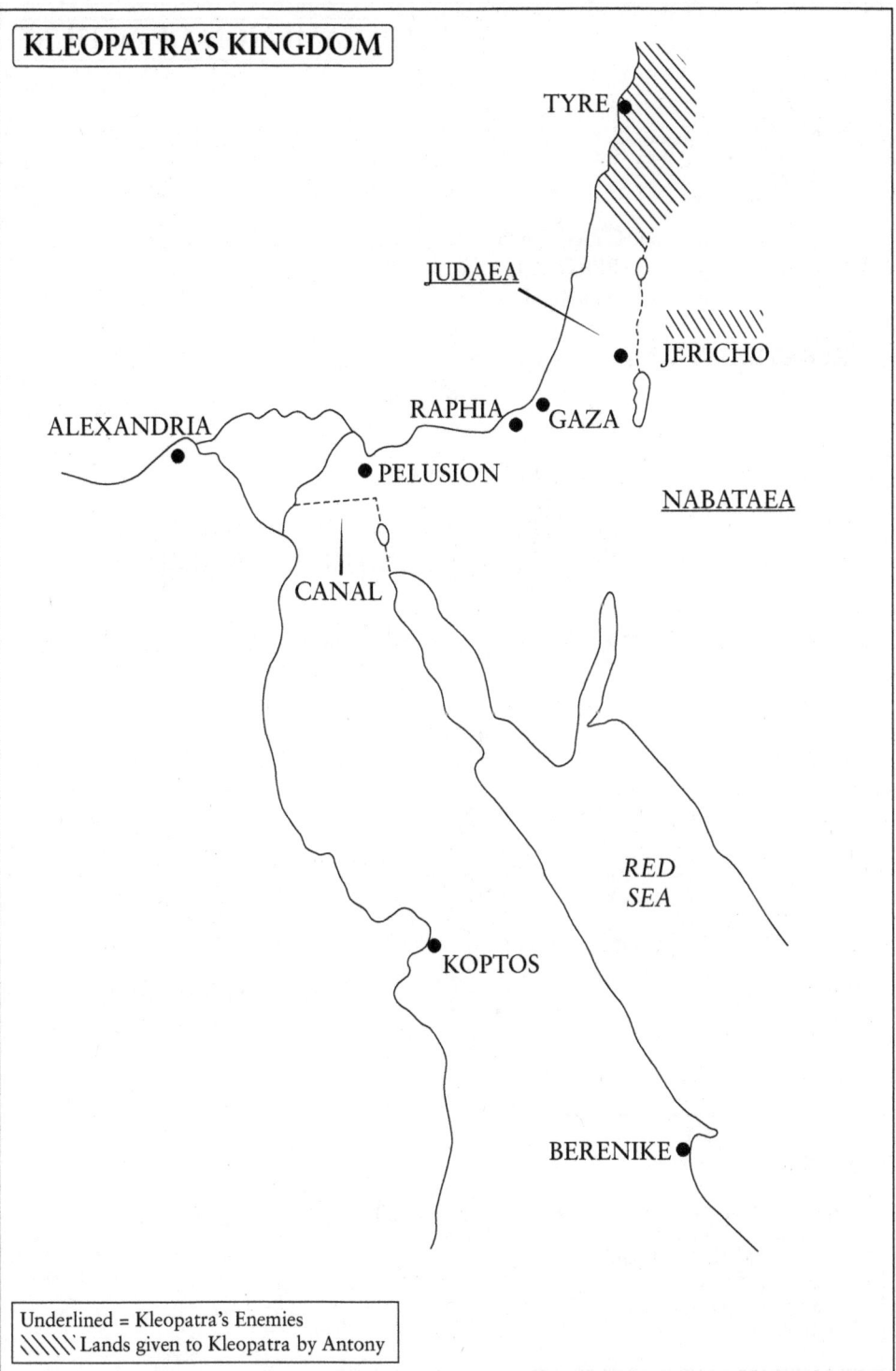

Introduction

This is the third of three books discussing the history of the Ptolemaic dynasty, whose members were rulers of Egypt between Alexander the Great and the Emperor Augustus, both conquerors of Egypt. It covers about a century of the dynasty and country from 145 BC to 30 BC, but on this occasion the theme, by contrast with the 'Rise' (the first volume) and the 'Apogee' (the second), is the steady decline and failure of the dynasty.

And it really is a story of incompetence, carelessness and defeat. In 145 BC, the last effective Ptolemy, Ptolemy VI, was killed in battle, and he was succeeded by his younger brother, Ptolemy VIII, who had attempted repeatedly to supplant his brother in ruling Egypt, and in between times had ruled as king in Cyrenaica. It ends at 30 BC with one of the least competent of the Ptolemies, Kleopatra, sometimes erroneously described as 'the Great', but who was much more concerned with her personal pleasures than the well-being and future of the people over whom she ruled.

It is clear that in some respects, the Ptolemaic kingdom had declined into sclerosis. The direct line of the monarchy had broken in 80 BC, and from then on for half a century, there was a continuous muddle over who should rule amid a deeply unpleasant and murderous succession of barely competent kings and queens. On top of this there was the interference of Roman Republican politicians whose main aim was to secure control of some of the Ptolemaic wealth – one may surely use the words 'steal' and 'blackmail' to describe their methods of extortion – in order to pursue their own political aims in Italy. And the Ptolemies were not strong enough to resist their demands.

This third volume, therefore, is a deeply unhappy account of an originally efficient, but autocratic, regime in Egypt as it declined into confusion and chaos. Not a pleasant story to tell, but one that will, of course, bring home lessons to anyone who has lived through a similar decline by any other country, ancient or modern.

Chapter 1

The Arrival of Ptolemy VIII

The death of Ptolemy VI Philopator in the fighting in Syria in 145 left the succession to the Ptolemaic throne uncertain.[1] He had fathered three children by his sister/wife Kleopatra II, but his son, Ptolemy Eupator, had died seven years before; the boy had been promoted as 'pharaoh' before his death, which presumably meant he was recognised as the successor to his father.[2] This position now fell to his brother, who was still a child: he is often referred to as Ptolemy Neos Philometor, or as Ptolemy VII; he had been briefly recognised as joint king with his uncle, it seems, in the interval after his father's death.[3]

Ptolemy VI had been on campaign in northern Syria when he was struck by an enemy weapon, fell off his horse, was hacked at by his enemies, and his skull was broken; he was then unconscious for several days. He recovered his senses briefly, but the only reaction he is known to have shown was satisfaction at the death of Alexander Balas, his former son-in-law and now mortal enemy, whose severed head was shown to him.[4] Ptolemy died soon after, during an unsuccessful operation, without discussing his successor, presumably either because he had been assured that he was not going to die, or he knew that his son had been clearly nominated as that successor.

So there were two, perhaps three, possible successors to him: first was his seven-year-old son, Neos Philometor; second, there was Ptolemy VI's sister and widow, Kleopatra II, who could succeed either as the reigning queen or as a regent for her son (her mother's life as a widow in just such positions provided a clear precedent for this); third, there was Ptolemy VIII, Kleopatra II and Ptolemy VI's brother, who was currently king in Cyrene, reigning there after several failed attempts to dislodge his brother from the throne of Egypt. He was widely disliked, but he was a capable, if ruthless, ruler, and he was an adult male.

Exactly how a decision was reached is not known, though Kleopatra II must have been involved, as were the chief men in the government in Alexandria, and perhaps the citizens of Alexandria who had driven Ptolemy VIII out of the city and the kingship once already.[5] The news of the death of Ptolemy VI will have reached the city within perhaps only two or three days, and the discussions will then have taken several more days. Some dated documents imply that there was an interregnum of three weeks,[6] but we do not know whether this was counted from Ptolemy VI's death, his injury, or the moment when the news of either of these conditions reached Alexandria. One consideration that had to be borne in mind was that if Ptolemy VIII was excluded, he would undoubtedly make a serious attempt to secure the throne, by any means he could use, including violence, and he clearly had support within the city – the prospect of a female regency and a child king was unsettling.

Ptolemy VIII had attempted to sieze the throne two or three times already, and without Ptolemy VI's cunning to block him, he would this time probably succeed. It was resolved – by whom or what group we do not know – that envoys would go from the city to invite the brother to accede to the throne. By keeping the invitation polite, perhaps it was hoped that Ptolemy VIII would reciprocate.[7] A marriage to his sister, the widowed Kleopatra II, was included, possibly without her consent, either as an offer or as a condition.

It was therefore three weeks after Ptolemy VI's death, if not more, before Ptolemy VIII arrived in Alexandria to take up the kingship. This period is perhaps somewhat longer than he might have expected if he had been the automatic and immediate choice. The invitation was by no means unanimous, opposition coming from, among others, Kleopatra II. He reacted at once with a purge to remove antagonists and proven enemies, of which he had no doubt accumulated a fair number in his previous career. Now, anyone who had argued against his accession would have been added to that list.[8]

His first actions were aimed at ensuring that there were no competitors for his position. The surviving son of Ptolemy VI, Neos Philomator, was the main one, but the king's mother was another. She apparently kept the boy with her, but she would know that her dynastic duty was to marry the new king; indeed, Justin, in his account of the formal invitation for him to go to Alexandria to take up the kingship, explicitly states that the invitation included an offer of her in marriage.[9]

Kleopatra was the daughter of a king and therefore carried with her a claim to the throne, which any man she married would acquire also; she had in fact been the co-ruler under Ptolemy VI. Therefore, she could not be allowed to marry anyone but a member of the royal family, and the custom within the Ptolemaic family was that such a princess should marry the king, or remain unmarried and live in a sort of seclusion. Consequently, Ptolemy began, not by directing his ire at his sister or his nephew, who was his heir since he had no children of his own, but at those courtiers who had argued for the accession of the boy (which would include a regency for Kleopatra). This is glossed by Diodoros, or perhaps more likely by the official Ptolemaic publicity, as people who were plotting against him; this is then further explained as illegal, or as false charges. However, the measures he took are to be explained; it was clearly a purge of the new king's enemies, both recent and from longer ago.[10]

The new king is thus said to have taken a series of measures as soon as he arrived in Alexandria. According to Justin, they were: first, the elimination of those who had supported his nephew's candidacy, defined as 'the leading citizens'; then, the wedding with his sister was organised and effected, during which he is said to have killed the boy 'in his mother's arms', and then entered his sister's bed 'still dripping with the gore of her son'. The only other source for this initial part of Ptolemy's reign, Diodoros, partly echoes Justin, but is more detailed and more believable, and omits the murder of the boy king. In fact, other sources indicate that the boy lived on for at least three more years. Justin's account is therefore at least partly wrong.

Diodoros repeats the purge of the king's opponents, but his words suggest it was more selective than Justin implies. Both claim that Ptolemy's actions were illegal, but he was an autocrat, and the concept of limiting the king's powers of life and death was not one that existed in the Hellenistic world, and certainly not amongst the Ptolemies. Both historians perhaps acquired the idea from the same source, which is probably Polybios, who was hardly an objective reporter on Egyptian affairs at this point, but Justin in particular embellishes the tale elaborately and unpleasantly.[11]

The killing of the boy king 'in his mother's arms' provides a distinct historical problem. Such an act, at a wedding feast, is highly unlikely, unless he was pre-empting a rival action by his sister/wife. It is known that Kleopatra had recently opposed Ptolemy's accession, and if so, the killing could only have been in order to prevent her son becoming king, with herself as regent. Possibly her aim was to make her son joint king along with her new brother/husband, and herself joint ruler with them – a resumption of the situation with Ptolemy VI. One may also note that, if Justin's account is accurate, it was the second time a murder of this type had taken place in the

Ptolemaic dynasty – Ptolemy Keraunos killed the two children of Arsinoe II at their wedding in 279 in Thessalonike; given that Ptolemy VII certainly survived for several years after his mother's remarriage, it is evident that it was from this episode that Justin took his details. Justin's whole account is thus suspect, and it would seem to be a matter of imagination and plagiarism rather than reportage.

There was another precedent for this particular succession situation, however – that of the Seleukid king Antiochos IV in 175–170, who had succeeded his murdered brother, and then married his widow and adopted his stepson as his heir. Then, after five years, by which time his wife had given birth to his own son, he had the stepson murdered. This was only thirty years earlier, and was no doubt a well-known incident in Alexandrian royal circles – after all, they had become familiar with the character of Antiochos IV at first hand, and the case had been well publicised by Egyptian regents in the preparation for the Sixth Syrian War. For the moment, however, the young Ptolemy (who is sometimes reckoned as Ptolemy VII, and counted as one of the kings, occupying the gap, the 'interregnum', between his father and his brother) was safe enough. Until Kleopatra produced a son for Ptolemy VIII, he was the only male of the family apart from Ptolemy VIII himself.

The king did gain a distinctly unpopular reputation later in his reign, being accused from the start of 'illegal' killings, and it would seem that the assumption was that he had started as he meant to go on. The purge of his opponents is quite believable, given his history and the disputation involved, but the boy was about seven years old – too old to have been 'in his mother's arms' – and in 144/143 he was named as priest of Alexander and the deified Ptolemies.[12] By that time, Kleopatra II, married to her younger brother soon after his accession, had given birth to their son. Ptolemy was visiting Memphis for his formal (Egyptian) coronation at the time of the birth, and the boy became known as Ptolemy Memphites as a result.[13] The story in Justin thus collapses: it is clearly misdated and compiled from a concoction of imagination and past events.

On the other hand, the charge that Ptolemy indulged in a purge of his internal enemies as soon as he acceded can be accepted, though without the gory embellishments of Justin. One group he turned on was the professors in the library, who were driven out of the city.[14] The head of the library had been Aristarchos of Samothrake; he is recorded as dying the next year in Cyprus.[15] That is, the purge of the library had taken place in 145, or perhaps in 144, though it was not so drastic as to force the men out of Ptolemy's lands altogether, for Ptolemy was also king in Cyprus, and that is where Aristarchos went. Here again is a clue to the unpleasant reputation of the king, for the professors were no doubt resentful at having to leave their comfortable sinecures, and had the ability, from their fame, and with their rhetorical abilities, to make their resentfulness known and widely publicised. It is certainly assumed in modern discussions that the effect had been 'sensationally exaggerated'.[16] One might add that, given that the professors were very liable to intervene in political affairs from their positions of privilege, Ptolemy would have been glad of an excuse to remove them, if not silence them; he was solving two problems – pushing criticism away and saving money, with a single gesture; most economical. It may not have been as unpopular and resented an action as modern academics assume: popular resentment at the comfortable lives of the professors, supported by tax funds, was no doubt rife, and could be easily worked up by government propaganda.

Ptolemy is described also as confiscating the houses left empty by those who fled the city in the face, and fear, of his purge.[17] No doubt, their abandoned properties were then sold for the benefit of the royal treasury, just as the expulsion of the professors will have saved that treasury their considerable salaries. This may be a sign that the resources of the king, when Ptolemy VIII took over, were much reduced, and the king was once again solving two problems with a single act – expelling and impoverishing internal enemies, and replenishing the treasury. He is recorded, a little later, in about 140, as being unable to pay his mercenaries because 'his funds were low', a condition that he experienced in 145 and had not improved in the meantime.[18] Ptolemy VI's campaign in 145 in Syria had been noticeably peaceful for the most part – possibly a sign of that shortage of funds.

There are also other signs, which may well indicate a continuing shortage of cash in the public treasury. The most expensive part of any ancient government was the army, and in this case, the military occupation of Syria. (Ptolemy VI must have known money problems as well; perhaps he expected to be able to solve them by the taxation of Syria.) In the aftermath of Ptolemy VI's death, the unexpectedly victorious troops of Demetrios II moved against the Ptolemaic occupation of the old Ptolemaic province of Koele Syria and Palestine. They gained control of the Ptolemaic elephants, who had presumably been marched to the north in the anticipation of a battle; the Ptolemaic soldiers either withdrew or were chased out – as Josephos says, they went 'back to Alexandria'.¹⁹ Demetrios II is recorded as being at Ptolemais-Ake in Palestine during the withdrawal, or perhaps one should say, near the end of the withdrawal.²⁰ His presence there implies that he was following on the retreating Ptolemaic forces, and securing control as they evacuated. He met the Maccabee Jonathan, the current leader of the Jewish insurrection in upland Palestine, who was besieging Jerusalem at the time. The city was held by a mixed force of 'Macedonian' soldiers, who must have been the Ptolemaic garrison installed by Ptolemy VI, and Jews who were inimical to the Maccabean aims of a new Jewish state.²¹

The three weeks it took to bring Ptolemy VIII from Cyrene to Alexandria must be increased by the time following Ptolemy VI's death before any instructions and the invitation came, and several more days at least will have passed before Ptolemy VIII could issue new orders. This will have added up to at least a month and a half, during which the Ptolemaic soldiers were without orders, and perhaps without pay, although Kleopatra II and Ptolemy VII could have been said to be ruling at that point.

The army in Syria consisted of the usual Ptolemaic mix of a fairly small regular force, mercenaries hired for the duration of the war, and an unknown number of cleruchs and militia embodied for the occasion. Of these, probably the mercenaries were the most important group, the others being either too few (the regulars) or less competent (the cleruchs and the militia). This heterogeneous force had little or no cohesion and probably little loyalty to the new king or to the urban government in Alexandria, unless some were from that city; also, the troops were presumably not paid in that period after Ptolemy VI's death (and possibly before). As in all armies that occupy conquered territory, the men most likely lived on confiscated supplies and loot. In the absence of orders to stand firm, some appear at least to have begun to move towards home. The cleruchs and the militia were no doubt the first to begin leaving, being probably the last to be paid; the mercenaries, noting the death of the king who had hired them, would have begun looking for alternative employment. There was some fighting against the approaching Seleukid forces – Josephos claims that Demetrios 'began to destroy the troops of Ptolemy'²² – but no details are recorded. Josephos is more interested in the Jewish attack on Ptolemy's forces in Jerusalem. No doubt, as the occupation forces thinned out, its commanders would take due note and begin to organise the withdrawal officially, so that it took place in an orderly fashion – and their troops did not disappear.

That the withdrawal was fully in accord with the new government's intentions was reinforced when Ptolemy VIII ordered that the Ptolemaic posts in the Aegean – the island of Thera, Itanos in Crete, and Methana in the Peloponnese – were to be abandoned and the garrison troops brought back to Egypt.

This is to a degree an assumption. There is no source that states the Aegean withdrawal as a fact. An inscription dated to 145 exists from Thera, but there seems nothing from Methana. It has been suggested that Itanos agreed to an alliance of sorts with Ptolemy and to have maintained that alliance after the withdrawal of the Ptolemaic forces. Its function had been partly as a watch post in always turbulent Crete, and partly as a naval base. The withdrawal has also been dated to late in Ptolemy VI's reign, which would be a sign that he was consolidating his armed forces in the face of the war in Syria. Either way, it is clear that the Ptolemaic forces left Itanos; evidence for their presence in Thera ceases after 145, and, if these places were abandoned, Methana, afar off on the Peloponnesian coast, was no longer useful or even viable.[23]

The withdrawal of the Ptolemaic presence in the Aegean was, of course, a significant geopolitical event. It came not only in the aftermath of Ptolemy VI's death (although if the hint from the evidence in Itanos is accepted, it was perhaps under way even earlier), but also at the moment when other Ptolemaic forces were being pulled out of Syria. Perhaps more importantly, it was the year after the definitive Roman subjugation of Macedon and Greece. The Ptolemaic Aegean bases had been a signal thatced the Egyptian kings retained ambitions in the Aegean region, and of the areas they had fought to dominate throughout the third century. This had been a major factor in their political thinking since Ptolemy I's time. But the Roman advance between 148 and 146 had foreclosed on any attempt to do so from then on; interference in Greece was now far too dangerous a game to be indulged in by a shaky new Ptolemaic regime.

Ptolemy VIII's reaction to this new situation, in Greece as in Syria, evident in his purge of internal enemies, his royal marriage, his preservation of Ptolemy VII, and his withdrawal of force from Syria and Palestine, had evidently included the confirmation, even the initiation, of the abandonment of the island bases as well. The alliance with Itanos, which was perhaps copied also with Thera and Methana (though there is no evidence either way), actually meant nothing, and never produced any activity. The

Ptolemies had abandoned any ambitions in the Aegean and Greece. It was a decisive withdrawal.

This withdrawal, and the other measures, would make a significant reduction in the burden on the Ptolemaic finances. The mercenaries would need to be paid off, and the number of men retained was much reduced, though probably some would accept payment in kind by taking up cleruchies in Egypt. The cleruchs had their plots of land for their support; whatever pay they were given while embodied would cease when they were sent back to Egypt and were dismissed; similarly, with the militia who had been called up. That would leave only the regular naval and military forces to be paid for; they could not be dispensed with, but certainly could be reduced in number, again possibly by the allocation of cleruchic plots. (And in fact paying these forces was always the last item in the treasury's priorities, so that unpaid and hungry soldiers became a common internal security problem.) The regular Ptolemaic army was relatively small.

One group, commanded by two Jewish officers, Onias and Dositheos, and presumably composed, at least in part, of Jews enlisted from those who were living in Egypt, had taken Kleopatra's part in the succession problem – and so, probably, also her son's. This was dealt with by a purge of the Jewish forces and people, and reprisals against the community generally – possibly at a later time and separately than the other purges.[24] Again, this would reduce government expenses. Presumably, the regular army was used, which would also keep it busy.

The birth of Ptolemy Memphites in 144[25] was a dynastic event of the first importance, for until then, Ptolemy VIII had no male heir other than his stepson, Neos Philometor. Ptolemy's coronation, coinciding with the birth of his son, was therefore a double celebration. On the other hand, in order to secure the marriage with his sister, she had to be given the same political status, as an equal with the king, as she had enjoyed with Ptolemy VI; the birth of a male heir in effect will have demoted her, and now the new child was a threat to her son. During the late 140s, having survived the early childhood years, Memphites was called 'successor to the king' in inscriptions on the temple of Edfu; thereby he climbed past his older cousin/half-brother.[26]

Ptolemy and Kleopatra are recorded as attending the dedication ceremony of the temple at Edfu in 142.[27] Its construction had begun in 237, but work had naturally ceased between 207 and 185 when Edfu came under rebel control. Most of the recent work had been done under Ptolemy VI, but his brother and sister managed to take the credit. This was a temple in the Egyptian architectural style, but was built by the Macedonian kings, who made sure this became clear in the inscriptions, and as such, it was inevitably a symbol of Ptolemaic rule.

It was in the same year, 142, that Ptolemy VI's child probably died. The presumption must be that he was murdered, and perhaps the journey to the south of Egypt had been in part the opportunity for the boy's killing, distance lending Ptolemy a claim to innocence.[28]

Ptolemy also visited other places in the Egyptian *chora* in these first years of his reign. He went to Memphis, of course, for his coronation, and to Edfu in the south for the temple dedication there. He is recorded at Hermonthis, in the south, also in 144, and in the Fayum, all in the same year as his coronation.[29] This was both a celebration and a visit deliberately engineered for him to be seen; no doubt, he would be expected to carry out ceremonies such as that at Edfu, receive petitions, and generously rectify his subjects' problems. He was a new king, already with an unpleasant reputation, whose accession had been recently validated by coronation, and he was showing himself to his subjects. The dense population of Greeks and Macedonian cleruchs in the Fayum must have been a particular target; the visits to Hermonthis and Edfu will have involved a long voyage up the Nile, and the opportunity to be seen in all the towns and cities along the way. Hermonthis was opposite Thebes and here again he was available to be seen by his new subjects, emphasising his succession to the king who had finally put down the great Egyptian revolt. One must assume that Thebes was also on his itinerary.

Interpreted as it is here, this was a necessary course of action to establish his position, rather than as a revenge and paranoid mission by the new king; Ptolemy VIII, that is, was taking the measures he felt necessary amid his dynastic concerns, carrying out the ceremonies expected of a king, and purging inveterate enemies. This all implies also that he was, now if not earlier, an accomplished politician, knowing what he wanted to achieve and devising acceptable methods of reaching those goals. It is particularly noticeable that more than once he was able to accomplish those goals by a sort of indirection, rather than a more blunt approach. It seems probable that his overall announced intention was to recruit the royal finances by reducing expenditure, which served him as the reason for his withdrawal of the overseas garrisons (rather than the now all too near presence of Rome in Greece), and for the reduction of the army. He protected Kleopatra II's son, at least for several years, while marrying her, and, at a fairly late age for a woman, making her pregnant with his own son.

This frenzy of political activity, which, of course, took place mostly in his first year, aroused opposition, to add to that he had faced after his earlier career and his disputed accession. Such opposition he no doubt expected. He reacted as any autocrat would, by selectively killing particularly obnoxious opponents and by exiling other opponents who were not as vulnerable. How many were killed in his first year is not known (the sources are all extremely vague, probably implying more deaths than were actually inflicted), but it seems to have worked, and at least by mid-144, he was fully in control and remained so for several years without serious further challenge. His reputation for unpleasantness may be in part due to his behaviour, but presumably, much of it can be attributed to the complaints of his enemies, which included a number of wealthy men, whose possessions had been confiscated, and to the articulate professors expelled from the library and from their salaries.

Ptolemy VII, Kleopatra's son, died some time in 142 or later. It is assumed that his stepfather had him murdered, though this is based on the account of the boy's murder amid the wedding celebrations of Ptolemy VIII and Kleopatra II, which was clearly an invention (it appears only in Justin, a late source). By 142, the boy was ten years old and had already served as the Priest of Alexander. Ptolemy VIII now had a son of his own who had survived his early years, so Ptolemy VII Neos Philometor may have become redundant. He was evidently in that case a prime target for a quiet murder. By that time, Kleopatra II was about forty years old, and was unlikely to be able to produce another child. Ptolemy VIII began relations with her daughter – another child of Ptolemy VI and so his niece. This was another Kleopatra (III); the liaison began soon after the birth of Ptolemy Memphites in late 144.[30] What this 'liaison' amounted to is unclear, but by 141/140, he had married her.

Modified shock is expressed at this, but more because, once he and Kleopatra III were married in 141/140, he had two wives, who were his sister and her daughter. But the marriage is only unusual, not surprising, given the marital practices of both the Ptolemies and the Seleukids during this time. The death of Ptolemy VII (presumed to have taken place before this marriage) left the dynasty once more with only the king and a single male heir (Ptolemy Memphites). The marriage to Kleopatra III was probably made specifically in order to generate more children, presumably boys as 'spares' (in the jargon of the British royal family) in case of the early death of Memphites. In this, the marriage was a success, and Kleopatra produced five children, two boys and three girls, in the next years. It could be assumed therefore that the dynasty was now safe.

Ptolemy VIII also had another son, Ptolemy, called Apion, by a non-royal woman called Eirene, to whom he was not formally married.[31] Her non-royal status put her son out of the calculations for the dynasty's future. It appears that she was from Cyrene, so no doubt, this liaison had been conducted while Ptolemy VIII ruled in that city before 145, and the boy was presumably born before that year. His whereabouts after 145 are not clear, but probably he lived at the royal court, as would be his right as the king's acknowledged son. His father evidently had affection for him and he survived all the turmoil in the court for the next fifty years – no doubt his non-dynastic status will have helped in this by providing some protection.

Ptolemy VIII, in his pursuit of legitimate male offspring, had entangled himself in a complex marital web. A concubine, a sister-wife, a niece-wife, and eventually seven children, six of them legitimate in a dynastic sense, resulted from his quest. Perhaps only this last element, the children, would have been counted as marking a success. The two Kleopatras are said to have hated each other, which would not be surprising, but which may in fact be an assumption from male imaginings. Ptolemy did his best by regarding both women as equal in royal status.

Ptolemy's solution to the problem of producing an heir was certainly ratified by dynastic practice. Only a royal woman could marry a Ptolemaic king, and royal princesses were generally prevented from marrying outside the royal family. This excluded Ptolemy Apion's mother, and therefore Apion also, from the succession, and since Kleopatra II was probably unable to have more children after the birth of Memphites, Ptolemy required a new wife. Of all the women in Egypt, only Kleopatra III was available and of sufficient status and age to take her mother's place. He could have put Kleopatra II aside, sending her to a remote town as a divorcee (like Arsinoe I by Ptolemy II, sent into internal exile in the Egyptian south), but she remained at court (like Ptolemy I's two wives). That is, there were family precedents for all sorts of solutions to these dynastic problems, but the one he chose – and it was surely Ptolemy's own decision – was to include both women in his court as equals of each other and of himself. Whether they actually did hate each other may be taken as likely, but not proven, though it is surely likely that they quarrelled.

And, of course, the other reason for keeping Kleopatra II close was that she had already attempted to thwart Ptolemy VIII's ambition to be king in Egypt, and the only way to control her ambition was to control her. The other solution was to order her execution or murder, and this was clearly not acceptable; as the daughter of the still well-remembered Ptolemy VI, such an action might produce an Alexandrian riot. (One reason for having doubts about the possible murder of Ptolemy Eupator is exactly this consideration: the son of Ptolemy VI will have inherited a part of his father's goodwill, and to murder him would clearly increase Ptolemy VIII's unpopularity.)

It may have been this display of dynastic ambition, or, more likely, the continuing resentment of Ptolemy's exiled victims, that produced the inevitable attack on Ptolemy's position. He had made it inevitable by driving many of his enemies out of Egypt, and perhaps by killing others. There were clearly enough exiles to form a military group and a set of plotters. The marital antics of the court may have eroded the king's prestige, such as it was, and possibly Kleopatra II was annoyed enough at the new marriage to link herself with the exiles; she would be one of the beneficiaries if the plot succeeded.

The leading man from Greece amongst the exiles in Egypt was Galaistes. He was the son of a former king of Athamania, Amynander, who ruled a minor kingdom sandwiched between Thessaly and Epeiros. By 141 or thereabouts, he was at the head of an assembled group of exiles and set about an expedition to overthrow Ptolemy VIII.

Galaistes had been employed by Ptolemy VI as a commander of the Alexandrian garrison, and had accompanied the king during the expedition into Syria. Clearly a capable man, he had been rewarded by the gifts of lands in Egypt in the normal way. Ptolemy VIII, however, faced by such a man loyal to his dead brother, could not accept his presence and prominence, and had turned on him. He was driven into exile, then the lands given him by Ptolemy VI were confiscated. The confiscations took place by September 144, by which time Galaistes was living in Greece.[32]

By 144, he had formed a plot, using a boy who he claimed was a son of Ptolemy VI, and who, he claimed, had been entrusted to him by that king; therefore, he should be the legitimate king of Egypt. He produced him in public wearing a diadem, the normal headgear of a king. This has led to the assumption that the supposed mother of the pretender, Kleopatra II, was a supporter of Galaistes' attempted coup. There is no evidence for this in the ancient sources. It has also been assumed, contradicting such an assumption, that one of Galaistes' aims was to marry Kleopatra III and become regent for the pretender's kingship, or perhaps king himself.[33] This supposes that Kleopatra III was not yet married to Ptolemy VIII – though, if Galaistes succeeded in his expedition, Ptolemy would have been his first victim, and Kleopatra III, whether or not by then a widow, would be available; on marriage to her, her new husband would be in line to be king. (This scenario, again, can be paralleled in Seleukid court history, when Heliodoros, the king's minister, killed Seleukos IV and is said to have aimed to marry Queen Laodike.)

Ptolemy VIII had gained the loyalty of one of Ptolemy VI's military commanders, Hierax, who had been one of those involved in the promotion of him as 'King of Asia' during the Syrian campaign. He and Galaistes had thus been colleagues in that war, but in this case, they emerged on opposite sides. Galaistes' actual movements are unknown, but he certainly seems to have set out for Egypt. Whether he landed there is not recorded, but he had apparently taken advantage of discontent amongst the mercenaries in Egypt, who had not been paid recently; they indicated their preference for Galaistes' candidate and his plot. This presumes that the mercenaries and the plotters had contacted one another beforehand, and that Galaistes had made acceptable promises to the soldiers. The linkage of plot and mercenaries, however, failed, for Hierax paid, or promised to pay, their wages out of his own resources, because 'Ptolemy's funds were low'. This ended any action by the mercenaries, who could see that a promise by a government official who was in favour with the sitting king was much preferable to one from the plotters: Galaistes' plot therefore failed.[34]

It may be that one of the results of this episode was that Ptolemy VIII married Kleopatra III, for the exact date of the marriage is not clear, and it could be that it followed rather than preceded the plot – the nearest calculation puts it in 141 or 140. The plot and its family ramifications may well have highlighted the possibilities inherent in the existence of Kleopatra III in an unmarried state. Marriage to her, willingly or not, would be one way to annex her to Galaistes or Ptolemy's cause. As an unmarried royal princess, the only marriage she would be permitted would be with the king, or another man of the dynasty (though there were none); if she chose to marry outside the dynasty – say, to Galaistes, who was certainly of royal descent in Greece, and so may have counted as eligible – her husband would gain a claim to the throne, a threat that Galaistes alone might well not be thought to pose. Hence, Galaistes' apparent aim to marry her himself, and Ptolemy VIII's marriage coup by seizing her for his own purpose.

That Ptolemy VIII and Kleopatra III were almost as closely related as Ptolemy VIII and Kleopatra II was no bar after over a century of sibling marriages in the Ptolemaic family. That the result was a king with two wives simultaneously was not unparalleled in the dynasty either. Ptolemy VIII at one point in his life wrote his memoirs (*hypomnemon*) and included in it a list of the mistresses and concubines of Ptolemy II amid a long series of other subjects;[35] his knowledge of the family's history would be available if any criticism was levelled at his marital practices – although given his reputation, such criticism would only be produced well away from the court and Egypt, if the author wished to stay alive. The account in his memoirs was, however, clearly self-serving, highlighting the marital practices of his predecessor to excuse his own. If anyone within his reach complained, or laughed at him, well, there were precedents for the drastic elimination of the critics of royal marriages in the dynasty.

The story of Galaistes' plot highlights a number of items that illuminate aspects of the new situation in Egypt, which followed the withdrawal from Syria and the Aegean, and the arrival of Ptolemy VIII. In making promises to the soldiers, Hierax had revealed that he had better financial resources than did the king, for the royal treasury was too low to produce their pay; he was probably not the only Ptolemaic aristocratic millionaire able to do the same. Neither the regular army nor the militia feature in the story, which emphasises – along with the absence of royal resources – that the main armed force of the kingdom actually comprised mercenaries, and little else. Hierax's wealth was probably not unique amongst the Egyptian aristocracy, which implies that the wealth of Egypt was being carefully diverted into private hands. The tax yield was thus no doubt low. (This was not a new problem; it had existed in the time of Ptolemy V, when the likelihood that the king would shake down the aristocracy in order to finance a new war had led to his murder. The implication is that even then the royal treasury was unable to finance a war, but the aristocracy was.)

The idea of the king who had 'abandoned himself to the most shameful pleasures', as Diodoros claims,[36] is not a sufficient characterisation. His authoring of his memoirs highlights an aspect of Ptolemy VIII that is echoed in other details. He had been a friend and colleague of Aristarchos, the head of the library whom he had expelled; they had co-operated on studies, and Ptolemy made a study of Homer. And it highlights also the later reaction of the king to the revelation of the sea route to India (see Chapter 5). Ptolemy VIII was clearly a complex character, a glutton, fond of 'shameful pleasures', and a ruthless politician, but a man capable of managing a household with two wives of equal status who disliked each other. To regard him as merely an obese tyrant is not enough.

Chapter 2

The Shadow of Rome

During the Ptolemaic succession crisis of 145–144, a Roman called Thermus was in Alexandria.[1] Numerous problems beset this notice: who was he? what was he there for? how long did he stay? how official was he? did he have any effect on the outcome of the crisis? ... and so on. None of these issues can in fact be resolved except by speculation and guesswork, and that process has produced suggested answers varying from total rejection of any effect the man might have had to his complete absorption in the process of the crisis.

We may say, almost certainly, that he was a Roman and was probably a member of the Minucius family, the only family to use the *cognomen* Thermus. In that case, he was either Q. (Quintus) Minucius Thermus, who had been praetor back in 164, or his brother Lucius, who does not appear to have held any of the Roman magistracies, although he was the legate and was attacked by Cato in a speech in about 181.[2] Neither of these was in any way a notable career, even if their father, also Quintus, was a distinguished consul and military commander in the 190s, until he was killed fighting in Thrace in 188. A man who had been praetor twenty years before, and his brother, whose only office was as a legate, were not going to carry much weight either in Alexandria or in Rome.

If this man, whoever he was, could influence Ptolemy VIII, as is usually assumed to be his purpose since he was in Alexandria during the first period of the king's installation, it could only be in a private capacity, or, if official, he was an observer, reporting back to Rome. The Senate did have a tradition of sending men of such rank to be in Alexandria in times of crisis – Numisius several decades before, for example; none of these had any great official standing, or any effect on events in Egypt. It is perhaps best to see them as senatorial reporters, charged with sending information of events back to Rome. We are not entitled to go any further than that. There is no indication that 'Thermus' was involved in affecting events in Alexandria, nor in those of Ptolemy VIII.

Identifying the man is, however, the question that has preoccupied most historians, to the exclusion of discussing his effects – although Lampela does speculate.³ L. Thermus is usually taken as his identity, but the only Lucius in the whole second century is the legate attacked by Cato in 181. He and Quintus, his brother, (praetor in 164) were the sons of the Quintus killed in Thrace in 188. They were thus born sometime before that date. The target of Cato in 181 must have been at least in his twenties, so in his sixties by 145; his praetor brother was not much younger. It seems doubtful that the Senate would send men of such age to Alexandria, men who had, it seems, only some distant and tangential experience of Ptolemaic affairs, or none at all. Lucius did have form in interfering in Ptolemaic affairs, however, in particular in 154, when he and four other Romans were given a quinquereme each to escort Ptolemy VIII in his latest attempt to seize Egypt, an expedition that was a spectacular failure, Ptolemy ending up as his brother's prisoner.⁴ It is this proximity to the events of 145 that suggests he was again in contact with the new king.

Ptolemy's accession, of course, happened chronologically just after the paroxysm of Roman violence which resulted in the conquest of Macedon in 149–148, in the conquest of Greece and the destruction of Corinth in 146, and in the conquest and destruction of Carthage in 149–146. In Macedon, a pretender, a private soldier called Andriskos, claimed the Macedonian kingship and succeeded in establishing himself for several months after having defeated a Roman legion. Andriskos was the point man for a wider plot involving Syria, some of the Attalids (mainly Macedonian exiles in Asia, refugees from Roman influence), and Thracian kings (including the daughter of Philip V, who was married to a Thracian king). The Roman sack of Corinth, until then one of the most prestigious and wealthiest of Greek cities, came in the same year as the conquest of Carthage, and involved both cities' total destruction. Both of these events came relatively close to Ptolemy and to Egypt: Carthage was the neighbour to Cyrenaica, Ptolemy VIII's kingdom at the time; Greece and Macedon were no more than two or three days' sail from Alexandria, and within a day's walk from the Ptolemaic base at Methana.

That post at Methana, only 50 kilometres from Corinth, was also a neighbour of the Achaian League, which had been Rome's principal enemy in Greece in this war. Although Rome maintained only an exiguous garrison force in Greece after the war, this was altogether too close to Methana, for any recrudescence of fighting would probably involve that city, and its presence would attack diplomatic suggestions for Ptolemaic support from all sides. The other two Ptolemaic posts, at Thera and Itanos, were further away from Roman direct power in Greece, but Thera was a conspicuously useful naval base, and in the event of a naval war in the Aegean, a Roman admiral could well demand the use of the base and might be very difficult to refuse. This would therefore probably involve the kingdom in a Greek war. Itanos, at the extreme eastern end of Crete, was already involved in Cretan wars, and was dangerously close to Rhodes, which already had been punished by Rome for having remained neutral. It was a useful naval base situated in a strategic position, and was a town from which recruiters could reach into the Cretan mercenary market. These conditions surely operated, along with the question of cost noted in the last chapter, to persuade Ptolemy VIII to pull out of all three Greek bases.

Ptolemy was, of course, fairly familiar with Rome, having visited the city more than once in his earlier attempts to displace his brother. He had passed through Greece and southern Asia Minor and Cyprus during those same campaigns, and on one occasion, as he recorded in his memoirs, he had visited Numidia and met King Massinissa (who died in 148, so the visit took place before he became king in Egypt, probably about 155).[5] The visit probably took place after his final visit to Rome (and Ptolemy before 145 probably considered himself to be in exile from Egypt). It was unusual for a Hellenistic king to be so familiar with much of the Mediterranean. Only exiles – such as the Seleukid Antiochos IV – had the opportunity to visit other lands. Kings only very rarely ventured out of their kingdom, mostly no doubt from fear of being unseated by internal enemies while they were away. No obvious political reason for a meeting of Ptolemy and Massinissa can be supplied, except perhaps an exchange of views on how to deal with Rome; the best assumption is that Ptolemy was a curious fellow, willing to visit various places simply to see them. Of course, it is also the fact that as king in Cyrene he was a neighbour of Massinissa in Libya, so maybe some sort of mutual problem existed, but any conjecture is unprovable. Personal curiosity seems the most likely explanation for his visit.

Whatever the achievements, or not, of the 'Thermus' who was resident in, or visiting, Alexandria in 145–144, it paled by comparison with the high-powered visit by a delegation of three Romans in about 140. And yet, the achievements of this later delegation were of as little note as those of

Thermus. The personnel of the group were L. Cornelius Scipio Aemilianus, the conqueror and destroyer of Carthage, Sp. Mummius, the brother of the conqueror of Achaia and destroyer of Corinth, and L. Caecilius Metellus, whose brother had conquered the Macedonian King/pretender Andriskos/Philip VI. The presence of such an august and ferocious group could only be interpreted as some sort of a Roman threat in any state where they turned up. They were accompanied by a set of Greek intellectuals, including Panaetios and possibly Polybios. This time the group was an official embassy of investigation, such as might be assumed, on a less exalted political scale, of Thermus five years before. Egypt was their first destination on their Grand Tour: they were to go on to Syria, Cyprus, Rhodes, the Attalid kingdom, and Greece and Macedonia.

The date of the visit is difficult to sort out.[6] They met Attalos II, who died in 138, which makes that the latest possible date. His kingdom was one of the last places they visited – they went on to Greece and Macedonia afterwards. Their journey had been fairly leisurely: in Egypt, they sailed upriver to Memphis and spent some time as tourists in Alexandria. The year 142 is ruled out because in that year Scipio was censor in Rome and Metellus was consul, both offices demanding their presence in the city all the year. Therefore, either the tour took place before 142, and so during 144–143, or after 142, and so within the period 141–138. Some would like it to be connected with Galaistes' attempted *putsch* in 144, but little other than the order of fragments in Diodoros suggests that, and as such is not a reliable guide, given Diodoros' practice of concentrating on one story at a time, and his liability to switch back in time for the next one. It seems that the delegation ostentatiously avoided becoming involved in local affairs, in Syria as well as in Egypt. In Astin's discussion, the only example of their effect is his suggestion that they advocated the recognition by Rome of Antiochos VII in Syria, and yet Antiochos became king only after the delegation had left Syria (and this was hardly something Rome could offer). And yet the very friendliness of the relationship with Ptolemy VIII might imply that the delegation was giving public, if limited, support to the king, who had had to struggle for years to acquire his kingdom, and had recently repelled the attempted coup by Galaistes. It seems likely, on the whole, that the most acceptable period during which the journey took place was 141–138, although there is a strong argument for the earlier period.

The journey therefore could either have followed closely on Ptolemy VIII's seizure of power and his purges in 145–144, or on his survival of Galaistes' attempt, and the occupation of Roman magistracies by two of the tourists. In Syria, it would have coincided with decade of turbulence when Demetrios II was forced into competing against the pretender/usurper Tryphon. Alternatively, if after 142, it will have succeeded Galaistes' attempt (though even the date of that event is not clear), and in Syria with Demetrios II's expedition against the Parthians, the emergence of Antiochos VII and the elimination of Tryphon. Whichever date is chosen, they were investigating a complex series of internal problems in every kingdom they visited. All we can do is to discuss the visit to Egypt in terms of the visitors' actions there.

It does not seem as if they involved themselves in the kingdom's internal affairs – other than by their very presence, which obviously underlined Roman support for Ptolemy VIII. This support was not unexpected. He had been Rome's favoured candidate for the Ptolemaic kingship for twenty years, and, if it meant anything, Thermus' presence in Alexandria in 145 implied that the relationship continued; if this was L. Minucius Thermus, he had already supported Ptolemy's attempt in 154. The arrival of the three men, in this new delegation, each associated with an episode of Roman conquest of extreme brutality, was clearly to be taken as another indication of Roman support for the similar, if rather different, brutality of Ptolemy VIII. His blood-soaked reputation for killing his opponents was a minor matter to the destroyers of Carthage and Corinth, who were responsible for the killing of tens of thousands of Carthaginians, Greeks and Macedonians.

Egypt was the first call on the carefully deliberate route of the three men's tour. Landing at Alexandria, they were met by Ptolemy VIII in person, wearing, so it is said, a near-transparent gown, which all too obviously displayed his fat belly.[7] He moved, obviously, slowly, and was very clearly out of condition; the contrast with the stern (and presumably fit) Romans was clearly deliberate on both sides. In the next days, the Romans toured the city's sites, including the Palace, where presumably they stayed, the Pharos and the Treasury, and made a study of the strategic situation of Alexandria and its harbour – the public could not help noticing this, even if they were normally acting touristy. Wealth was on display conspicuously, in marked contrast with the emptiness of the Treasury at the time of Galaistes' threat.[8]

How impressed the Romans were is not obvious, but it may be assumed that Ptolemy's purposes in this display were multiple. He would want to emphasise the wealth of the kingdom, to display his political control – they walked the city openly, tourists themselves touring to display themselves – and to emphasise that the city, notorious for its riots, was peaceful. They sailed up the Nile to Memphis, during which the Romans were certainly impressed by the wealth and productivity they could see, and the density of the population, all implying a rich kingdom. But what was not on display, it seems, were the armed forces at Ptolemy's disposal, although there were no doubt guards at the Palace, and they noted the 'strong defensive position' of the country, defended by deserts to east and west, and by the (rather decayed) navy based in Alexandria.[9] The wealthy city and the diligence and productivity of the population, however, would be sufficient to suggest a kingdom of some notable power, given that wealth and a large population was the basis for military success. Such sharp politicians and soldiers as the Romans would also not ignore the politics of the kingdom any more than they would its strategic situation.

Ptolemy VIII himself may or may not have impressed the Romans, and Diodoros comments on the unsuitableness of the kings for such a rich land, and even if the king's physical appearance was somewhat repellent, that did not necessarily apply to his brain and his cunning. The kingdom itself did impress, and it will have been clear that Ptolemy was in control of his kingdom; this was especially obvious if the visit came soon after the failure of Galaistes' attempt. And if so this will have been a quite satisfactory conclusion for both sides in the visit: Ptolemy was assured by Galaistes' failure that he had shown his control at home, and could see that the presence of such a notorious group meant that he retained the political support – at a distance, to be sure – of the Roman Republic.

The Romans could see that any problems in Egypt would be internal, for there was clearly no indication that Ptolemy was contemplating any aggressive moves outside his kingdom, and that was emphasised by the absence of any military display (even if, or even more, if the Ptolemaic army was as run down as its fleet). He was unusual amongst the Ptolemaic kings, showing absolutely no ambition to attack anyone. His withdrawal of Ptolemaic forces from Syria and from the Aegean would assure Rome of that also. Probably by the time of the visit (if it took place in the second possible period), Ptolemy's marriage to Kleopatra III had also already taken place.[10] The remaining doubt in his internal policies was the question of the succession; a new marriage would, however, imply more children soon, who would supplant or complement Ptolemy Memphites. The death of Ptolemy Eupator, which had probably occurred in 142 or 141, had opened the way for Ptolemy VIII's own children to inherit.

Ptolemy had carried off the visit well enough. His personal appearance – fat, flabby, slow, and unfit – had been displayed, and this vision had had its own purpose. It cannot be doubted that displaying his physical disabilities in such a way was quite deliberate, and was intended to emphasise the lack of aggressiveness in his foreign policy – a man so fat and slow as Ptolemy VIII was hardly to be found in a military stance.

So the Roman delegation could go on their travels confident that under Ptolemy VIII, Egypt was a powerful entity, at least in wealth and production, it was peaceful, its king was unaggressive, and with the succession secure, and the challenge of Galaistes thwarted, it seemed stable. It was also powerful, in so far as that was possible, but by no means was Ptolemy aiming at conquest. There was no call for Rome to interfere in Egyptian affairs, and this again may be assumed to be one of Ptolemy's purposes during the visit. Visiting Syria, as they did soon after, will have emphasised this to the delegation. The country had been embroiled in civil and foreign wars for a decade and more. To the Romans this will have provided a satisfying view of Ptolemaic quiescence, while the Syrian turmoil looked terminal in about 140; it had suffered usurpations and invasions, and was in process of losing control of its eastern empire.

The Seleukid kingdom was certainly the most powerful and potentially threatening kingdom in the east, and to see it in such a mess was reassuring for the Romans; they would assume that no danger to them threatened from Syria. The delegation had gone from Alexandria on a visit to Cyprus, then to Syria, then Rhodes. A visit to Attalos II at Pergamon was followed by a visit to Greece and Macedonia, now a formal Roman province. They were back in Rome sometime in 138.

The Roman delegation may not have been particularly interested in Syria, though since little of their activity there is recorded, we cannot be certain. Ptolemy VIII, king of the neighbouring state, with which it had been at war only recently, on the other hand, had no choice but to be watchful of events there. In Ptolemy's lifetime, his kingdom had been invaded by Seleukid armies and occupied for a year or so, and although the invaders had withdrawn, they had helped themselves to as much loot as they could carry on their way out. Ptolemy's own armies had been used to invade and occupy Syria for an even longer period. Furthermore, his niece Kleopatra Thea had been married to the usurper Alexander Balas, who had been installed as king in Syria partly by the machinations of Ptolemy VI, and she had then been unceremoniously transferred to Alexander's enemy, Demetrios II, as his wife by Ptolemy VI's decision. Kleopatra Thea had been only the second Ptolemaic princess to be married to a non-Ptolemaic husband in two centuries. The first of such marriages, by Berenike, the daughter of Ptolemy II, to Antiochos II, had resulted in a war and her own murder and that of her infant son; the evidence of Syria in the 140s was that Kleopatra Thea might be achieving the same result.

Ptolemy VIII had to be watchful, partly because Kleopatra Thea was his niece – though he never displayed any family feeling for her – but more because the husband of a Ptolemaic princess could mount a strong dynastic claim to the Ptolemaic throne, although probably only in a time of instability in Egypt – and she had a succession of three husbands. This was why these princesses were normally married to a Ptolemaic king, or were secluded, and left unmarried.

Kleopatra Thea was, so far as can be understood, no more than a hapless puppet of her husbands, Alexander Balas and Demetrios II, during the 140s. She had been married at about the age of fifteen to Alexander Balas; they had one son, Antiochos, who was taken to be fostered with an Arab chieftain, Zabdiel, when war developed in 147. King Alexander was killed in 145, executed by a pair of Demetrios' men with Zabdiel's permission,[11] by which time Kleopatra Thea had been transferred to Demetrios II, and then her father Ptolemy VI was killed in battle.[12] Demetrios faced a rebellion led by Diodotos of Kasiana, who had been one of Ptolemy VI's ministers, and had been the joint promoter of him as 'king in Asia', at Antioch in 145.[13] Diodotos took over the protection of the child Antiochos and proclaimed him king as Antiochos VI, in opposition to Demetrios. The boy died in 142 – his enemies claimed that Diodotos poisoned him – at which point Diodotos took the vacant kingship to himself, as King Tryphon.[14]

This was the situation when the Roman delegation arrived on their visit of inspection. Tryphon had gained control of a considerable part of the Seleukid land in Syria – he gained Antioch in 143, though he had to burn the city to do so. Demetrios held most of the rest, but it seems that his marriage to Kleopatra Thea, though it had produced two children, was not happy. In 141, Demetrios abandoned the fight in Syria and went east to combat the attacks of the Parthians, who had invaded Babylonia; and yet in Syria, Tryphon made no more progress despite Demetrios' absence, and Kleopatra Thea holed up in Seleukeia-in-Pieria.[15]

How deeply the Roman delegation investigated all this is unknown, but they reached Syria by way of a stay in Cyprus, and the obvious way into Syria from there is by ship to Seleukeia. If they were in Alexandria in 140, then later in that year is the most likely time of their investigations in Syria – and no doubt Kleopatra Thea was one of their early sources of information. Whether they got to see Tryphon is unknown; they certainly will have interviewed Demetrios II, and Antiochos VII was in exile until 138 (though he was apparently residing at Side, on the Pamphylian coast just north of Cyprus, and perfectly accessible).[16]

Kleopatra Thea in Seleukeia-in-Pieria was effectively independent and the queen of the city. Demetrios I had meanwhile pursued his campaign in Babylonia; he was not, it seems safe to say, a particularly good commander, and in 139 he was defeated and captured by the Parthians.[17] He was kept in a comfortable prison somewhere in Iran, and one of his comforts was a new wife, Rhodogune, a daughter of the Parthian King Mithradates; they had two children.[18]

In Syria, while he was away in the east, his brother Antiochos arrived from his exile in Side, and was accepted by Kleopatra as her new, third, husband. It is unknown whether she had received information about Demetrios' new 'marriage' (to Rhodogune – if they were ever married in any legal sense); it seems unlikely she was bothered either way. It was in fact her duty to choose a new husband to be king in the circumstances of Demetrios' absence. Antiochos turned out to be a highly competent commander, and succeeded, in only a year or so, in suppressing Tryphon, who died fighting in battle, and destroying his conspiracy.[19] By 138, Antiochos and Kleopatra Thea were ruling most of Seleukid Syria from Gaza to the Taurus Mountains. (In the next years, they had five children.) By this time, the Roman delegation had returned to Rome – which is generally taken to be in 138. The political situation in Syria had by then been sorted out, but the capture of Demetrios had allowed the Parthians to secure control of all Babylonia.

Egypt was judged to be a powerful kingdom, and Kleopatra II and Kleopatra III appear to have settled down, if not in amity, then in a mutual accommodation, though this was unlikely to last. Kleopatra III (like her cousin Kleopatra Thea) was producing children with great regularity – five were born between 138 and 131 to each of these women. This meant that the succession issue in both kingdoms was probably settled, except for two problems: the multiplicity of children posed a problem in itself, and the three Kleopatras began to assert themselves.

This period, specifically 138–133, is a blank in the records of the Ptolemaic kingdom in political terms. Elsewhere, however, things were developing for the worse in Asia Minor, and one of the consequences was that the Roman menace, as personified in 140 by the three men in the Roman delegation, became very different and grave from 133.

Attalos II of Pergamon died in 138 and was succeeded by his nephew, Attalos III, but he lasted only five years. For some unknown reason he made a will in which he bequeathed his kingdom to Rome. This was a practice invented by Ptolemy VIII while he was king in Cyrenaica, when he was under dire threat. He claimed to have survived an assassination attempt, which he blamed on his brother Ptolemy VI, but which may have been by Cyrenians, with whom he was unpopular, to say the least. This had happened when he was about to go to Rome; he feared, not unjustly, that his Cyrenaican kingdom would be in danger from his brother while he was away. He thus made a will, or perhaps issued it as a decree, which assigned his kingdom to Rome in the event of his death. It was a political gesture designed to ward off the threat he feared, but it was in effect cancelled by his marriage to Kleopatra II in 145, and the production of their son Memphites. The Romans probably never knew that they were being used in such a way. Ptolemy VI was probably informed – indeed, there was no point in the will unless Ptolemy VI knew about it. The wording was set up in an inscription in Cyrene detailing his promise publicly, where it was later discovered by archaeologists.[20]

Now Attalos III was using the same device. It may have been because he had no children of his own (which had been Ptolemy VIII's situation when he made his will), but there were certainly other members of the Attalid family still available, and presumably Attalos feared that he would be overthrown or assassinated. It is likely that, under normal circumstances, the bequest to the Romans would be evaded or refused, and that one of the existing Attalids would be permitted to be king. But in Rome, when Attalos died in 133, the situation was by no means normal. Unxpectedly, Attalos' bequest was accepted.[21]

This was a windfall for the Republic; the resources it produced were funnelled into the internal dispute concerning colonisation – the settlement of needy Romans and discharged Roman soldiers – that then concerned Rome.[22] In the east, the result was a new and decisive extension of Roman power into Asia Minor, a matter that greatly enhanced Roman power and wealth, but also added to Rome's involvement in Asia Minor, and brought it substantial difficulties there.

In particular, the idea of being subject to Roman power was repugnant to many inhabitants, and an Attalid son, an illegitimate child of Attalos II, Aristonikos, set himself up as King Eumenes III. The subsequent war lasted until 129, and the settlement imposed by Rome effectively dismantled the Attalid kingdom – the Greek cities and the major colonial cities were made autonomous, the rest of the territory was divided, with Rome taking only about half of the former kingdom, the area near the Aegean. In the interior there followed a generation of disputes and quarrels over the rest of the former kingdom.[23]

For the existing Great Powers, the Seleukid and Ptolemaic kingdoms, this was a major extension of the Roman reach, not only by Rome's territorial growth, but still more in the resources it could wield; this was clearly ominous. Rome's greater resources now included a notable increase in its naval strength, since many of the cities of the Aegean coast and islands had some naval power, and by pulling them all together, which several Roman governors did in the next fifty years, a serious naval force could be accumulated to add to Rome's own formidable navy, or be used in place of that navy if the Roman Senate did not sanction its use. Roman dominance of the eastern Mediterranean was clearly enhanced.

In Syria, meanwhile, the disappearance of Demetrios II into Parthian captivity in 139 had resulted in his brother seizing power, as Antiochos VII. Having succeeded in this he then married his brother's wife, Kleopatra Thea, the daughter of Ptolemy VI, the assumption being, one supposes, that Demetrios II was finished. This was the lady's third royal marriage, and all had produced children, all of whom might be thought to have some claim to both the Seleukid and Egyptian kingships. (And Demetrios had sired children in his imprisonment, who might, at a stretch, be included in the Seleukid succession.)

These political developments were dangerous. Rome, with its internal problems, had become even more unpredictable than before, both in the revolutionary developments in Italy from 133, and when Attalos III's death and legacy had produced a new war; the Attalid pretender Aristonikos fought with some vigour and persistence to secure his supposed inheritance. In Syria, Antiochos VII, like his brother, fought to remove Tryphon, although unlike his brother, he was successful. Eventually, again like Demetrios, he went east to fight the Parthians, and in 129 he was killed in battle.[24] Also in 129, 'Eumenes III' died, and, as it happened, so did Scipio Aemilianus. Out of Iran, Demetrios II escaped from his captivity and returned to the throne of Syria.[25] Unfortunately for him, he was greeted with repugnance by Kleopatra Thea, still in mourning for Antiochos. Apparently resuming marital relations with Demetrios after several years with Antiochos was something she was not prepared to do. She locked herself into the city of Ptolemais-Ake and refused to allow him to enter. By that time also, the Ptolemies had fallen into their own dynastic civil war, accompanied by more rebellions, so with both Egypt and Syria in political difficulties, and Rome having advanced substantially from the Adriatic to Central Asia Minor in only thirteen years, but, still struggling with an internal crisis of its own, the stage was set for more fighting.

Chapter 3

Civil War and Rebellions

The extended, century-long crisis that afflicted the Ptolemaic kingdom and dynasty from 132 onwards was in part the result of the continuing dynastic dispute of the previous years, although the sources do not provide any information about them between 142 and the beginning of the civil war. The dispute that began in 132 and quickly developed into a civil war was between Ptolemy VIII and Kleopatra III on the one side and Kleopatra II on the other. It is evident from the sequence of events, so far as they can be discerned, that both parties had considerable support inside Egypt, but it is also clear that there was another aspect in that there were native Egyptians who hankered for independence on the lines of the seceding kingdom that had governed Thebes and the south for two decades half a century before, and that both the Alexandrian population and the Egyptians in the *chora* were more than willing to assert themselves against the Ptolemaic regime.

The power of the king had been reduced. The case of the general Hierax who could pay, out of his own resources, the wages of a disaffected set of mercenaries has been noted earlier, and it was not the first time that it had become clear that the Greco-Macedonian aristocracy had succeeded in becoming very rich, to the extent in addition that the king's treasury was less than well filled. This contrast between private wealth and public shortage was in part the result of the diversion of public resources into private control. The ramifications of such a redistribution of wealth resulted in, amongst other things, the unsettlement of class and ethnic relations. Add to this the memory of the success for a generation of the native pharaohs in holding on to their independence in the south, the new assertiveness of the Egyptian peasantry, which had not been the case in the first Ptolemaic century, then it is clear that the relations of kings, aristocrats and the peasantry had changed, and this was a phenomenon that all needed to keep in mind.

Ptolemy VIII deliberately cultivated support from the native Egyptian population. The priests and the temples were seen as the key to this. These had been among the supporters of the great rebellion, and were still the king's key to communication with the rest of the Egyptians. A general amnesty was one of his first measures, in 145/144,[1] and priests and temples had their privileges reconfirmed, also their resources.[2] Ptolemy and Kleopatra II were publicised, in decrees and sculptures, as joint kings, with the traditional Egyptian titles.[3] All these measures were taken early in Ptolemy's reign; their benefit emerged sometime later.

That is to say, in the new dynastic crisis that began in 132, the kings, queens, and their children were not the only participants. The Greco-Macedonian aristocracy were already involved, and Ptolemy VIII had now summoned the native Egyptian population to support him. So there were interventions from outsiders acting autonomously and from the general population of Egypt, the native Egyptians and the Alexandrians. This crisis was therefore of a different type than earlier ones in which Ptolemy VIII, in particular, had been involved. He had, of course, disputed the smooth succession process in the family ever since he was a teenager. Such behaviour was, it seems, infectious, encouraging the outsiders to become involved, and set the pattern for conducting such crises for the future. From 132 onwards, the dynasty may be said to have been constantly in crisis until its very end. In addition, there was the repeated involvement of the Seleukid state and family – another set of outsiders. They became much involved in Egypt and in the Ptolemaic family, thanks in part to the marriages of Kleopatra Thea to a succession of various Seleukid kings, and to her children, who were as disputatious a group as their Ptolemaic cousins.

It is, however, one thing to assume that the crisis that began in 132 was a continuation of the bad relations between the king and his wives that was evident in 145–140, as is generally assumed, and another to demonstrate that continuation. No doubt, these family unpleasantnesses did continue, although there is no indication that they did so between 142 and 132. We are entitled therefore to assume that, after 142, when Kleopatra II's son Eupator probably died, and Kleopatra III's first son was born (the later Ptolemy IX), the relations of the family were more or less tranquil. The assumption is that Kleopatra II was angered by Ptolemy VIII's marriage to her daughter, Kleopatra III. The two women were mother and daughter, after all, but it is only male historians, ancient and modern, who assume that they were enemies.

By 142, when the first child of the new marriage was born, Kleopatra II was over forty years old, and she was unlikely to have any more children. If Ptolemy Eupator did die in 142, the succession was reduced yet again to a single child, Ptolemy Memphites, and this was dynastically dangerous. If Ptolemy VIII was to have more children he must marry again, and given the practices of Ptolemaic marriages, only his niece was a suitable wife. There is a comment in the ancient sources that he raped the girl, who was in her mid-teens when Ptolemy took her as his wife, but again, we have to take such reports with care – neither of the sources on the matter (Justin and Livy) are reliable on Ptolemaic family affairs.[4]

It is therefore mainly assumption that the royal family was dysfunctional, based on misogyny and the later attitudes during the civil warfare. If so, it was possibly the visit of the Roman delegation in 140/139 that had its effect in this, for it would have been both discourteous and disastrous if the family disagreements had been aired in front of the visitors. From then on for several years, there is no sign that relations were anything but quiet. There is no evidence either way, of course, but such disputes as happened before and after this gap in the record did attract record-keeping (and writerly imaginations), and to a degree the absence of such records may be a sign of the relative peacefulness in the palace for several years.

So if that interpretation may be provisionally accepted, the reason for the eruption into civil war in 132 has to be sought in a new situation that came about in that year, not simply in a continuation of the old, hypothetical, bad relations. What happened in 132 was that Kleopatra II attempted to seize power at the expense of her brother/husband. Since she had opposed his return to Alexandria back in 145 and now staged a *coup d'état* aimed at unseating him, it is reasonable to assume that 'antagonism' between them is perhaps the least opprobrious term to use, although there is little or no evidence of it until 132. By this time, however, the dynastic set of people involved had increased considerably – Ptolemy Memphites, the five children of Ptolemy VIII and Kleopatra III, who included two boys, and Ptolemy Apion, the eldest of them all, as well as the king and his two wives.

Memphites was the senior heir, and the two sons of Kleopatra III were not much younger than him; the future Ptolemy IX, their eldest son, had been born in 142, only a couple of years after Memphites, and that may well be the year in which Ptolemy Eupator, son of Ptolemy VI and Kleopatra II, had died, or been killed. The other children of Kleopatra III were born in the next six years.⁵ As the boys grew up, the tension within the family would have increased. Memphites, as the son of Kleopatra II, may be assumed to have been favoured by her; the two sons of Kleopatra III both will have been favoured by their mother, although it appears that, at least later, she favoured the younger before the elder. It was within Ptolemy VIII's power to choose his own heir, not necessarily nominating the oldest son – there were precedents in the dynasty for several methods of choosing, and for promoting a younger son. No doubt, like the cunning politician he was, and probably beset by pressures from several directions, including both of his wives, he made no announcement of any choice; to choose was to choose even more trouble.

Kleopatra II's *coup d'état* in 132 may be interpreted best as her attempt to circumvent this situation. It appears that Ptolemy Memphites had been sent to Cyrene, possibly by Ptolemy VIII, who was king there still. The boy was about twelve or thirteen years old by this time, almost old enough to be associated with his father as king, if not to take power personally. Elevation to king was a ceremony that would need to be performed in Egypt, preferably at Memphis or Alexandria. Being sent to Cyrene would suggest that Memphites was being groomed as king in Cyrenaica, a post that his father had held for many years. As such, he would be set up in semi-independence, possibly as a subordinate of Ptolemy in Egypt – but the distance was such that effective independence would be the result, as Ptolemy VIII, and earlier Cyrenaican viceroys, had shown.

Ptolemy Memphites in Cyrene has not attracted much attention, but his situation surely requires it. Whitehorne suggests that he was sent there by his mother as a refuge,⁶ but as Ptolemy VIII's heir, his permission was presumably needed. Considering the place as a refuge presupposes that it was common knowledge in the court that Ptolemy VIII was considering killing Memphites, for which, once again, there is no evidence, only presumption. And, as was shown later, as a 'refuge' it was insufficient, since Ptolemy was king in both Cyrenaica and Egypt. We do not know when he was sent there, but it was clearly not long before the events of 132. And if the heir to the Ptolemaic kingship was sent to Cyrene, possibly on a permanent basis, this was a major political event. It has to be accounted for, and the obvious reason was to install him there as king.

The installation of Memphites as king in Cyrene might allow Kleopatra II to go there with him, or be sent there, as his regent. The advantage to

Ptolemy VIII would be that both would then be separated from the Alexandrian court, and from him. Since Kleopatra II had considerable support amongst the Alexandrians, this move would not only get mother and son out of the court, but would sever Kleopatra from her main source of political support in Egypt. It would thus also clear the way for Ptolemy VIII's children by Kleopatra III to become his recognised heirs for Egypt. Such a scheme would not be surprising; Ptolemy had the cunning to arrange it, while proclaiming that Memphites in Cyrene was a promotion. Ptolemy was by then about fifty years of age, and must have been thinking for some time of organising the succession. He could reasonably assume that the exile of mother and son to Cyrene (as she will perhaps have formulated it) would be seen by Kleopatra as extremely unpleasant. But only Memphites went to Cyrene, Kleopatra stayed in Alexandria, and Ptolemy VIII certainly did not expect her violent reaction.

It may have been the prospect of this dynastic coup by the king that provoked Kleopatra II to make her own attempt to seize power; this is speculative, of course, as is much of this interpretation, since no reasons other than the continuing antagonism within the family is ever recorded in the ancient sources. But the results of her move were sufficiently violent and widespread to suggest that her coup was planned, and that the tensions in the royal court were mirrored by similar tensions in the city and the country.

The dating of events is less than certain, but Kleopatra's move appears to have been made shortly after the start of the thirty-ninth year of Ptolemy VIII's rule, which began on 11 November 132;[7] the king then maintained his position, under pressure, for several months. No information exists as to the development of the fighting, but the decisive event came late in 131, when the Alexandrians stormed the royal palace in the city; in the fighting, the palace itself caught fire.[8]

Ptolemy, taking Kleopatra III and their children with him, left the city and went to Cyprus. There he could recruit forces, partly from the Ptolemaic forces already in the island, and partly from his access there to the mercenary market in Greece and Asia Minor.[9] It appears that Kleopatra II was at the time in the Egyptian south, or at least that she had gathered support there, as indicated by the documents from the area dated by her 'Year 2'.[10] When Ptolemy left Alexandria, in August 131, she had herself proclaimed as the ruling queen, apparently backdating her reign to 132/131.[11]

Ptolemy was now threatened by two measures – his sister's proclamation of her own rule, which was in effect his deposition, and the possibility that she would bring Memphites back to Egypt and make him king jointly with her. The existence of a king in Egypt could well rally more support for Kleopatra. This may, in fact, have been her intention, but the absence of Memphites from Egypt impelled her to proclaim herself first, rather suggesting that the whole process happened unexpectedly, to her as to Ptolemy. Ptolemy VIII, however, could not accept this. He summoned the boy to Cyprus from Cyrene, which he must have done even before Kleopatra's self-proclamation, given the distances involved. Either with encouragement from Kleopatra, or spontaneously, the Alexandrians then overthrew Ptolemy's statues, and Kleopatra began a new year-count for the new reign. These actions amounted to a renewed deposition of Ptolemy. He reacted by murdering Memphites, dismembering him, and sending the pieces to Kleopatra in Alexandria as a birthday present. Not to be outdone in a demonstration of tasteless unpleasantness, she put the parts on public display, apparently expecting the sight to stimulate the anger of the population even more.[12]

The two rivals competed also in adopting new names. Ptolemy already had taken the name *Euergetes*, and now he and his wife became *Theoi Euergetai*; Kleopatra II took the name *Theoi Philometor Soteira*. These names were intended to recall earlier Ptolemies' names and grandeur, although it is perhaps unlikely that the names would have been recalled in any detail by even the Greek Macedonians in the population. Ptolemy's favour had been detailed earlier towards the native Egyptians, their priests, their temples and their administrators, and this produced dividends in this crisis, since he seems to have gained much support from them. In 130 or 131, one Egyptian, Paos, was promoted to the post of *strategos* of the Thebaid, in effect, the governor-general of the south, although who it was that promoted him is not known.[13]

This appointment came soon after another Egyptian, Harsiese, appears to have made an attempt to seize power in the south region – possibly Paos' appointment was in response to Harsiese's appeal to native Egyptians in the area. It certainly came in the period following one in which documents were dated by Kleopatra II's 'Year 2'. Harsiese did not last long, if he did gain any political traction in the first place. Whenever he did, he cannot have been regarded too seriously since he was simply sent into internal exile at el-Hibeh.[14] The appointment of Paos then brought the area decisively into Ptolemy VIII's camp.

By that time, also, in 130, Ptolemy had gathered his forces in Cyprus and returned to Egypt. It seems he avoided Alexandria, and headed straight for Memphis, which again suggests a reliance to some extent on the support of the native Egyptians.[15] At the same time, he appointed his own priests of Alexander and the Deified Ptolemies. This was the most senior Greco-Macedonian priesthood, and was normally based in Alexandria; this new succession of priests operated it seems at Memphis. He was stating in this that he was the rightful king, in whose power was the appointment of these priests; those in office in Alexandria, appointed by Kleopatra II, were thus, he was claiming, illegitimate, and so Kleopatra was not a rightful king. He was making an appeal to the Greco-Macedonian population in this gesture, and insisting that the processes of his own depositions were invalid. Alexander was a well-regarded king, even amongst the Egyptians, and Ptolemy was thus also turning once again to their support; he named his second son by Kleopatra III (later Ptolemy X) Alexander in an attempt to draw on the old king's charisma.[16]

The king's actions and arrival evidently stimulated a widespread revival of his authority in Egypt, judging by a considerable number of documents dated to 130 and 129, which were dated by the years of his reign. In the south, however, Paos had to campaign to reduce the city of Hermonthis, which resisted him for several months.[17] And for several years, Alexandria continued to resist the returned king, and to support Kleopatra II.

The Ptolemaic kingdom was thus, once more, divided between the queen ruling in Alexandria and the king in control of the *chora*, a situation reminiscent of that in 169–168, with the invasion of Antiochos IV. And once more, the city showed that even without access to the resources of Egypt outside the city walls, it was capable of surviving. It was a major port and a rich city, and it was found relatively easy to supply it with food from abroad; it was also particularly the base for the surviving Ptolemaic fleet, which would also be available. And in another echo of Antiochos' invasion, there was a new threat to Ptolemy VIII from Syria.

While the Ptolemaic kingdom was sliding into division and civil war, the third husband of Kleopatra Thea, Antiochos VII of the Seleukid dynasty, was beginning a serious attempt to reconquer the lands recently taken by the Parthians. He began in 131, and by 129 his army was in occupation of Babylonia and much of eastern Iran, and had penetrated as far as the satrapy of Parthia, which had given the mixed population of the Parthian kingdom their common name.¹⁸ In the winter of 130/129, the Parthian king Phraates II was faced with a dilemma. He was clearly losing the war, and, as is the way of these things, he was also now at the same time being threatened by nomad invaders, the Sakae, from the east, exploiting the momentary Parthian weakness. He made two decisions, first to make a series of winter attacks on the Seleukid forces, which were spread out in garrisons for their winter quarters, and second, to release Demetrios II, Antiochos' brother, from his comfortable imprisonment in hopes of disrupting Antiochos' regime in Syria. Demetrios, despite his comfort, his Parthian princess-wife, and the children he had by her, had at least twice before made escape attempts. The Parthian king's purpose in releasing him was, of course, to create confusion amongst the Seleukid army, and as soon as he was out of his prison, a Parthian detachment followed him.

The first part of the plan succeeded. The Seleukid army was, according to Justin, 80,000 men strong and was accompanied by '300,000' camp followers. The figures, as usual, need not be accepted as anywhere near accurate, but the army was clearly numerous, and would certainly be accompanied by 'cooks and bakers',¹⁹ to quote Justin, and even perhaps 'entertainers', although this is deleted in some translations. After all, Alexander's campaign two centuries before had been similarly provided with servants. But the sheer size of the occupation forces will have imposed a great burden on the Iranian population, and made it widely detested – there is no sign of any loyalty to the Seleukid regime in Iran, unlike in Babylonia – and this will have compelled the forces to be dispersed into separating garrisons, and so made them vulnerable.

Separate attacks in the winter on the divided Seleukid army caused confusion and produced Parthian victories. One perhaps unexpected result, though, was that an ambush was laid for him and King Antiochos was killed in the fighting. On this news, the order was given to reimprison Demetrios, but, by now an expert escaper, he had moved much faster than expected, and he outrode those who followed and pursued him. He reached Syria during 129, when he reassumed the kingship, and tried to reclaim Kleopatra Thea as his wife.²⁰

Many thousands of the Seleukid troops were captured. This included a daughter of Demetrios II and Kleopatra Thea called Laodike, who had been accompanying Antiochos in the campaign; she was taken into Phraates' harem.²¹ A son of Antiochos and Kleopatra Thea had been on the expedition also, and appears to have been captured and brought up in the Parthian court.²² The captured troops were taken to the eastern border of the Parthian kingdom and were there supposed to defend it against the Saka nomad attack. However, when they had been marshalled and the first attack came, they turned on the Parthian commanders, and killed King Phraates.²³ How many of them then escaped back to Syria is not known, nor is the fate of Laodike and her half-brother, but if she produced a child – which is presumably why she was in the king's harem – this was one more Seleukid to add to the growing list of possible claimants to the kingship, which already included the children of Demetrios and Antiochos, and the children Demetrios had fathered in his captivity.

He faced a crop of major difficulties when he got back to Syria. The Seleukid army that had gone to the east had been destroyed, its survivors came back to Syria few in number and slowly, and the population of Syria reacted with shock and extravagant mourning.²⁴ Demetrios had never been popular, having depended first on Ptolemaic support and then on a group of greedy mercenaries, before he rode off to fight in the east, where he disappeared into defeat and capture. (He had grown a beard in his captivity, and kept it on his return, so distinguishing himself from the rest of the population.) And his wife refused to have anything to do with him – the contrast with Antiochos, his younger brother, was perhaps too strong.

Apart from these internal and personal problems, he also confronted several international difficulties. The Parthians, strangely enough, were the least of them, for Phraates found that he had to turn to the east to face invasions from Baktria, in which he died at the hands of his captive soldiers, probably the next year; his successor, his cousin Artabanus, had to fight all through his short reign,²⁵ and was also killed in battle against the Sakae – the third Parthian king to die in battle in the past fifteen years. So the threat from the east was deflected. Under normal circumstances, this would have been a good moment to make a serious attempt to recover the territories lost to the Parthians, but it was rather too much for the men of Syria who would have to set off, after two defeats, for the third time to do that.

Instead, Demetrios, when he examined the situation in the eastern Mediterranean, found that there were other opportunities. In his time as pretender and king from more than a dozen years before, the Romans had advanced to take over Macedon and western Asia Minor, and in the process had constructed, or planned out, two of their great roads – the Via Egnatia from the Adriatic almost to the Hellespont, and the Via Aquillia from the

Hellespont to Side in eastern Pamphylia.[26] The existence of these roads, along which it was intended that Roman forces should march when necessary, was obviously a threat to all in Asia Minor and to Seleukid Syria. Together they brought Syria within a relatively easy march of a Roman army from Italy. In addition, the Roman control of the Aegean increased its naval strength considerably. Rome had become, for the first time, the dominating power in the Middle Sea, the eastern basis as well as the western. A cool consideration would have concluded that, in time, Rome would advance even further.

Demetrios may well have made such a calculation. The kingdom he returned to was considerably diminished, not just by the conquest of Babylonia and Iran by the Parthians, but by the secession of several parts of Syria. In the north, Kommagene detached itself into an independent kingdom, the governor taking over as king;[27] on the Phoenician coast, the city of Arados, based on an offshore island and controlling a stretch of the adjacent coast, similarly made itself independent. It cannot have been a surprise to anyone in Syria that this had happened, since Arados had several times already attempted to increase its autonomy; it chose a crisis of the kingdom to take the final step.[28] In the south, the Judaean uplands was inhabited by another group, the Jews, who had been among those aiming for independence. A contingent of their forces had been conscripted by Antiochos to fight in Parthia, but had escaped, like Demetrios, from the Parthian vengeance; for thirty years they had been fighting and scheming to achieve that independence, and the survival of their army now allowed them to achieve it.[29]

In such a situation the obvious thing for a king to do would be to campaign to recover control of these seceding fragments, as the Ptolemies had done when the south of Egypt set itself up as an independent pharaonic regime. Detaching fragments, little more than city states, often based on well-defended cities, was a practice that could well become infectious (and did so a few years later). Instead, Demetrios responded to an appeal that came out of Egypt.

By 130, the dispute between Ptolemy VIII and Kleopatra II had reached a stalemate, Ptolemy controlling most of the countryside, Kleopatra the city of Alexandria. Kleopatra turned to her son-in-law Demetrios for help. She promised to marry him and so make him king in Egypt.[30] (That both were already married was by this time, after the marriages of both families in the previous half-century, clearly no obstacle, though no doubt one of the victims of Demetrios' success, should he achieve it, would be Ptolemy VIII.)

Demetrios responded to the appeal by gathering an army in Syria and marching towards Egypt. This has caused considerable surprise, astonishment and scorn amongst historians, given the problems Demetrios already faced, but it was clearly a rational decision. His ultimate aim would be to unite Syria and Egypt into a single state, which would stretch from Cyrenaica to the Taurus Mountains and Mesopotamia. Only a state of such wealth and extent and populousness would be able to survive in a world where Rome ruled from Spain to Asia Minor and Parthia, if it survived the nomad attacks, from Babylonia to the border of India. The secessionist fragments in Syria could then easily be dealt with, and the Parthians, suffering large casualties in their nomad wars, and who had almost succumbed to Antiochos VII's invasion, could be defeated by the joint power of a united Syria-and-Egypt.

The issue of such a process, of course, been raised in 145 by Ptolemy VI, who had himself accepted the title of 'King of Asia' (as well as Egypt). The idea had presumably been in the back of political minds ever since. It was a seductive thought, which, if successful, would revive the power of the Macedonian kingdoms, if only by allowing a united kingdom to focus on outside threats, and away from their age-old mutual antagonism. The countries were both vigorous and populous, and it is possible, even likely, that the idea of unity had been mulled over by Demetrios in his captivity. He certainly reacted very quickly to Kleopatra's invitation. The exact details of the future arrangements were apparently not discussed, though it does seem that a marriage of Demetrios with Kleopatra II was to be the basis of the union. Demetrios may well have not wanted to consider the political details; if he won by destroying Ptolemy VIII, he would be in a position to dictate the terms.

Such a situation ignored all too many problems, of course, including Ptolemy VIII and his children, Kleopatra III, Kleopatra Thea and her children, not to mention Demetrios' two children by Rhodogune. Then there was the question of his acceptance by the Egyptians, in the city, and in the *chora*, which was loyal to Ptolemy. And it wholly ignored the cunning and capability of intrigue of Ptolemy VIII.

Demetrios set off on his expedition in the spring of 128, having reached Syria in his escape the previous summer or autumn. Six or eight months is a reasonable period in which the appeal from Kleopatra II arrived, arrangements were made, and Demetrios could gather an army. He marched along the traditional invasion route along the north coast of Sinai and then met the perennial obstacle of the fortress of Pelusion and its surrounding subsidiary forts, which had long blocked invasions of Egypt.[31]

And at that point his plans began to go awry. Pelusion was under the control of the forces of Ptolemy VIII, and Demetrios' troops were compelled to camp in the desert, presumably blocked by the fortress complex. This initial check, of course, gave those opposed to his plans the time to take measures to thwart him. In Syria, his wife proclaimed one of her children as a rival king, and at Pelusion, the army mutinied. In Syria, first the Antiochenes, then the Apamaeans, repudiated Demetrios' authority. The arrival of the body of Antiochos VII, in a silver casket donated by the Parthians, emphasised the contrast between the two brothers.[32] And in Egypt, Ptolemy VIII, who had hardly been seriously threatened by Demetrios' attack, came up with a repeat of his brother's successful ploy against Demetrios I twenty years before.

Kleopatra Thea's promotion of one of her sons as king is not actually altogether certain. The evidence is the existence of a single coin in the name of 'King Antiochos', which would seem to be Kleopatra's second son by Demetrios, who was later Antiochos VIII. The date is claimed to be 128, which would make the king a usurper against Demetrios. But the image on the coin is probably not of Antiochos in 128 – he would be in his early teens by that date and the image is of a much younger child. The dating therefore is not conclusive. Yet such a usurpation fits well into the situation at the time.[33] It might have been a reaction to the news of the defeat and death of Antiochos VII, or to the revolt of Antioch (when the coin was minted), or to Demetrios' defeat in Egypt. Whatever date is chosen, his 'reign' at this time did not last more than the time it took them to mint the coin.

It may have been this act that stimulated Ptolemy VIII to promote his own usurper. He located an Egyptian Greek, a son of a merchant called Promachos, whom he designated as Alexander, and was claimed to be the son of Alexander Balas, an earlier usurper, and therefore supposedly also another child of Kleopatra Thea – Ptolemy VIII would seem to have had a sense of humour. Alternatively, he was said to be an adopted son of Antiochos VII, who had never been heard of before. No doubt, the contradictions were intentional and deliberately confusing, for no one ever seems to have accepted him as a legitimate king, only as a convenient tool with which to oppose Demetrios. He was accepted briefly as king in Syria, but only so long as Demetrios was his opponent; then he was dropped. He was sent into Syria with an army, presumably of Ptolemaic mercenaries, in order to thwart Demetrios' attack on Egypt.[34]

This move was successful. Demetrios' army mutinied against the conditions it was enduring in the desert camp. Kleopatra Thea sent two of her sons into exile for safety (just as Demetrios I had sent Demetrios and Antiochos away for the same reason). One of them was a son of Demetrios (Antiochos VIII, later) who was sent to Kyzikos, a powerful independent city on the Sea of Marmara; the other was a son of Antiochos VII (Antiochos IX, later), who was sent to Athens.[35] The other children remained with her, presumably in Ptolemais-Ake, where she is recorded as living during Demetrios' renewed reign. Alexander, nicknamed Zabeinas ('bought', so transparently bogus was he), was able to maintain his position in Syria for several years.

Ptolemy's ploy was successful in destroying his enemies' plans, but it also destroyed any possibility of achieving a unification of the two kingdoms of Egypt and Syria. And yet, that was all of a piece with his earlier policies. He was never willing to go to war, until forced, never interested in conquest, or in foreign policy, other than, as with Demetrios, in deflecting his enemies. He clearly, in a crisis, always thought first of a devious way of avoiding the trouble rather than meeting it, seeking every time for an intelligent and inexpensive solution.

Alexander Zabeinas in Syria gathered enough support to defeat Demetrios in battle near Damascus (in 127/126).[36] Demetrios' lack of popularity, and perhaps his lack of much of an army after the mutiny, was no doubt the cause of his defeat. Alexander, however, was just as unpopular. Demetrios was joined at some point by Kleopatra II, who had left Alexandria after Demetrios' failure to reach Egypt. She took her treasure with her but his defeat thwarted her plans as well; she seems then to have gone to Kleopatra Thea.[37] Demetrios sought refuge with his wife in Ptolemais-Ake, but she shut the gates on him. He turned north to seek refuge in the city of Tyre, but there he was murdered by the governor, possibly on instructions from Kleopatra Thea.[38] At much the same time, Ptolemy VIII, with Kleopatra II absent in Syria, was able to gain control of Alexandria.[39] He then indulged himself in the destruction of a set of opponents, including burning many young men to death, whom he had shut into the gymnasium and then burned the place down.[40]

Kleopatra II, her options having run out, made a pragmatic decision to seek a reconciliation with Ptolemy VIII and Kleopatra III; this she achieved over the course of the next few years, possibly using the treasure she had removed as a lure. This, of course, solved Ptolemy's problem; he could then abandon Alexander Zabeinas, who struggled on with little success until 123, when he was captured and executed.[41] The reconciliation was in place by 124 when the Egyptian government had been returned to the triple monarchy of Ptolemy VIII, Kleopatra II, and Kleopatra III.[42] In Syria, after Demetrios' death, Kleopatra Thea had promoted her eldest son by Demetrios as Seleukos V, but he soon objected to her claim to equal or superior authority, and she had him killed.[43] She now called back her next son by Demetrios, Antiochos VIII, from Kyzikos and made him king; they ruled jointly until 121, when Antiochos began to manifest the same wish for authority as his dead brother. But he did not fall into the same trap; when Kleopatra Thea offered him a drink when he returned heated and thirsty from a hunt, he insisted that she drank it; as he had supposed, it was poisoned so she it was who died.[44]

It was not until he had stamped out the opposition (necessarily concentrated in the city of Alexandria) that, at his leisure, Ptolemy VIII issued an amnesty decree in 118, in the name of all three rulers.[45] The decree was directed above all at the native Egyptian population, and particularly the priests, as usual, whose lands and offices were confirmed; the *machimoi*'s plots of land were also confirmed in the same way as the cleruchic lands, and unpaid taxes were forgiven. All these measures, and others, were in fact largely traditional, a similar set of forgivenesses having been promulgated in early pharaonic times, and were essentially aimed at restoring public quiet. Of course, another major purpose was to restore respect for the rulers, after the civil war that they had inspired and conducted at the expense of all Egyptians. And perhaps as a gesture to Kleopatra II, Ptolemy Memphites, murdered and dismembered, was added as a god to the list attached to the priesthood of Alexander and the Deified Ptolemies.[46]

Chapter 4

The Red Sea and the Way to India

The Greeks and Romans were as self-centred and as pleased with themselves as were any other people. They believed that they had achieved things no one else had achieved, and ignored, belittled or disbelieved evidence to the contrary. Modern historians studying these peoples are as equally convinced that the subjects they study were extraordinary and did things in an extraordinary way, and had achieved extraordinary things. There was, of course, nothing necessarily wrong in this, but such an attitude requires them to ignore other peoples' achievements both in their importance and in their priority.

Take, for example, the roads apparently 'constructed' by Egnatius and Aquillius in Macedon and Asia Minor; these roads already existed, from time immemorial; all the Romans did was to name them, formalise them, and mark them with milestones – some of these are still in position and legible – and perhaps signposts. A further example would be Alexander the Great's campaigns, which in some accounts are described as 'explorations', although he never went out of known territory. One would not believe from many modern accounts that he was travelling well-trodden roads and reaching well-known places. Such places may not have been known to the Greeks and Macedonians who stayed at home, or even to most of those who marched with the king, but the furthest places that he reached were perfectly familiar to the Persians he was fighting, and both Central Asia and the Indus Valley were known territories to them, and had been occupied by them. Of a certainty, Alexander will have reconnoitred and researched the areas he was approaching by questioning knowledgeable Persians before setting out to campaign there. He did not 'discover' these areas any more than the Greek visitors to India 'discovered' that country; even so, he has been included in one book as an 'explorer'.[1]

The subject of this chapter is the exploitation, by the Ptolemaic Greek state, of the Red Sea and the Indian Ocean. Part of this story has been discussed in earlier parts of this account, and the quest for elephants and ivory along the Red Sea coasts is a familiar story, at least to students of the Hellenistic world. But that earlier Ptolemaic exploitation of the Red Sea trade, and associated particularly with Kings Ptolemy II and III, was hardly a new discovery – the Pharaohs had sent out similar expeditions, if not for elephants then for other goods, notably gold and ivory, during the previous 3,000 years, and the Greeks and Macedonians who came to rule Egypt from 330 BC onwards could have found this out by a fairly superficial investigation. Their tame Egyptian historian, the priest Manetho, could have told them, for example, of the expeditions sent by Queen Hatshepsut.[2]

And so it is also with the question of the 'discovery' of the Indian Ocean and its weather problem – the monsoons. None of this was new to the people who sailed those waters. The coastal route from India westwards had been known, at least to the voyagers, since the Bronze Age, if not earlier. There is ample evidence, from archaeology, that there was a substantial trade between western India and southern Arabia and the Gulf during that time.[3] When Nearchos the Cretan sailed from the mouth of the Indus River to the Persian Gulf he was following a sea route well known; the only surprise is that he apparently never met any local sea craft, although after Alexander's horrific campaign in the Indus Valley, it seems quite likely that the Indians and the Iranians were keeping their heads down and their ships in port to avoid contact with such brutal strangers.[4] The routes east from India to the peninsulas and islands of Southeast Asia were also well frequented by Indian sailors and merchants, particularly those from southern India, and there were to be Indian-type kingdoms established there in the near future. It is not known, however, if any Hellenistic sailors reached that far to the east, although some Romans certainly did.[5]

In summary, therefore, we know that Indians sailed west into the Persian Gulf and along the South Arabian coast from about 2500 BC at least, and it is reasonable to suppose that Babylonians and Arabs went the other way; we know that the Egyptians sailed from the northern Red Sea to the Bab el-Mandeb and perhaps beyond – so to the land they called Punt – from about that same date or earlier. This does not seem to be have resulted in any worthwhile exchange of sailing information, at least none that is recorded, probably because the skills required were those of illiterate sailors; it did, however, lead to a worthwhile exchange of goods at the entrepots in southern Arabia such as Eudaimon Arabia (Aden) and Muza (Mocha) in the Bab el-Mandeb region and Yemen. It is evident that neither side felt the need to pursue their voyages beyond the strait, perhaps because the trade goods they sought were fully available in the South Arabian ports, and the more distant voyages – along the Arabian and Iranian coasts – or for the Indian sailors along the Red Sea coast, were unfamiliar and difficult. It was possible to trade at the strait, so why go any further?

From the point of view of the Ptolemaic government in the third and second centuries, the trade of the Red Sea lands would seem to have been only a secondary consideration. The exploitation of the Red Sea lands was focused mainly on the African side, on the search for gold, and on the acquisition of elephants for warfare, and of their ivory for trade and decoration. The Arabian coastlands, at least in the south, were major sources of incense, valued above all for religious celebrations, but there was already a well-established trade in these goods, carried in caravans – using donkeys at first, until camels could be used – from the southern lands where the incense was harvested, along the road parallel to the sea coast, from the Yemen through Mecca and Medina and into North Arabia and Palestine. This was so well developed a trade that Alexander was able to send a vast quantity of incense to Macedon from Gaza, which developed into the major port for the export of incense, after he conquered that city.[6] It was being organised by the Nabataeans, who were extending their political influence along the trade route, and reached out to Gaza, of which they acquired control. Some incense trade by sea also developed, or existed, during the Ptolemaic period – the Nabataeans certainly had such a trade by the end of the Ptolemaic period – but it was given no priority, since there was a reliable trade by land. During that time, goods from India reached Egypt partly, no doubt, by that same land route and carried in caravans, or by trade from Babylonia, or even by sea along the Red Sea, but it made little impact in the records of the period.

The name of Eudoxos of Kyzikos is associated primarily with the 'discovery' of the ability to join the two parts of the voyage into one, that along the Red Sea, and that from Arabia to India. He was visiting Egypt as an envoy from his city in connection with the celebration of the Koreia, a quadrennial religious festival to which delegates from many cities and countries were invited, one of the many such festivals held in the Hellenistic period. An ambassador like Eudoxos was a wealthy man of considerable importance in his home city, cultivated and educated, the sort of man who could negotiate for his city at the highest level, say, with kings. He stayed on after his embassy was completed, and when invited, took the opportunity to sail up the Nile on King Ptolemy VIII's invitation.[7]

The date of this visit is unclear, but it was presumably after the political settlement that was concluded in 124 between Ptolemy VIII and Kleopatra II to bring the civil war to an end, but before 116 when the king died. No record of the king sailing up the Nile to his southern border is known, although a visit to the Bucheum at Hermonthis near Thebes in 119 is recorded.[8] The year 118 is generally accepted for Eudoxos' later voyage to India, which would fit well with the other indications.

During the Nile cruise an Indian, who turned out to be a ship's captain – or said he was – was found, half dead and starved, by some of Ptolemy's soldiers on patrol along the coast. He had been sent on to the king 'by the garrison of the Red Sea', who had apparently found him on the stranded ship, had been puzzled by him, and had been unable to understand him. It is of interest that they had forwarded this package, not necessarily to the king himself, but he reached Ptolemy because he happened to be in the region at the time. Possibly, he was at the office of the Governor General of the Thebaid, which would be the soldiers' obvious reporting point, and in this accidental way, the king therefore took a personal interest in the cas. And so did Eudoxos, who was with the king at the time.

Strabo gives this information in his *Geography*. He also expressed deep scepticism over the whole story, listing a long series of questions that he thought it raised, some of them frivolous, but some others very much to the point, although it is clear that he had started disbelieving the account and had only developed his objections afterwards.[9] Very much the same attitude had been taken by Herodotos to the story of the voyage of a sailor who claimed to have rounded Africa in the seventh century BC.[10] In both cases, it is the reason for the disbelief that actually highlights details that are convincing the most historians: in Herodotos, it is the report that the sailors saw the sun rising on their right hand on their return voyage; in Strabo, it is the fact that the shipwrecked sailor was cared for and then agreed to pilot a return voyage, no doubt because it was the only way he could see of getting home again.

The sailor recovered and, apparently quite quickly, learned enough Greek to explain himself. This is not really too surprising. As a sailor he will have had a smattering of several Indian, Arabian and Iranian languages, and he possibly had some Greek already, which was a language spoken in parts of

India at the time – there had been Greek-speaking kings ruling in northern India until a generation before these events. (And although 'Greek' is what he is said to have learned, he may have known other current languages, such as Arabic, which would also be known at Ptolemy's court.) His explanation was that his crew had died of starvation when the ship 'lost its way', and he was the only survivor. There is no explanation of where the ship was wrecked, other than it was discovered in the 'Arabian Gulf', that is, the Red Sea. It is evident that he did not tell the whole story – as a lone survivor, it looks very much that he may have been abandoned by his crew rather than that they died on him – or, of course, that he abandoned them.

In particular, the story is very vague about where he was actually found. The 'Arabian Gulf' is fairly unspecific, and 'the garrison of the Red Sea', who were the soldiers who rescued him, could be from any one of a number of Ptolemaic ports along the African coast of that sea. The southernmost Ptolemaic port, Adulis, for example, would be garrisoned by men familiar with the Bab el-Mandeb, which was close by, and would probably know about the entrepots of Muza and Eudaimon on the Arabian coast. But they would hardly have sent him all the way to Egypt from there; it thus appears that he had sailed a good way north along the Red Sea before being wrecked.

That he came to southern Egypt from the Red Sea suggests that he was forwarded from one of the posts strung along the northern part of the sea, Berenike being the obvious one, but there are other ports even further north. The Ptolemaic garrison, or rather presumably the commander thereof, would have perhaps looked with some suspicion upon a man who could not speak Greek. Rather than making a decision himself, he would more likely have referred the matter up the official bureaucratic ladder. And yet the question then is, how did the sailor end up so far north? We do not know, but the story more or less hangs together, reserving the point that he probably did not necessarily tell the whole truth; there was no need for the captain to have explained everything or that Poseidonios, whose account Strabo was quoting, necessarily included all possible details – or even that Strabo was entirely accurate or complete in his summary.

It is the reaction of Eudoxos and of King Ptolemy that is as interesting as the Indian captain's story. Eudoxos was evidently fired with the desire to take the Indian home and see how the voyage from Egypt to India took place – 'he was known to admire the peculiarities of a region' – that is, he was a born tourist and explorer. And the king, perhaps with some understanding of the wealth of the trade involved, was interested enough to provide him with a ship, a crew and trade goods – 'presents', presumably for the local Indian rulers Eudoxos was to meet; with all this he sent him on his way. Eudoxos succeeded, or rather his Indian refugee captain succeeded, in getting his ship to India, where Eudoxos, a skilled trader, sold the 'presents' that the king had provided, and bought 'a cargo of perfumes and precious stones' to bring back.

Again, however, we are not informed as to where in India they landed, just as the Red Sea port the Indian reached is not known. Despite these gaps in the story there seems no reason to doubt the essential facts that Eudoxos captained a Ptolemaic merchant ship on the first known direct voyage from Egypt to India, piloted by an experienced Indian ship's captain. Since it was a royal voyage, funded by the king, the products with which they returned were taken by the king (although how much of the profits were earlier pocketed by the crew and Eudoxos is not known).

Eudoxos' report to the king (which he presumably made, even if his cargo had been appropriated, a result he would have expected) did not, of course, include information about the Indian Ocean wind system. No doubt, the Indian captain-pilot knew all about the regular monsoon winds, but he may well have kept that information to himself; certainly, Eudoxos did not learn of the whole system of winds in this first voyage, and the Indian captain did not enlighten him. The prospect of regular voyages by Egyptian merchants to Indian ports would undercut the captain's trading prospects – he had clearly been reticent in a number of areas. But another voyager, one who was more sea savvy, worked it out fairly soon. This was Hippalos, who gave his name to the wind system.

It seems that Hippalos, unlike the Indian captain, did broadcast his 'discovery', which led to his name being attached to the wind system, but it was only one of the possibilities that came out of the voyages. Pliny points out that Hippalos' destination in India was Patala, beside the Indus Delta. This had been the port from which Nearchos had sailed two centuries earlier, and it was not one that need be approached by a monsoon; instead, it was clearly reached as easily, and perhaps more safely, by a coastwise voyage. However, further investigation of the winds revealed a slightly different route that took the trader to Sigaros, which was in the Gulf of Cambay, a predecessor of Barygaza and of the later Surat. Still more discoveries then followed to reveal yet another route even further to the south, which took the ships to southern Indian ports, in Kerala and round the southern Cape Comorin to

Coromandel. The port that is particularly noted here was Muziris, though it was said to be difficult to approach because of coastal mudbanks. This sequence of revelations is familiar from the explorations of the sixteenth and seventeenth centuries AD: the first voyage is relatively slow and even unsuccessful, but it led to a known trading port. Its importance was that it opened up various possibilities so that later voyagers had the confidence to seek out different, richer, quicker and more profitable routes.[11]

This was an achievement of Ptolemaic Greek and Egyptian sailors and merchants over an unknown period, and with an unknown but probably significant contribution from Indian and Arabic sailors. By the time Pliny was summarising the information he had[12] – in the mid-first century AD – the whole system was clearly well known, and he knew when and how the winds blew, so that the voyage from Berenike on the Red Sea coast should start before 13 January, and preferably in December, in order for the ship to be able to return during the same year. But the scheme certainly took some work and some time to sort out, probably with as little help from the Indian merchants as they would provide. Hippalos was thus merely the first Greek to detect the overall system; it was then soon being exploited by other merchants.

Strabo suggests that about twenty ships a year made the voyage to India in the Ptolemaic time,[13] and implies that the sailors then regarded the voyages as too dangerous. This trade was perhaps royally financed, with official fleets, and will not account for private or clandestine voyages. Some such unofficial involvement rather suggests itself, because in the reign of Augustus, when Strabo visited Egypt with Aulus Gellius in 25 BC, he could report that 120 'Roman' ships made the voyage to India each year.[14] Either the voyage had suddenly become much safer and more profitable, or many more sailors were suddenly involved. Also, it could be that many more had been making the voyages earlier, without publicity – the Ptolemaic tax inspectors would then be avoided. It was a sufficiently familiar voyage for Queen Cleopatra to plan to evacuate her son Caesarion to India for safety when the Roman conquerors arrived.[15]

Eudoxos sailed on a second voyage to India.[16] This time he was financed by Kleopatra III, who had taken over political control in Egypt soon after the death of Ptolemy VIII in 116, and in the name of her son Ptolemy IX Soter. (It is more complicated than that, but it will be dealt with in the next chapter.) Exactly when the second voyage took place is not certain. The royal family was going through a new crisis following the death of Ptolemy VIII, and the voyage to India was not something within their priorities. It was also a larger expedition (which, since the first was only a single ship, does not necessarily mean a great deal). The ships, therefore, sailed sometime after 116, probably several years after. They reached India, but on their return at least one of the ships, the one carrying Eudoxos, was blown past the entrance to the Red Sea and made a landfall somewhere on the coast of Somalia.

This landfall may well have been at Ras Hafun, a projecting cape 100 miles south of Cape Guardafui, which is the easternmost extension of Africa. Excavations have found an array of successive, but apparently temporary, camp sites there, interpreted as possibly a place where ships' companies waited for a change in the monsoon, though it could also have been a temporary fair, an informal site for exchanging Egyptian and Indian goods well away from tax collectors. The Ras certainly would provide some shelter and could be a base for further explorations south along the African coast.

Eudoxos displayed his ingenuity once more by trading exotic foods (exotic to the inhabitants, that is – Mediterranean products such as figs) in exchange for a supply of water and the services of pilots. The mention of pilots clearly implies that this was an active port, although they could have been local experienced sailors, not professional pilots. He found the prow of a European ship that had been wrecked there earlier, and took it away with him. He then successfully returned to Alexandria, after the winds turned favourable, which suggests he might have sailed from the Red Sea through the canal that had been cut from the Nile to the Red Sea two centuries earlier (and remained in use until the ninth century), or alternatively, he had disembarked at Berenike, crossed to the Nile at Koptos, then sailed down the river. By this time, Kleopatra III was no longer in power, according to Strabo, though she had retained control even after quarrelling with Ptolemy IX, who had fled from Egypt to Cyprus, so this information is not useful in dating the voyage and its ending – though a date after 100 BC is probable. Eudoxos clearly knew what would happen when he arrived, and he had secreted some of the profits of the voyage; this was discovered and 'he was again deprived of everything' – but this is probably what he expected anyway. No doubt, he talked himself out of punishment – he was a plausible fellow. Strabo, in one of his sceptical points, complains that he had not been punished for this delinquency. Eudoxos, however, had succeeded in his main task, and the government did recover his profitable trade goods. Perhaps a first theft, on the first voyage, had finally been discovered and a new and more rigorous search of his ships had been made. (And perhaps the customs men had not found everything.)[17]

He kept the salvaged prow, however – it was scarcely valuable in itself to the finance department – and had it identified by sailors in the city market place. It had a figure of a horse carved on it and the sailors verified this as typical of ships from Gades in Spain. Eudoxos went home to Kyzikos, then set out on a series of attempts to examine the route that he conjectured 'must have' been followed by the Gaditan ship, that is, round Africa. The problem was, of course, that he had no evidence that the original ship had made such a voyage to get to Somalia; it could have been sailed through the Nile–Red Sea canal and along the Red Sea – and the sailors in Alexandria could have been wrong, or could have been deliberately misleading him. He spent the rest of his life on this quest, incurring suspicion from kings and merchants, until finally he did not return from yet another voyage.[18] (Strabo added some more sceptical questions on this to his original list concerning the first voyage.)

The occurrence of incidental – or accidental – discoveries were the two crucial elements in Eudoxos' story. First, there was the rescue of the starving Indian ship's captain, and his presence with the king to whom the man was brought for examination; this led directly to the deliberate implementation and exploitation of the direct sea route to India thanks to the king's interest. Second, there was Eudoxos' own accidental visit to the king's court, and to the Somali coast on his second voyage, which produced the curious figurehead, and his enthusiasm for further exploration.

Eudoxos' discoveries were not of new lands, that is, of unknown lands. India was a well-known and fairly frequently visited country and several of its Greek visitors had published books describing it, including men who had been in the employ of Ptolemaic kings; as an educated and curious man, no doubt Eudoxos consulted these. Somalia was already known, on the evidence of the carved prow of the Gaditan ship – which even if not precisely 'Gaditan', was certainly European in origin and construction – and from the discoveries he made at Ras Hafun. But in both cases, it was the willingness of the Egyptian Greek merchants to exploit these accidental 'discoveries' that ensured they entered general knowledge. The direct voyage to India became the normal voyage route within a few years, especially once Hippalos' 'discovery' of the wind pattern was publicised.

In fact, it is possible to go further, but not in denigrating Eudoxos' achievement, which, together with Hippalos, was clearly decisive in expanding trading opportunities, though as 'discoverer' he cannot be counted. Decades ago, Sir Mortimer Wheeler excavated at Arikamedu on the Coromandel (eastern) coast of South India, and identified it as a port at which merchants from the Roman Empire traded, the evidence being mainly Roman coins and Italian 'Arretine' pottery.[19] More recent re-examinations of the products of the dig in the light of later work have refined and extended his conclusions. In particular, for the purpose of this account, it appears that there is some evidence for trade between the Mediterranean and South India for some time before Eudoxos' voyages.[20] This means that it was already in use by Mediterranean sailors before Eudoxos or, less likely, that the goods from Egypt reached southern India by a series of individual and successive voyages. Certainly, our starving Indian ship's captain had sailed from India to the Red Sea, and was able to pilot Eudoxos' ship back to India, using Hippalos' winds, before that man described them. It looks as though both men were some decades behind the Indian, and possibly some Greek and Egyptian sailors, in utilising the monsoon winds.[21] Even if this clandestine voyaging and trade counts as denigrating Eudoxos' and Hippalos' work, it remains vital that they publicised it, and that Ptolemy VIII provided ships and finance to exploit their revelations on a major and official scale.

The Somali coast had been, in all probability, explored in part from Egypt earlier, for it was the land the earlier Egyptians called Punt, and there is plenty of evidence that they had visited it repeatedly. The *Periplus* records that they were at least three stations along the coast of the former British Somaliland (Auletes = Zeila, Malao = Berbera and Mussollum) – '*auletes*' being one of the names of Ptolemy VIII – and a post with the telling name of Aromaton Emporia on Cape Guardafui itself. These were known in the first century AD and no doubt even earlier. A Ptolemaic post had been established in the area in the third century BC. These occupied the coast east of Djibouti to the Cape.

The Somali coast was nothing like as attractive, or as productive, as India or even Arabia, and was scarcely exploited for some time. The original Ptolemaic purpose in the Red Sea had been to collect ivory, gold and elephants, and even if their ships passed Cape Guardafui, the products of Somalia were not interesting enough to warrant exploitation. And yet, within a century and a half of Eudoxos' visit, in the *Periplus* there is clear knowledge of the East African coast as far as the later Zanzibar and perhaps beyond. Again, the example of Eudoxos and his accidental 'discovery' was eventually followed up. It was only when such men as Eudoxos and Hippalos became involved that this next stage was undertaken. Both men combined avocations as independent merchants and freelance explorers, and as such they were evidently willing to examine the possibilities of an unknown coast or a unknown climate. (One must also include Ptolemy VIII, who was clearly willing to be persuaded, and to finance Eudoxos' first voyage, and Kleopatra III, who financed the even more expensive second voyage.)

Eudoxos' successes in the Indian voyages took some time to produce wider results, for his second voyage, undertaken some years after the first, was still to a large extent exploratory. It took place perhaps about 100 BC – the usually suggested date is before 107 BC – and it was only after that voyage that the trade developed. Strabo reckoned that twenty ships were making the annual voyage to India before the Roman conquest of Egypt (in 30 BC), but that 120 sailed there annually by 25 BC. It is possible that the expansion in the trade was rather greater than these figures imply and almost certainly the expansion was less than sudden. It was no doubt expanding since 100 BC, the approximate date of Eudoxos' second voyage, though probably in an erratic way, dependent on the demand for the products of the trade in Egypt, but if the trade had the capacity to employ 120 ships after Rome's intervention, the number of vessels employed earlier was likely approaching that number. But one effect of the trade itself was the emergent use of more robust ships.

The effects of the revelation of the possibility of direct trade with India were considerable, as one would expect. The first results applied to the merchants in Egypt who wished to become involved, and at once, they discerned a major problem. The voyages, particularly those using the southwest monsoon across the Arabian Sea towards southern India, was somewhat difficult and stormy, and required sturdy ships. This is one part of the trade that was new and was the main Greek contribution to the system. The shipwrecked Indian ship's captain brought to the king appears to have taken Eudoxos to one of the northern Indian ports on his return voyage, to Patala by the Indus Delta or Sigaros on the Gulf of Cambay. The monsoon winds in the north tended to be the lesser violent part of this monsoon; those crossing the Arabian Sea further south were too violent for the small and less robust Indian ships.

The Greek ships now coming into use had been the type that had been constructed in Mediterranean shipyards for centuries, and were stronger in build and had better sailors than those that had developed in the Indian Ocean. This was partly because of the practices of Greek and Roman sea warfare, which demanded strong and well-built vessels, and whose builders transferred their skills to transport ships. It was also partly due to the possible sudden violence in the Mediterranean weather. Both of these conditions needed strong, seaworthy ships. In the Indian Ocean it was the practice not to sail at all at the height of the south-west monsoon, and because of the danger, insurance cover was not available.

It was those sturdy Greek ships that were now entering the Indian seas and were able to use the sea route directly across the Arabian Sea, where many local craft were too flimsy to risk the violence of the monsoon. Indian sailormen, such as our shipwrecked captain, were perhaps more confident in sailing from India westwards on the gentler north-east monsoon than from the Bab el-Mandeb eastwards – but Greek ships could cope well with both voyages.[22]

The trade that developed was almost entirely in luxuries – silk, spices, precious stones, perfumes – high-value, low-volume and low-weight goods, which also promised a high profit margin. For in practice, low value goods were often not easy to preserve on long voyages. But the intervention of Greek ships had wider effects than providing pleasant luxuries for a small percentage of the inhabitants of the Mediterranean world. The trade to and from India was a new type of maritime activity for the merchants and sailors, primarily from Egypt, who were involved. First of all, it required a large amount of capital even to get started, partly for the ships, but also to fund the cargoes, which were expensive to purchase in the first place. Those cargoes, spices and the rest, appear to have been shared by any number of merchants, and perhaps each merchant spread his goods between several ships, just in case, and, of course, insured the goods as well.

Geographically, the rise of this new oceanic trade had effects in Arabia, Egypt and East Africa, and eventually in Rome. The Arabian trade in incense was a well-established one, but mainly along the land routes from Yemen and its neighbourhood towards southern Palestine and Babylonia, where the goods were distributed. This was a trade that had funded the development of political systems at both ends – in the Yemen, and in Nabataea. The Yemeni end had produced a series of competing kingdoms.

There had been four of these kingdoms originally, though probably these were produced by the union or conquest of smaller states. In the late first century BC, these four had become consolidated into one, the kingdom of Himyar. It is difficult to dissociate this political development from the effects of the diversion of some of the incense trade from the land route to the sea. It is impossible in the state of the evidence to describe this process, but it was probably connected with the rise of the port of Qana, on the Arabian Sea coast of Arabia, in the final century BC, an attractive export port for the markets. The end of competition between the kingdoms would no doubt contribute to a deliberate increase in prices, in the normal capitalistic and governmental way.[23]

At the other end of the land route, the kingdom of the Nabataeans emerged in the mid-second century BC, at the time when the Seleukid kingdom had entered its long, painful and terminal decline. It was based, like Himyar, on a major port, in this case Gaza, and on effectively monopolising a large part of the incense trade. It spread its political control from Damascus to Madain Saleh in North Arabia, so that all routes to the Mediterranean ports from inland Arabia were under its effective control. It also concentrated therefore on the lands along the Red Sea, at least the northern part of that sea, and by the time of the Roman conquest of Egypt, it had developed a seagoing fleet capable of tackling the Egyptian naval forces in the Red Sea.[24]

To a degree these effects in Arabia are speculative, but since both Himyar and Nabataea depended on exploiting the incense trade, and grew rich on it, it seems reasonable to assume that it had a great deal to do with their rise in importance. Egypt, of course, also benefited. First was the employment provided for sailors, merchants and shipbuilders, then the profits that were gained by the merchants (not, of course, by the sailors), and these were skimmed by the Egyptian government's taxes when the products arrived at the Egyptian ports. It is evident that Egypt was a much wealthier kingdom in the first century BC than it had been in the mid-second, when Ptolemy VIII could be outspent by one of his officials. It seems obvious that one of the sources of that wealth (much of which went to Rome in tribute and political bribes) was due to the development of a new and exceedingly rich trade.[25]

Eudoxos' visit to the northern Somali coast may have stimulated others to explore the trading possibilities of East Africa, but his experiences – hiring pilots, for example – would imply that in doing so the 'explorers' were linking into an existing trading system. The *Periplus* was able, in the mid-first century AD, to list and briefly describe a string of coastal settlements from Cape Guardafui to about the area of modern Zanzibar, whose small archipelago of islands provides a useful navigation point.[26] It seems likely that the most notable port along the coast, Rhapta, at the southern end of the system, lay beyond Zanzibar, but it has not been satisfactorily located on the ground, and has been suggested to have been at several different locations, from one of Zanzibar's islands to Madagascar.[27]

This expansion along the coast coincided with the explosive expansion of Bantu peoples out of West Africa, some of whom reached East Africa during the first two centuries AD, though the advance groups probably reached East Africa in the first century BC.[28] Connecting the two events seems an impossible conjecture, but between them the two movements populated the whole region south of Ethiopia with farmers as well as the earlier pastoralists, and settlements developed along the ocean coast. Interaction between migrants and sea traders was inevitable, but probably did not develop properly until Muslim times, though it was Ptolemaic mercantile enterprise that is one of the strands of history for the whole area.

The revenue from the Indian trade is impossible to calculate. For a start, it is not clear when the trade really got going. The dating of Eudoxos to 118 for his first voyage, and after 116 for the second, and perhaps 110 or 100 or later for Hippalos, is not the start of the trade, but only marks a series of exploratory voyages that may or may not have turned a profit. Nor is it obvious that all the ships who sailed from the Red Sea returned to Egyptian ports. On these early years of the trade, we are very much in the dark. One item of information that may be relevant is that King Ptolemy Auletes had an annual income of 12,500 talents during his reign (80–51 BC). Of course, this sum includes revenues from various sources, but it is larger than that under Ptolemy II in the third century BC, and the one extra source for royal revenue since that time was the customs duties generated by the Indian trade.

The ports of destination in Egypt, their major market, to which the ships from the east headed, were those that had been developed in the third century for landing the elephants captured in the southern Red Sea lands – Berenike and Myos Hormos, in particular. These had effectively fallen out of use when the south was part of the pharaonic seceding state in the Thebaid from 207 to 185. Then in the second century, the demand for elephants was less than before, partly because it may be that enough of them had been brought to Egypt to establish a breeding group, and partly because African elephants were of little use against the larger and stronger Indians. But it seems that these ports were revived in the first century BC. The appointment of an officer as *strategos* of the Red and Indian seas, which post was in existence by 62, when an official called Kallimachos held the office until 49 BC, suggests that the Ptolemaic government saw a profit in trade in these seas, and was also perhaps conscious of the need to combat piracy that would threaten the Indian ships.

The appearance of this office – which may have existed before 62 BC – coincides with the reign of Ptolemy Auletes and with the refurbishment of the Red Sea ports, which is very suggestive. It may have been this king in whose reign the Indian trade at last became especially notable and profitable. The naming of the post at Zeila after him suggests a renewed interest. But Kleopatra VII's reign, which followed (from 51 BC), was one of heavy taxation, which may have damaged the Indian trade, and of a good deal of internal violence that would do the same. This may be an explanation for Strabo's comment that the number of ships sailing to India with only about twenty under the Ptolemies, but rose to 120 by 25 BC, in so far as either figure is anywhere near accurate. It may have been encouraged by the brief lightening of taxation under Augustus to allow Egypt to stage some sort of economic recovery, and the end of the endemic state violence that would also restrict trade.

It may also be pointed out that at the other end of the trade system, in India, there is very little evidence indeed of any trade during the Ptolemaic period. In the subsequent Roman period, there is certainly evidence, from written sources by Roman writers to archaeological finds and a whole collection of Roman gold coins found in India marking the trade imbalance, which had to be rectified by the export of Roman gold. But for Ptolemaic remains there are a few bits of pottery, and occasional coins (which is not evidence of trade, only that somebody dropped that coin later); indeed, Indian historians pay little attention to this trade, whether from nationalist attitudes or lack of source material in Indian texts is not altogether clear. But most historians do not ignore something that is obvious, and it has to be said that the source material for the Indian trade is almost entirely Western; exaggeration may well have taken place, not to mention speculation and invention.

The reign of Ptolemy VIII, or rather the last few years of that reign, therefore, saw a revival of Ptolemaic activity in the Red Sea that led on directly to the expansion of that activity as far as India and along the East African coast under his several successors. It cannot, however, be asserted convincingly that Ptolemy himself had much to do with this expansion. Unlike the hunts for elephants two centuries before, the Ptolemaic encouragement and participation in the trade was no more than permissive – and exploitative, of course. That is, Ptolemy VIII gave permission and equipment so that Eudoxos could sail to India to return the Indian captain to his home. Later, Kleopatra III financed a second expedition. Only at some distance in time after 100 BC did the Indian trade begin to grow in importance.

Nevertheless, this minimal participation in the new eastern trade by the Ptolemies reveals something in particular about Ptolemy VIII. He is generally portrayed as a fat, self-indulgent, cruel king; this is probably no more than anti-Ptolemy scurrility, and certainly has elements of exaggeration. It must be recalled that he was an author, though his quality is impossible to judge, and here and there, we have indications of his interest in other intellectual matters, his friendship with Aristarchos, for example, or his visit to see King Massinissa. It is to his credit that he quickly understood the significance of the arrival at his court of the starving Indian ship's captain, and either agreed that Eudoxos should be financed in a return voyage or picked out Eudoxos as the most useful man around to conduct that voyage. Ptolemy VIII is thus not quite the fat, scantily dressed, buffoon of our sources. And such a judgment must lie alongside his careful political practices, and his unaggressive foreign policy, if it was also in contrast to his turbulent personal and family relationships.

Chapter 5

A Confusion of Rulers

Ptolemy VIII and Kleopatra II concluded their peace agreement in 124. This is indicated by the dating formula on written documents, by which Ptolemy, Kleopatra II and Kleopatra III were all indicated as joint rulers for several years.[1] The precise reason, or reasons, for reaching an agreement, by which they returned to their original triune joint rule, which is sometimes described as a 'reconciliation', is, or are, unknown, but several can be conjectured, as can some of the terms included. There is no reason to believe that the three were in any way friendly, but both Ptolemy and Kleopatra II were now getting old, in their sixties, and the civil war they had been fighting had dwindled to nothing since Ptolemy had gained control of Alexandria in 127, when Kleopatra II left for refuge in Syria.

In Syria, Kleopatra Thea, daughter of Ptolemy VI and widow of Antiochos VII and Demetrios II, had murdered her son Seleukos V in 126,[2] and perhaps had instigated the murder of her husband Demetrios II at much the same time. For a while, her image alone appeared on the coins, but later it appeared alongside that of her next son (by Demetrios II). This was Antiochos VIII, nicknamed Grypos from his hooked nose. She was therefore, despite her murders of her husband and her son, holding to the strict hereditary system. It was with Kleopatra Thea that Kleopatra II took refuge.

The combination of Kleopatra II and Kleopatra Thea (mother and daughter, of course) may well be the link that brought Ptolemy into the peace process. He had promoted Alexander Zabeinas as king in the Seleukid kingdom back in 128, but by 124 that problem had shifted. It was no longer the issue of preventing an invasion of Egypt by Demetrios II – who was now dead – and Alexander was still unexpectedly fighting; he was able to last longer than expected, no doubt, because there was no Seleukid adult (apart from Kleopatra Thea, originally a Ptolemaic scion) available to dispute the throne with him. With the death of Demetrios II in 126, his purpose, from Ptolemy's point of view, was ended. Demetrios' death also relieved Kleopatra Thea of the threat of facing a renewal of her marriage, while her son King

Antiochos VIII Grypos (the replacement for Seleukos V) was a compliant youth, at least for the moment, devoted as he was to hunting. The civil war in Egypt was now over, but the civil war in Syria sputtered on for a short while longer. Ptolemy VIII, with exquisite ruthlessness, possibly as part of the agreement with his wife, abandoned Alexander, his protégé, and, to make all clear, sent a Ptolemaic military contingent to assist in destroying him.[3] This all meant that the peace agreement that returned Kleopatra II to the palace in Alexandria had also involved the Seleukid royal house, and promoted the end of the civil war there as well as in Egypt.

It may be, of course, that Kleopatra Thea had complained about Alexander's continuing presence in her (as she would by now have called it) kingdom, and she had the military resources, and the example before her of Demetrios' invasion, to be able to make life difficult for Ptolemy – possibly by sending Kleopatra II along with a Seleukid army to reclaim her heritage. (Although her military resources were apparently not sufficient to tackle Alexander, or perhaps he had much better support, given Kleopatra Thea's murderous disposition.) Given the history of these people, it is highly unlikely that the 'reconciliation' that had resulted was any such thing; it was no more than a new, and no doubt fragile, political arrangement, an attempt to return to the old familiar system.

Kleopatra II returned to the joint palace in Alexandria, which she shared with Ptolemy VIII and Kleopatra III and their children, but not to any real power; Ptolemy VIII had arranged the peace, and had won the civil war, so he was now in complete authority in Egypt. Kleopatra Thea was also relieved of the threat of Alexander. Peace resulted, both internationally and internally, in both kingdoms.

This was the background for Ptolemy VIII's sponsorship of Eudoxos and his exploration of the Indian sea route in 119/118 (see Chapter 4). It is unlikely that he would have taken such a step, which involved a significant expenditure of money from the treasury, and no guarantee of a return on his investment, if the royal dispute had still continued. As it was, not only was Eudoxos able to go on his voyage to India and to return with profit, but Ptolemy also issued, six years after the end of the royal disputation (that is, in 118), amnesty decrees that sought to deal with some of the aftermath of the recent fighting in Egypt.[4]

The king could, of course, have issued these decrees, or a version of them, when Kleopatra II had left Alexandria, several years before, when it would have been a clear mark, and a proclamation, of his victory, for the decrees were the sign that the fighting was over. They were not, therefore, issued because the royal dispute had ended, but more likely because that dispute had entailed a long set of other internal issues that needed to be addressed. The size of the problem may be suggested by the elapse of six years between the peace agreement and the amnesty. Rather than investigating and solving all of these problems, disputes and difficulties, the decrees evidently sought to wipe the slate clean, including forgiving unpaid taxes, which, given the problems of Egyptian royal finances, may well have hurt. This was the lazy method to a solution, of course, and it meant that a similar set of problems would collect over the next years, including more failures to pay taxes, or rather there would be an increased need to use force to collect them; anyone who had stolen land from another, or from the state, could both keep his ill-gotten gains, and attempt to do the same again, in the reasonable assumption that he would benefit from yet another amnesty decree.

The issue of problem repetition, because they were not properly attended to in the first place, would not necessarily become obvious for some years, and given Ptolemy VIII's age (he was well over sixty years of age in 118 – Kleopatra II was even older), he probably did not expect to have to confront them, even if he did realise what the result would be – and he surely did; it was not difficult to comprehend. He must have considered those issues were resolved, at least for the moment – and that the future was not his concern, an attitude that was recorded elsewhere. But what was not solved by the 'reconciliation' agreement was the antagonism within the royal family. It was, by 124, a decade since Ptolemy VIII had murdered Kleopatra II's son Ptolemy Memphites – not something she would find it easy to forgive, presumably – and one of the terms of the peace agreement was to add his name to the list of Deified Ptolemies celebrated by the priest of Alexander.[5] At the same time, the two lines of priests of Alexander, one in Alexandria and one 'in the king's camp', which had been a feature of the royal *chora* during the dispute, were amalgamated into the normal one. The records of the priesthood are in fact empty from 132 to 120.

This was possibly a conciliatory gesture by Ptolemy, though he was hardly known for such gestures, or it was, perhaps more likely, part of Kleopatra II's price for making peace with him. She clearly had useful cards to play if she chose. There was no need for Ptolemy to make such a concession unless he was compelled, particularly since he was, by adding the boy's name to the deified list, in effect admitting to blasphemy of the worst sort, the killing, notably, of a potential god. It must have been difficult for him to accept this, and as such, it hardly amounted to a reconciliation; it was more an item in a peace treaty between independent powers. And it was a sign that the enmities within the family continued, not that they had been resolved.

Ptolemy VIII also had to deal with his other wife, Kleopatra III. She was scheming to secure the future succession. At least she did not have to shoulder any stepchildren out of her way, since the children of Kleopatra II and Ptolemy VI had been killed (except for Kleopatra Thea, who was well catered for in Syria, and would not last for long, anyway). But Kleopatra III had two sons, eventually to be Kings Ptolemy IX and Ptolemy X. Ptolemy IX was the elder, aged twenty-four in 118; he had been given the surname Soter, as a reference to the first of the family to be king. The second, however, was given the name Alexander – a ruler even more exalted in political and Egyptian memory. In 118, Kleopatra III persuaded Ptolemy VIII to appoint her eldest child as governor general of Cyprus, and he was provided also with a complete set of official posts: *strategos*, *nauarchos* and *archiereus*, that is, commander of the army, commander of the fleet, and chief priest, as if being the eldest son of the king was not enough.[6] When he took over in the island, the existing *strategos*, Helenos, was demoted to *tropeos*, 'helper' of Ptolemy, though no doubt he did the bulk of the real work.

The purpose of Ptolemy IX's promotion could be said to be to give the young man the experience of governing, and this was often the purpose of promoting the eldest royal sons. But here it seems that the main purpose was to move him out of the royal court and away from Alexandria, so that the way was opened for his (younger) brother to be made the successor to his father Ptolemy VIII in Egypt. It was the same ploy that had moved Ptolemy Memphites to Cyrene, and may have been intended to have the same result. That is, the old and continuing enmities within the royal family had been supplemented by a new one. If there was a more certain way of promoting a new civil dynastic war, no one could have found one.

This appointment took place probably in 118, in the year of the amnesty decrees, and only a year or so before Ptolemy VIII's death (which took place on 28 July 116);[7] that coincidence rather implies that he was ailing by then, and was expected to die fairly soon. It appears, however, that, whatever his state of health, Ptolemy knew exactly what he was doing, for he also planned that Ptolemy Apion, his son by the concubine Eirene, should go to rule in Cyrenaica. With one son in Cyrenaica, and one in post in Cyprus, the empire was likely to be safe for the moment – unless these subordinates shifted into independence. So the appointment to Cyprus was presumably not necessarily such an exile as it might seem. To keep his three sons apart might have been Ptolemy's solution to preventing the expected fighting between him and his wives.

He had also recently disposed of two of his three daughters. The second, Kleopatra IV, had been married to her brother Ptolemy IX Soter some time before, when both were children; they had a daughter, Berenike, born about 115.[8] In 124/123, Ptolemy VIII's eldest daughter, Tryphaina, was married to Antiochos VIII Grypos of the Seleukid family at the time when Ptolemy reversed his Syrian policy to remove Alexander Zabeinas; we may thereupon assume that this marriage was another part of the political agreement that settled peace in both Syria and Egypt – it was perhaps part of the price Kleopatra Thea exacted.[9] The third girl, Selene, had remained unmarried for the present. Having been born in the early 130s, though, she was certainly of marriageable age by 117. As a Ptolemaic princess, however, she could only be married to a Ptolemy or to a reigning king, and only her youngest brother, Ptolemy X, was available, unless yet another Seleukid was chosen (or even Ptolemy Apion); but Ptolemy X was apparently married already, although his wife's name is not known, and perhaps he refused to add a second wife, or to divorce his first. If so, it would make a nice change.

The sequence of appointments and marriages, which took place between 124 and 118, was clearly organised by Ptolemy VIII with the purpose of arranging the succession in an acceptable and accepted way, and of disposing of possible problems beforehand. The weak part in the scheme was the choice of Ptolemy X as his successor in Egypt, apparently at Kleopatra III's behest, since he was her favourite child. This involved displacing the elder brother, who had been holding offices and posts that indicated he had been seen as the 'crown prince' for some years.[10] But even the choice of a younger son as successor was not without precedent in the family, for Ptolemy II had been chosen as his heir by Ptolemy I instead of his elder half-brother Keraunos. (On the other hand, this expedient had not been repeated, and male primogeniture had been the rule since then, through six generations.)

The result of the new choice was a serious division in the family. The imposition of the surnames Soter and Alexander on the brothers was a clear sign that the king was highly conscious of his heritage – he had even composed a book on the subject. Ptolemy IX may not have liked being superseded by his brother, and no doubt he complained, but it was a decision well within the king's competence, even if he was doing so to please one of his wives, which seems to be the case, or even to spite the other wife, which is perfectly possible. And yet Ptolemy IX did have a legitimate complaint, in that he had for several years been recognised as the king's successor, and was now being deprived of the results of that expectation, and superseded by a much less experienced heir.

The family agreement of 124 that brought to an end the civil warfare in both Syria and Egypt is never detailed in any source, but several of those details are evident from the measures taken when the main participants, Ptolemy VIII and Kleopatra II, concluded their agreement in that year, and some have emerged from the discussion in this chapter so far. First, we may instance the return of Kleopatra II to Alexandria and to her position as a ruling queen along with her brother and her daughter, obviously an attempt to return to the dynastic compromise that had existed before the civil war. The deification of Ptolemy Memphites would seem to be another item in this agreement, no doubt insisted on by Kleopatra II. Third was the joint Seleukid-Ptolemaic military expedition to suppress the awkwardly persistent Alexander Zabeinas – Ptolemy had promoted him in the first place and it was to a degree his responsibility to suppress him. The marriage of Tryphaina, Ptolemy VIII's eldest daughter, to Antiochos VIII Grypos, was probably also part of the treaty. (Eldest Ptolemaic daughters were usually reserved for marriage to their brother.) These were the main obvious terms, but there were other issues that derived from the agreement, including the question of the Ptolemaic succession (and perhaps that of the Seleukid succession also), and also the government of Cyprus and Cyrenaica. The former at least seems to have been involved in the settlement. Ptolemy VIII may well have felt some satisfaction that he had sorted out so many problems.

However, much of this was abandoned by Kleopatra III when Ptolemy VIII died in 116. His will apparently did not specify the successor, other than that the kingship was to be decided by Kleopatra III, and she was to install as king whichever of her sons she should choose; in other words, he was confirming the exile to Cyprus of Ptolemy IX.[11] The concession to Kleopatra III may have been a desperate measure designed to prevent trouble after his death, but with Ptolemy VIII's recent plans ignored as soon as he was dead, all his dispositions, of Cyprus and Cyrenaica as well as Egypt, now failed. And he had set up a situation in the royal family that inevitably led to more disputes.

The sources for subsequent events are confused and somewhat contradictory,[12] no doubt the reflection of the confused situation and of the propaganda messages produced from all sides. It appears that the news of Ptolemy VIII's death, and that Kleopatra III was to be the executor of his will, brought immediate opposition. Kleopatra II, still alive and angry, objected, and perhaps relished an opportunity to displace her daughter from power; she had no personal interest in the heirs, since they were all Kleopatra III's children, but no doubt she was keen to thwart her daughter, and to upset whatever plans her husband had made. In Syria, Kleopatra Thea had scrupulously adhered to primogeniture despite having murdered and attempted to murder her children – and herself was now dead at the hand of her son. Kleopatra II could appeal to the normal tradition that the eldest son of a deceased king should inherit. She could also appeal to the Alexandrians, and to the army, that a more mature king was required. (The age of Ptolemy X is not actually clear, but he was certainly some years younger than his brother, perhaps by half a dozen years.) The Alexandrians had supported Kleopatra II in the recent civil war, and even before in the succession wars of the past, and they now came out to support her again. They were supported by elements of the army, which were in Alexandria, in order to block Kleopatra III. The result of the crisis was that Ptolemy IX Soter was installed as king in Alexandria, and the two queens continued in their roles as joint rulers with him.[13] So the previous triple arrangement was continued, but with Ptolemy IX replacing his father.[14] Ptolemy X Alexander was thus sidelined, no doubt angry at being thwarted of his father's intention. This arrangement was in existence by October of 116, according to papyrus documents, but that is only the earliest reference in a document; it could have been organised and instituted earlier.

The disappointed Ptolemy X Alexander was sent to govern Cyprus in his brother's place.[15] Ptolemy Apion was not allowed to take up his proposed role as king in Cyrenaica, where the inscriptions indicate that Ptolemy IX governed for several years.[16] This shuffling of positions had to be changed yet again before the end of the year, because Kleopatra II died in November or December of 116. So from then on there were, once more, two rulers, Queen Kleopatra III and King Ptolemy IX – his mother is always named first, and clearly she had the greater authority. The king gathered nicknames, like his father – Lathyrus ('chick-pea') and Physkon ('fatty'), which latter had applied to his father also; their grossness was perhaps genetic. The placing of the queen ahead of her son reflected their relative power in the state.

Ptolemy IX, perhaps in a vain attempt to secure some power from his mother's grasp, became the priest of Alexander and the Deified Ptolemies (who now included his murdered half-brother Memphites) in 116. This was a union of the kingship and the most prestigious priesthood, an unprecedented concentration, and was an obvious attempt to consolidate and increase his royal authority, probably deliberately engineered by Ptolemy to distinguish himself from his dominating mother – he also went on a long visit to the south, as far as Elephantine Island, to sacrifice to the 'Great God Nile', travelling alone, or at least without his mother.[17] Kleopatra had acquired a number of cults in southern Egypt since 145, in her own attempt to elevate herself. Perhaps Ptolemy was emulating her. Another priesthood for her was established in 130, when she had been expelled from Alexandria with her husband; she was also worshipped as identical with the goddess Isis. The earlier priesthoods were developed as part of her rivalry with her mother, then later in competition with her son; as a woman she could not become priest of Alexander, hence the multiplication of other cults, associating her with various gods. It was a family duel, priesthoods at ten paces.[18]

It is curious that Kleopatra III should suddenly emerge in her new role as an active ruler, after almost thirty years of being overwhelmed by her husband, but perhaps she had learned the main lessons of ruling from him. Certainly, she could be as cruel. It also suggests that she had been ambitious for such power all along; she had thus followed her mother and her cousin Kleopatra Thea as well as her husband. The many priesthoods developed for her imply a multiplication of sponsorships of priests and temples, building up her own clientele. She emerged from the succession crisis of 116 as the dominant force, but with her favoured son, Ptolemy X Alexander, consigned to Cyprus, and her less favoured son, Ptolemy IX Soter, as her governing partner in Alexandria.

Cyprus had become more important within the Ptolemaic scheme of things in the previous half-century, ever since the Seleukids Antiochos IV and then Demetrios I had vainly attempted to seize it, and since the Ptolemaic posts in the Aegean were abandoned in 145. It functioned as a forward defence for Egypt by sea, as a source of several minerals, a shipbuilding centre, and as a base for further expeditions, for example against Asia Minor or Syria. It also served as a refuge for exiled Ptolemies, and a place to dump unwanted aristocrats and unrequired intellectuals, like Aristarchos. At some point, perhaps in the last few years before Ptolemy IX was briefly ruler of the island in 118–116, the main naval base and the governing centre had been moved from Salamis on the east coast to Paphos on the west.[19] This was no doubt a reaction to the arrival of Roman power in the Aegean, since in naval terms the Roman naval forces were the most obvious threat, and the Aegean bases, which might have kept an eye on Roman activities, had gone. At Paphos, the ships were 100 miles closer to the main threat than in Salamis. There was also a growth of piracy in the region, originally fuelled by the Seleukid civil wars in the 140s, and now there were pirate bases in Kilikia just to the north of Cyprus, and in Crete to the west.[20] The island also, as it soon became clear, had a substantial military garrison; Kilikia, besides being a base for pirates, was also a major source of mercenaries, who probably composed the major part of the military forces in the island.[21]

The series of governors of Cyprus in the reign of Ptolemy VIII is known.[22] The first was a man called Seleukos of Rhodes, who had been associated with Ptolemy VI in Alexandria in the 150s. He was appointed as Cypriot *strategos*, or governor general in 144 or 143, and held the post until 131. He was succeeded by an official called Krokos, who in turn was succeeded in 124 by Theodoros, the son of Seleukos, possibly the governor who preceded Krokos. Theoderos was in turn succeeded by Ptolemy IX in 118 on his appointment by Ptolemy VIII, probably at the instance of Kleopatra III.

The dates of the changes appear, in so far as they are accurate, to be in close relationship to the events in the dynasty at the time, and therefore are a clue as to the loyalties of Seleukos and Theodoros. Their periods in office coincide precisely with the times when Kleopatra II was in power in Egypt, and not just in Alexandria, between 145 and 131, and between 124 and 118. Seleukos ceased to govern Cyprus when Kleopatra began her rebellion in 131, and his son returned to that office in the year of the treaty between Ptolemy VIII and Kleopatra II, which brought her back to the palace in Alexandria and so in a position to influence such appointments. (Seleukos had a great-granddaughter by 131, so he was of a considerable age and it is doubtful if he survived for long after that date.) If this linkage is so, then Krokos was a creature of Ptolemy VIII, installed to displace Seleukos so as to be sure that the king retained control of Cyprus and its valuable garrison and ships; he had, after all, fled along with Kleopatra III to the island when

Kleopatra II began her rebellion, so he no doubt installed a new, but loyal, governor as soon as he arrived.[23]

The return of Seleukos' family to power in the island in 124 was thus yet another part of the dynastic agreement of that year, in which a loyal partisan of Kleopatra II displaced Ptolemy's man. And so we have yet a further explanation for the appointment of Ptolemy IX to the island in 118 – not just to gain governing experience, but to remove an official loyal to Kleopatra II from power in the island, and to allow Ptolemy VIII to gain relatively full control once more. No wonder Kleopatra II seized power again when Ptolemy VIII died, even if for no more than three or four months before her death; the eight years since her return had clearly been a tense time in the palace.

The deaths, within a few months, of Ptolemy VIII and Kleopatra II left Kleopatra III in power from the end of 116, and it was now her turn to dispose of the lives of her children as she wished. It appears that Ptolemy IX had been married to Kleopatra IV, his sister, since childhood; she now compelled them to be divorced, and Ptolemy was then married to his youngest sister, Selene. The purpose of this manoeuvre is unclear, though it is possible that Kleopatra IV was urging her husband to oppose her mother; presumably, she was now intended to marry Ptolemy X, but being a divorced princess, she was less under her mother's control and she decamped to Cyprus intent on pursuing her own scheme.

The Seleukid kingdom had seen a decade of peace after the destruction of Alexander Zabeinas, but in 114/113, a new internal war began, when Antiochos IX Kyzikenos, the son of Antiochos VII and Kleopatra Thea, emerged from exile in Kyzikos and claimed the throne from Antiochos VIII Grypos, who had been king since 126. It appears that Kleopatra IV's scheme was for her to marry Kyzikenos and so become queen in Syria in place of her divorced position as queen in Egypt. In Cyprus, she recruited a substantial armed force, presumably from among the mercenaries in the island, and perhaps from other mercenaries overseas such as Kilikia, and then took herself and her soldiers across to Syria.[24] There she was married to Kyzikenos. This certainly has the appearance of a pre-concerted move between them, for the arrival of Kleopatra's army from Cyprus was the signal for Antiochos, who cannot have had much of an army until then, to begin his (and Kleopatra's) attempt to claim the Seleukid monarchy.

Antiochos IX's initial attack was successful and he overran almost the whole of Seleukid Syria. But then, Grypos revived and recovered most of his kingdom. In 112, the war had settled into a siege of Antioch by Antiochos VIII's forces. Kleopatra IV was beleaguered inside the city. She was presumably unable to get out, or perhaps she had taken command of the defence. As a result, when Grypos' forces were successful in taking the city, Kleopatra had to take refuge in a temple, possibly at the holy grove of Daphne, hoping for sanctuary. But on the opposing side was her sister Tryphaina, Antiochos Grypos' wife, who insisted, possibly against her husband's wishes, that Kleopatra should be killed.[25] (Justin makes a long moan over this, but the details he includes are less than convincing.) Apart from Justin's curious justifications, it is fairly clear that the reason for Tryphaina's vengeance is that Kleopatra and her army had been instrumental in stimulating Kyzikenos' cause, and that Kleopatra herself had animated the defence of Antioch. If blame was to be cast, Kleopatra was the perfect victim. Antiochos, her husband, might complain, but he was Tryphaina's and Grypos' enemy already and there would be no doubt that if either Grypos or Kyzikenos had been captured by the enemy, the prisoner would have been killed. Tryphaina had faced the likelihood of death also if Kyzikenos had won, or at best exile, refugee status, and possible poverty. Her anger is quite understandable, if not her solution. Kleopatra III and Ptolemy IX could hardly complain either – and there is no indication that they did – since Kleopatra IV had cut her ties with them already. A revenge campaign must have seemed most unlikely given Tryphaina's justifications.

It is possible that Tryphaina's action, on the other hand, re-stimulated Antiochos Kyzikenos, for he recovered somewhat from his defeat, and in moving south again succeeded in capturing Tryphaina herself during the campaign. He, of course, had her executed, citing the need to appease the ghosts of his wife and her sister, though personal revenge is just as likely.[26] (He may also have lost the services of Kleopatra's army after she died.) In the Seleukid kingdom, therefore, two kings and three queens had been murdered in the past ten or so years.

Not surprisingly after these atrocities, the civil war in Syria became institutionalised and atrocities became endemic. It therefore lasted throughout the rest of the lives of the two rival kings; it was likened by Josephos to a wrestling match between equally matched contestants, neither of whom could either prevail or cease to fight.[27] Not only did the situation render the Seleukid kingdom internationally powerless, it opened the kingdom to interference from without.

For a time the Ptolemies were less aggressive, but just as unpleasantly disputatious among themselves (though Kleopatra III did finance Eudoxos' second voyage). Kleopatra IV had filched part of the Cypriot garrison for her Syrian adventure without any protest, so it seems, from Ptolemy Alexander, who was in control in the island, and who had claimed the title of king in defiance of his family.[28] The administration of the island in fact seems to have been in the hands of his *tropheos* ('helper'), a soldier called Helenos, who had not objected either. At that point, Helenos, who had been *strategos* before Ptolemy Alexander arrived, and had remained as his *tropheos*, now returned to the status of *strategos* he had held before Ptolemy's arrival.[29] These two might claim that Kleopatra IV had taken the troops away to Syria without their knowledge, but it is much more likely that they knew all along what was going on. How can a non-military woman take away a whole army without the two commanders, one of whom was an experienced military administrator, knowing about it? Ptolemy Alexander had himself been demoted, as he might have said, when he had to exchange Egypt for Cyprus in 116; he would undoubtedly relish the opportunity to act against his mother. The death of Kleopatra IV in Syria, of course, was almost as great a disaster to them as to Antiochos IX, supposing they were her allies, as her use of their army suggests, since a large part of the Cypriot garrison had disappeared with her. It has to be noted that, of the five kings in Egypt and Syria in the period after Ptolemy VIII's death, none showed any real regal energy or military ability, though the queens did exhibit a certain crude and unpleasant cruelty and strength.

The visit of Scipio Aemilianus and his colleagues to Egypt and the east in 140 and after may have had little result in political terms, as it was probably intended as an investigation rather than aimed at a diplomatic initiative. He did, however, mark the interest of Rome in Syria and Egypt, so that the turbulent dynastic members were fully preoccupied with their own affairs.

Aemilianus' visit may well have encouraged Roman merchants to trade with Egypt, and, not surprisingly, in a feedback loop, increased commerce with Egypt then attracted the attention of Roman senators. As it happens, of course, this period – the late second and early first centuries BC – is poor in historical sources, and it is probable that a number of senatorial visits may be missing from the record, while the visits of Roman merchants are rarely noted, unless they became involved in political affairs. But there are three records of Romans in Egypt between 130 and 112 that may exemplify what was going on.

During the troubles in Alexandria in 131–127, a group of Roman shipowners and merchants were caught up in the city's problems. They had no doubt arrived to trade, probably singly, but found they could not leave, for whatever reason. They were assisted to leave by Lochos, son of Kallimedes, a royal kinsman (and governor general of the Thebaid from 127/126),[30] acting it seems on behalf of Ptolemy VIII. Having escaped from the city – no doubt in the situation there any foreigner would be in danger from the Alexandrian rioters – they stopped off at Delos to set up an inscription to Apollo giving thanks to the king, Queen Kleopatra (III) and Lochos for their survival and escape.[31] The date is not stated, but the threat to them came at the time of the capture of the city, which was in 127, when Kleopatra II fled, carrying off the royal treasure.

Ten years later, a group of Romans were at Philae, in the far south of the country, and carved their names, in Latin, on a statue.[32] The date was 116, when there was trouble in Alexandria again, as a consequence of Ptolemy VIII's death, his will, in which he effectively abdicated responsibility for the future, and the death of Kleopatra II at the end of the year, and the tussle for power between the two women. But the *chora* was apparently safe for the Roman tourists, if that is what the graffiti artists were. They were certainly a long way from their arrival point (which was probably Alexandria) and had travelled all the way to the southern border of the kingdom.

These visits were by private individuals, but the third item is more formal, and is recorded this time on papyrus, a set of instructions by a local official, Hermias, to a subordinate in the Fayum, detailing the treatment to be provided to a Roman senator, L. Memmius, on his visit to the region in 112 BC. The accommodation was to be clean, the beds also, food was to be supplied, and 'titbits' were to be handed over for the delectation of the sacred crocodiles. He was visiting a region of dense Greek settlement, and to be given a glimpse of the exotic Egyptian religious practices. This has led to the visit being described as a tourist wander, which it clearly was in part, though it is unlikely that a Roman senator would be merely playing the tourist in Egypt in 112, and the fragmentary record that survives deals only with a single incident – we do not know where else he went, or what he did.[33] We can be reasonably sure, however, that, even if he was making a private visit, he would be reporting on events and the country to the Senate on his return to Rome. And the merchants who were helped by Ptolemaic officials would no doubt comment on this to all and sundry back in Rome, just as they publicised their gratitude in the inscription at Delos.

This was when the Syrian civil war was at its nastiest, and this clearly involved the Ptolemies at least at one remove, for a Ptolemaic princess had included herself in the situation. It would be natural that the Roman Senate would be interested in, even concerned about, the turmoil in the east, now that Greece and western Asia Minor were their territory. One must assume that Memmius was on an official senatorial visit, and the arrangements being made for his comfort have all the appearance of being intended as a way of displaying Egypt and its products, and as a touristic distraction for an inquisitive Roman official. It was also the case, no doubt, that he was being guided to certain places on his tour, and diverted from others. That is, his investigative intentions were understood in Egypt, and the bureaucracy was busy making sure that his report to the Senate was as favourable as the clerks could contrive.

A stalemated civil war in Syria would probably suit the Ptolemaic government of Kleopatra III perfectly, as long as the fighting did not spill over into Egypt, as it had with Demetrios II. If it did, of course, the Ptolemaic rulers had only themselves to blame for their interference. Kleopatra IV may have gone into Syria on her own initiative, but any Syrian king or queen could turn her professed reasons into acts of hostility if required. The effect in Syria of the stalemated civil war was thus to promote the continuing disintegration of that kingdom. This took the form of units of the kingdom acquiring, or taking, their independence, which is marked for modern researchers by their producing their own coins rather than the royal versions. The Phoenician cities were especially adept at this – Arados had been the first, and Tyre, Sidon and Tripolis went that route after 111 – but those in Palestine then followed.[34] The Jewish kingdom of the Maccabee dynasty, by its unrelenting hostility to the Seleukid state, was a prime agent in this integration. It also spread to the great cities of the north, where Seleukeia-in-Pieria was independent by 109.[35] The Ptolemies watched this with considerable interest, no doubt, but also some apprehension, and were always on the lookout for their own profit.

But the real concern of the Ptolemaic dynasty was with its own internal relationships. The removal of two of Kleopatra III's daughters in 112 and

111 left only a single daughter, Semele, who was married to Ptolemy IX; they had two sons. After their earlier disputes, Kleopatra III and Ptolemy IX were not compatible, unsurprisingly. We do not know the details but the decisive break came in 107. It is said that Ptolemy was plotting to overthrow Kleopatra; it is also said that this was a rumour spread by Kleopatra to provide a reason to oust Ptolemy. Whatever the truth (and one would rather credit the plot than the rumour), Ptolemy took the hint and fled to Cyprus. There he displaced Ptolemy X Alexander, who left the island and went to Pelusion in the eastern Delta, perhaps by arrangement with Kleopatra III, perhaps on his own initiative. But Kleopatra needed a king through whom to work, and took him back. Ptolemy IX meanwhile had left Semele and their children in Alexandria; the names of the two children are not known, though they are said to have been boys, and soon vanished.[36]

Ptolemy X therefore was now king in Egypt, with Kleopatra III's thumb firmly pressed on him. It is possible he was married to Semele on his arrival in Egypt, though this is not recorded – they certainly lived in the palace in Alexandria, and Kleopatra III ruled the roost there, and had form in juggling the marriages of her children. Meanwhile, Ptolemy IX took control in Cyprus, and also retained control of Cyrenaica. Once more, the family reshuffle, the royal game of wife-swapping, settled into a tense equilibrium, which lasted for several years.

Chapter 6

The 'War of Sceptres': A Final Syrian War

The displacement of Ptolemy IX Soter from Egypt and his brother from Cyprus in 107, so that they took each other's places, scarcely solved the Ptolemaic dynastic problem, probably because the real power remained with Kleopatra III in Alexandria. Similarly, the earlier murders of two of her daughters in Syria did not solve the Seleukid dynastic problem either, and the disputes between them all remained alive. And since they were – Ptolemaic and Seleukid kings and princes and queens – all related to each other in various ways, these domestic disputes in Egypt and Syria overlapped and reinforced each other in what amounted to a mutual war, both civil and international.

The result of this tangle is that it is a terribly complicated story, only partly known; in the absence of full sources, modern accounts tend to focus on one or other of the participants – Seleukid, Ptolemaic, Maccabee and Roman – so that only partial views of the events are discussed.[1] And into the mix comes the shift into independence of many cities and peoples in Syria, as the Seleukid kingdom disintegrated into a continuing, indeed never-ending, civil war, for this war was hardly a straightforward contest between Ptolemies and Seleukids as had been the case with the previous eight 'Syrian Wars'.[2]

Already while he was king in Egypt, Ptolemy IX had intervened in the warfare in Palestine when the leader of the Jewish state, John Hyrkanos, laid siege to the Macedonian colonial city of Samaria, beginning in 109 and lasting a full year – it was clearly a blockade rather than an active siege. Ptolemy sent a force of 6,000 Ptolemaic troops from Egypt to assist Antiochos Kyzikenos, who had been defeated by Hyrkanos' son in his first attempt to relieve the city.[3] Josephus says that Ptolemy sent this force to Syria against Kleopatra III's wishes. In the previous years these two had quarrelled severely enough so that Ptolemy had twice been expelled from Egypt by his mother – or had left to escape her – once in 110/109 and again in 108.[4] It appears that he moved to Cyrenaica, at least in his flight in 108, and probably stayed there until tempers had cooled.[5]

Kleopatra was probably correct to object to the expedition in Judaea, because Kyzikenos was defeated once again, even with the reinforcement of 6,000 Ptolemaic troops. He withdrew to Tripolis, and Samaria was then captured and razed to the ground at Hyrkanos' orders (November 108).[6]

It is possible that interference from Rome was involved here. Hyrkanos had earlier contacted Rome and Josephos claims that the two had made an alliance. For Rome, of course, this was a minor matter, but the city welcomed anything that weakened the Seleukid kingdom. It seems that Hyrkanos had activated this alliance in the crisis of Kyzikenos' attack, and Rome had responded with a *senatus consultum*, which was included by Josephus by mistake in a decree from Pergamon. It pretended to protect the Jewish state and ordered 'Antiochos son of Antiochos' to restore the lands he had taken, including Joppa.[7]

The identity of the 'Antiochos' mentioned must be Kyzikenos, and the details mentioned suggest that he had succeeded rather more in his attacks on Judaea than Josephus allows. And since Kyzikenos did in fact evacuate his conquests, however considerable they were, it may be that the Roman message had an effect. It may also be, of course, that Antiochos never heard of the Roman intervention, but retreated because his forces were being defeated; the coincidence of the appeal to Rome and his retreat therefore allowed the Jews to assume that their alliance with Rome was effective. There seems little reason for Kyzikenos to pay any attention to such feeble Roman demands.

This was one of the items on Kleopatra's charge sheet when Ptolemy IX made his third escape, this time to Cyprus, the year after, in 107, though most probably it was not the only cause of his exile, as Josephos claims. Kleopatra claimed to be, or at least acted as, the Egyptian ruler, placing her name before her sons' names on coins and in documents, and no doubt this subordination was the basic cause of their resentment. Ptolemy's decision to send Ptolemaic troops to Palestine was a clear attempt to escape his mother's authority, by acting on his own in and in defiance of her. No doubt, another cause of his need to escape was that Ptolemy IX Soter had conducted his own foreign policy, also without her approval. A display of independence like this was one that she could not tolerate; he possibly feared for his life while in her proximity. Ptolemy Soter, however, was also correct, if in a rather personal way, in that the best available route to power in Egypt was through the warfare in Syria. Kleopatra was clearly in full control in Egypt, hence Ptolemy's need to use foreign policy as his break for independence.

The victory of Hyrkanos at Samaria was a major step forward for the Jewish state. It had originated as a rebellion against Seleukid rule, and against Greek culture and religious practices. It was centred on the hills in the area of Jerusalem, and had developed into an expanding autonomous state, which moved into complete independence in 129, after the death of Antiochos VII in the Parthian War. Hyrkanos had loyally participated in support of Antiochos in the war in Iran, but had brought his troops out safely after the Seleukid defeat and had returned with his own forces, scarcely damaged, to Judaea.[8]

This gave him a political edge, because much of the Seleukid army in Iran had been killed, captured or dispersed, and the government was thereby disorganised, while the population generally was in shock. A good proportion of the survivors managed to return eventually, but the kingdom was very badly damaged, even so. Hyrkanos set about establishing his state's independence and slowly expanded his territory. One of his first acts had been to destroy the Samaritan temple on Mount Gerizim, above Samaria; refugees from this attack went to the city, which already had a considerable Samaritan population.[9] It was not only Seleukid rule and Greek culture that the resurgent Jews objected to.

Samaria had been a foundation of Alexander the Great's, who established a colony of Macedonians at the site. The Samaritans, a dissident Jewish sect who had killed the previous Macedonian governor, thereby provoking Alexander's attack, were subjected to Macedonian rule by the foundation of the city, but developed their own temple to the south, outside the city on Mount Gerizim. There were thus two reasons for Hyrkanos' attack on the city, to destroy the Samaritan community (he had already destroyed the temple), and to remove a well-fortified Seleukid city that was blocking his expansion northwards.[10]

With the conquest of Samaria, Hyrkanos had achieved a compact and defensible principality centred on the Judaean Highlands, with extensions eastward beyond the Jordan and to the west to Joppa (now relinquished by Kyzikenos) on the Mediterranean coast, which provided a valuable port for trade and communications. This territory thus separated the remaining Seleukid territories in the south into those north of Judaea, and those south of Joppa – but each of these areas was dotted now with cities that had asserted their independence, a fact usually visible now mainly by their practice of producing their own coinages. Gaza, for example, began coining its own currency in 104, and between it and Joppa on the coast there were at least two more independent states, Ashkelon and Strato's Tower.

Ptolemy Soter was pushed out of (or fled from) Egypt in late 107. He had to leave his wife, Selene, and their two children behind, though whether this was his choice, or at Kleopatra's insistence, is not known. But it did mean that Kleopatra had control of two Ptolemaic family members who were possible alternative kings to either Ptolemy IX or X.[11] The relationship of mother and son had been bad before he had sent troops to Palestine, and he had twice been expelled from Egypt, but now a rising in Alexandria, supposedly orchestrated by Kleopatra, finally persuaded him to leave,[12] and he went to Cyprus. This left the mercenary force he had loaned to Kyzikenos in Palestine, where it was taken over by Kyzikenos' commanders. It was, however, damaged by Maccabean guerilla attacks.[13]

Ptolemy X Alexander, who had ruled Cyprus for nine years, now finally moved to Egypt, summoned by his mother to take the place of Ptolemy IX Soter. It is likely, though not certain, that he had been ordered to Egypt already by Kleopatra before Ptolemy Soter left, and was waiting at Pelusion to complete his journey.[14] This fact, when known, would be a clear threat to Ptolemy IX's life, as well as his position.

Ptolemy Soter's arrival in Cyprus as a refugee from Egypt gave him access to the considerable armed force that was already assembled in the island, both naval and military. His mother, conscious of this, sent an expedition after him, which arrived early in 106 and seized the island, but not Ptolemy himself. He escaped to refuge in Seleukeia-in-Pieria, which had recently secured its own autonomy by agreement with Antiochos Kyzikenos.[15] Kleopatra's reaction to this was to execute the commander of the expeditionary force for this loss, and to suborn one of Ptolemy's own entourage to attempt to assassinate him. The first ploy succeeded, but the second failed.[16] This makes it clear that the aim had been to eliminate Ptolemy IX altogether, and that his removal out of Egypt was an escape indeed.

Presumably Kleopatra, too confident, then withdrew some at least of her own forces from the island, for Ptolemy was able to return in the autumn of 106 with a newly recruited force (or it may be the remains of the force he had lent to Kyzikenos) and succeeded in recovering his lost Cypriot kingdom. He was evidently in full control of the island by September 105.[17]

Ptolemy IX and Kleopatra III were now at open war with each other, and there was little chance of a reconciliation between them, after their hostile histories. Any political or military move by either of them has therefore to be seen in the light of this mutual hostility. Ptolemy spent a year establishing his control in Cyprus. He reorganised its administration, and, in particular, recruited more troops.[18] He was also, of course, looking to find a way to return to Egypt. The fact that he does not seem to have attempted a direct invasion of the country suggests that the defences were well equipped and alert.

He did have two possible alternatives to a direct attack. He ruled Cyrenaica – where he seems to have spent his short periods of exile from Egypt in the last few years – as well as Cyprus, and a march along the Mediterranean coast might well have been worth trying, or perhaps a landing on that coast near to Egypt, but either of these led through the desert for several days' march to end up at the all too well-fortified Alexandria. The alternative was to go through Palestine, which would involve a good deal of diplomacy with the various independent authorities there, and perhaps a good deal of fighting.

But an area with many independent states was also one in which there were continuing quarrels and disputes that an intervener could exploit. Ptolemy IX had gathered a large army – said to have been 30,000 men,[19] though no doubt this figure was subject to the usual exaggeration – and a fleet, and he presumably made this fact known to interested parties. Sure enough, an appeal for help came from the city of Ptolemais-Ake, which technically was still part of the Seleukid kingdom, though it was evidently, at least in these years, self-governing. It was being threatened by the Maccabean King Alexander Iannai, who was new to the kingship of the Jews, having succeeded his brother only the year before, and was clearly trying to establish himself, particularly as a military commander.[20] The city had responded with the appeal to Ptolemy for assistance. Ptolemy embarked his forces and sailed.

The Ptolemaians had promised him an alliance with themselves, and with Gaza, Zoilos, the ruler of Strato's Tower, and Sidon, 'and many others'. They may have exaggerated here – for Sidon and the 'others' never appear in the events – but there is no reason to doubt that the offensive that Iannai directed against the city was seen as a danger to all the rest. If he took the city he would then probably be able to capture a series of other, smaller Palestinian cities; Zoilos was already operating in support, though Josephos claims that he was doing so in hopes of making himself ruler in the city.[21]

On the voyage to Palestine, however, Ptolemy was informed that the city had changed its mind, or rather the faction that had advocated neutrality, and presumably believed that the city could defend itself without help, had defeated the party that had asked Ptolemy for help. The citizens evidently now felt that Ptolemy was quite likely to impose his own rule on the city if they let him in. (They had good reason to fear this, since Zoilos had apparently not hidden his own ambition to do the same; if one ally could plan a takeover, another could.) They now believed they had a good prospect of defeating Iannai's siege by themselves, and that their allies were not strong enough to impose themselves; Soter, with his unusually large army, was evidently therefore seen as dangerous.[22]

Despite this discouraging message, Ptolemy landed his army south of Ptolemais, at a place called Sykaminos, which is south of, but also below, Mount Carmel. This has been regarded as unlikely since it was an unsuitable place for the landing of a large force. Instead, it is proposed that he actually landed in the Bay of Haifa, to the north of Mount Carmel, which is certainly a more suitable landing place for a large army, and in fact it is only just north of Mount Carmel from Sykaminos. The bay is also a well-sheltered anchorage where his ships could remain in safety. It was also only 10 miles from Ptolemais.[23] Wherever he landed, he was being careful to do so well away from potential immediate enemies.

The landing took place in the midst of a series of independent and quarrelling states: inland was Iannai's Judaean territory, south were the series of independent states, Strato's Tower (under Zoilos, who also controlled Dor), Ashkelon, Gaza, with Joppa, part of the Iannai's kingdom, and Ptolemais to the north. Ptolemy was pushing himself into a complex political area. Not only that, but Iannai's army was sitting before Ptolemais itself. Ptolemy's landing was sufficiently far from both the city and the Judaean army that he had space and time to become properly established on shore before anyone could interfere.

The Seleukid rivals, Grypos and Kyzikenos, were neither of them making any real progress against the other, and when Ptolemy arrived, they were operating well to the north, so it seems; Grypos was evidently in control of Antioch and Seleukeia-in-Pieria and Kilikia, Kyzikenos' territory was to the south, bordering on Judaea in places. They did not involve themselves in the events in Palestine. Ptolemy could ignore them, just as Alexander Iannai apparently did. Ptolemy marched his army to Ptolemais, camped outside the city, and negotiated. He found that there were already a number of participants in the siege and the crisis generally. The city of Ptolemais was one, which Alexander Iannai and his Judaean army had been busy besieging, though they had not got very far, and the Judaean army did not have much skill in the way of siege expertise; Iannai withdrew it into the interior when Ptolemy Soter arrived. Zoilos, the ruler of Strato's Tower and the town of Dor, south along the coast, had taken fright at the prospect of Iannai's capture of Ptolemais and had allied himself with the city, and had brought his forces along to help. Gaza, just as fearful, had also joined the coalition.[24] And now, Ptolemy and his army had arrived. He was probably the strongest of all the participants, militarily at least. With all these authorities present, it was clearly a time for negotiation.

Alexander Iannai raised the siege when Ptolemy's army arrived, and Ptolemy was about to conclude an alliance with the city and with Zoilos. Ptolemy could for the moment ignore Ptolemais, which was no longer threatened. Ptolemy could, however, capture an easier target, the town of Strato's Tower, south of his landing place, which, along with the well-fortified town of Dor further south, constituted Zoilos' principality. He was present, of course, and an ally of Ptolemais, but the city was a formidable position for a besieger. Zoilos was now cast in the role of a victim. Negotiations with Ptolemy brought forth a plan from Iannai. Ptolemy, whose army had siege skill, would capture Strato's Tower, then hand it over to Iannai in return for 400 silver talents.[25] This seemed a useful bargain for both of them – Alexander could expand his kingdom without any effort, and Ptolemy could gain a helpful war chest for his campaign into Egypt. Whether either of them would honour these terms was, of course, doubtful; such a bargain between enemies was clearly subject to betrayal, and certainly, Iannai immediately betrayed Ptolemy.

Josephos' account is somewhat ambiguous as to the results of this pact. He says that Ptolemy Soter captured Zoilos himself, which, if they were still negotiating an alliance, would have been the necessary preliminary to the bargain being kept. But he does not say that the cities were handed over to Iannai, nor that he received the cash, though it is generally assumed that all this happened.[26] Iannai, however, clearly believed that diplomacy involved betrayal, and he did not like the thought that Ptolemy might establish himself militarily in Palestine; Soter had easily captured Strato's Tower, so it could hardly be held successfully by a Jewish garrison, if Ptolemy betrayed him as he was about to betray Ptolemy. Iannai contacted Kleopatra III in Egypt and invited her to invade Palestine to fight Ptolemy.[27] Presumably, he believed that Ptolemy was not going to go away, and perhaps that Kleopatra might well provide a useful reward.

Ptolemy discovered this intrigue and denounced Iannai, giving him a good excuse, if he wanted one, for holding on to Strato's Tower. Then he set off into the Palestinian interior with his army, leaving a detachment to blockade Ptolemais. He marched by way of Asochis, which he captured, and then attacked Sepphoris nearby, but failed to take it. He marched on into the Jordan Valley. He received supplies from a local chieftain, Theodoros of Amathos, who was no doubt as fearful of Jewish conquest as anybody else in the area. Ptolemy then encountered Iannai's army at Asophon, near Amathos. He put his army under the command of professional tactician Philostephanos, which made sense, since there is no sign that Ptolemy had any military training. Philostephanos got the Ptolemaic army across the Jordan without being interfered with, and then roundly defeated Iannai in the subsequent battle – the battle of Asophon. The defeated Jewish force was relentlessly pursued, and largely destroyed. The suggested casualties were 30,000 or 50,000, depending on which exaggeration is accepted.[28]

Ptolemy was now able to march without hindrance through Palestine, ravaging parts of Judaea and supposedly committing atrocities,[29] heading for Gaza. The detachment besieging Ptolemais, now that Iannai had withdrawn and been defeated, had probably not taken the city; probably it also had been withdrawn.[30]

In Egypt, Kleopatra III became rightly alarmed as his successes multiplied, and had been alerted by the message from Iannai, asking for the help of her army. Iannai's defeat at Asaphon will have speeded her response. Ptolemy IX Soter spent some time campaigning and ravaging Judaean territory – which probably means he was collecting supplies, and loot, rather than indulging in a relentless devastation, for he scarcely had time for much more; he then headed west to Gaza. It was during that time that Kleopatra and Ptolemy X Alexander and their army had arrived. She sent her forces against Soter's, and the two forces met and fought somewhere inland and north of Gaza, and it seems that Kleopatra's forces were defeated, but Soter then ignored her and moved on to camp at Gaza with his large and victorious army. This, of course, was the essential first move for any attack on Egypt, and it seemed that he was well on the way to beginning an invasion. This was now evidently his new purpose, or perhaps always had been, and both Kleopatra and Ptolemy Alexnader and their forces had been drawn to Palestine; Ptolemy Soter must have thought that the country was wide open to him – if he could get past Gaza and then Pelusion.

The speed of his conquests in Palestine did not mean that they were secure. In particular, Soter had made an enemy of Alexander Iannai, who could reconstitute his defeated army, composed mainly of amateurs, relatively quickly. (The massive casualties claimed to have been suffered by Iannai's army, stated by Josephos quoting earlier historians, did not prevent Iannai's early recovery.)[31] Apart from Gaza, Ptolemy had not taken control of any other cities or territories, apart from the relatively minor fortress town of Strato's Tower. He had in the process of his campaign collected a sufficient number of enemies in his campaign to put him in a precarious situation, despite his victorious army.

There were two obvious authorities in the region who could be persuaded to join with Kleopatra III against Ptolemy Soter. In the north was Antiochos Grypos, chosen no doubt because Kyzikenos was still, at least theoretically, allied with Soter, though the two Seleukid kings in effect blocked each other's movements. The other was Alexander Iannai, defeated, humiliated and seeking vengeance. She made preparations, sending 'part of her wealth and her grandsons' (Selene's children), to Kos for safety at the Asklepeion sanctuary there, and added her written testament to this cargo.[32] Then she used her surviving daughter, Selene, the divorced wife of Ptolemy Soter – this must have been a satisfying insult for Kleopatra to produce – to bring Grypos to her side. She sent Selene to him as a new wife, and they were quickly married,[33] though Grypos does not seem to have joined in the war; perhaps keeping him neutral was sufficient, while his fighting with Kyzikenos could keep both of them out of the way. The Seleukid internal war, quiescent it seems before Selene's arrival, resumed in 103/102, presumably by an infusion of Ptolemaic money or forces.

Ptolemy X Alexander was sent by sea from Alexandria with an armed force into Phoenicia.[34] No doubt, one of his tasks was to take Selene to her new husband; delivering her to Antiochos by using a fleet would be good diplomacy, and would emphasise and publicise their alliance. Ptolemy X also delivered reinforcements to Grypos' army, which was probably what reignited the Seleukid civil war, and prevented Kyzikenos, still reckoned to be Ptolemy IX's ally, from intervening in the war in the south.[35] It is assumed that Ptolemy Alexnader was intending to secure alliances with some of the independent Phoenician cities, such as Tyre and Sidon, though this is not confirmed in Josephos, the only fairly reliable, if biased, source, and in fact it seems quite unlikely – the cities are not recorded as involving themselves, any more than the Seleukid competitors did.

Alexander Iannai, on the other hand, clearly was contacted directly by Kleopatra. She herself sailed with another army and the main Ptolemaic fleet to Ptolemais-Ake, which she besieged and captured, though this will have taken some time. Excavations have found evidence, attributed to the end of the second century, of destruction that can be ascribed to the violent capture of the city.[36] Having possession of the main city of Palestine, of course, gave her control of a very useful piece in the game that was being played. She moved inland to the independent and neutral city of Skythopolis, where, by prearrangement, she met Iannai; they concluded a 'treaty of friendship'.[37] This was a fairly pointless exercise, and bore no military fruit – Alexander Iannai was as slippery as Kleopatra, and had no intention of tackling Ptolemy Soter's army again. But Kleopatra's presence in inland Palestine was a clear threat to Soter in front of Gaza.

Kleopatra III had usurped several positions normally held by men since driving Ptolemy Soter out of Egypt. In the first two years after his brother left, Ptolemy Alexander as king had remained quiet, perhaps pleased at his return to kingship in Egypt. As his brother's successor, he had also taken the office of priest of Alexander and the Deified Ptolemies in 107 and 106. But next year, 105/104, the priesthood was held by Kleopatra herself.[38] The queen was setting a series of precedents – a ruling queen (though with her sons as subordinate kings, installed at her choice), chief priest, and now, in Palestine, commander of an army in the field. (It was not actually all unprecedented, if one takes the Hellenistic period as a whole, however, for there had been women in all these positions or their equivalents at various times in the last two centuries, including some in the Ptolemaic kingdom.)

She had, however, also sent her son Ptolemy Alexander on his expedition with an army into Syria. Attention is usually directed to Kleopatra's activities because she had the main Ptolemaic army, and probably the main fleet, with her at Ptolemais-Ake, and it was she who conducted the negotiations with Alexander Iannai – and, of course, because she was queen. But Ptolemy X had campaigned with some success. He had delivered Selene to her new husband. Whether he had really been intended to bring Tyre and Sidon into Kleopatra's alliance is not clear; they had only recently, in the previous ten years or so, secured their own independence, and they would be very suspicious of an alliance with the queen, just as Ptolemais-Ake had been suspicious of Ptolemy IX's intentions. The fate of Zoilos, arrested by his coalition partner (and either killed or imprisoned) and his cities bought by his enemy, was a caution. Ptolemy had campaigned through northern Syria, and reached Damascus, probably at much the same time that Ptolemy IX was camped in front of Gaza, and while Kleopatra III was at Skythopolis.

The visit of Ptolemy Alexander to Damascus is in fact rather a surprise. It is not mentioned by Josephos, but it appears in a letter of Panobchounis, son of Phmois, one of a dossier of the Pathyris documents. In it he remarks as one of the details, but without any emphasis, that 'the king went to Damascus', where he left, or took, a company of men to the city. The date of the letter is 27 September 103.[39]

The 'king' here is obviously Ptolemy Alexander, who thus turns out to be unusually active. Damascus was one of the cities that were subject to Seleukid rule, and since Ptolemy went there with no more than a company of men, it was evidently expected to be friendly, and so we may assume it was in Grypos' area of Syria. He and his men marched from Ptolemais, or at least from the forces besieging that city; alternatively, they could have marched from northern Syria, but this was an even greater and more difficult distance.

What Ptolemy was doing there is not stated, but one assumption that has been made is that the visit was in some way connected with the 'Damascus Document', one of the Dead Sea Scrolls. G. Cohen makes this point and produced a number of possible explanations, though the connection with the Damascus Document is by no means made.[40] The least unlikely reason for Ptolemy's visit – all the possibilities are speculative – is that it had two purposes, to strengthen Grypos' hold on the city as part of the alliance forged with Grypos' marriage to Selene, either by delivering reinforcements, or by showing the flag of the alliance; it would also be seen as a threat to Ptolemy Soter, who was active to the south in Palestine, and on his way to, or at, Gaza by this time – and so it was also connected with the alliance Kleopatra III had made with Iannai at Skythopolis.

The essential point, however, is that Ptolemy Alexander reached Damascus with no more than 'a company of men'. He may have installed reinforcements for Grypos' garrison, but he would not be able to campaign any further in the face of armed opposition of any numbers. Even the inefficient Maccabean army would be able to take on a 'company' of Ptolemaic soldiers and win. So the purpose was not to bring serious reinforcements to the city, but was mainly symbolic, a signal to Grypos that his alliance with Kleopatra and Ptolemy Alexander was serious. But this event, which happened well before the date of the letter, since it was obviously well in the past by then, was overtaken by an advance by Ptolemy Soter from Gaza against Egypt.

So, by the late summer of 103, Ptolemy Alexander was in Damascus with a small force, Kleopatra III was in the Jordan Valley with an army, and had part of her army blockading Ptolemais-Ake; Ptolemy Soter was in, or approaching, Gaza, having defeated the Maccabean and Kleopatra's armies. His enemies, Kleopatra III and Alexander Iannai, had concluded their 'treaty of friendship' at Skythopolis. If the three Ptolemaic forces had actually been operating in concert, it might have been seen as a serious attempt to recover Ptolemaic rule over the old province of Koele Syria. It was almost certainly not the original intention of any of the Ptolemaic participants to reconstitute the old Ptolemaic Empire, but inevitably, in their campaigns in Syria and Palestine the idea would occur to them. Kleopatra, for one, reveals a great ambition in her later years as ruler, though the ambitions of her sons were more likely focused on Egypt and Cyprus than on reconquering Koele Syria. For Syria was by this time much fractured politically, and even the Ptolemaic armed forces in Syria were divided between several authorities. They were divided not just between the two kings and the queen, but between the generals in Cyprus, Cyrenaica and Egypt. Further, in Egypt the entrenched bureaucrats and aristocracies were very difficult to motivate into new activity, and so were holding up all initiatives. And yet, Ptolemaic Egypt being an autocracy, the *stasis* between the members of the royal family was the basic cause of the kingdom's clear decline.

The events that follow are sourced by the letters, already referred to, found at Pathyris in the Thebaid. They were written by men who had been ordered from their homes to the defences on the Mediterranean coast. One, referred to already, mentions events at Ptolemais, and refers to the king going to Damascus, but others were dated from Pelusion. This was the place that, properly garrisoned, was an almost impregnable defensive fortress for Egypt. It was a few days' march from Gaza – but that march was across the Sinai desert – and Ptolemy Soter at Gaza was an obvious threat to Egypt. By February 102, the men from Pathyris were writing home from Pelusion. It appears that Ptolemy Alexander was recalled from his campaign in Phoenicia to Egypt by sea while Soter was still preparing for his next expedition, or even before he reached Gaza. Once there, of course, Soter was stationary for a time, resting his troops after the Judaean campaign and maintaining his blockade or siege of the city; as it happened, he stayed there all the winter of 103/102.

Ptolemy Alexander therefore had the time to transfer himself and his forces from Phoenicia to Pelusion. Meanwhile, Kleopatra's army had captured Ptolemais and a garrison was installed there.[41] Alexander Iannai took the opportunity of Ptolemy Soter's installation at Gaza, with Kleopatra in control at Ptolemais, and Ptolemy Alexander at Pelusion with possibly most of the Ptolemaic forces, to evacuate his forces to Judaea, and then to campaign to extend his kingdom beyond the Jordan. He captured Gadara, which was the treasure store of Theodoros of Amathos, but soon lost it again.[42] However, he had long had his eye mainly on the towns along the Mediterranean coast, which were now dominated by Ptolemy Soter's army at Gaza. Until the Egyptian crisis was resolved, therefore, Iannai had to operate elsewhere; he found his *metier* in the capture of small, undefended towns, where his limited military abilities were not put under too much strain.

The letters found at Pathyris mentioned earlier, together with some inscriptions, provide information that expands that provided by Josephos, and from an Egyptian point of view, whereas Josephos is largely focused on events in the Jewish community. The troops who were mobilised for the defence of Egypt in the north were, in this case, of course, brought up from the south, which explains that the mobilisation was countrywide. In addition, from the names of the men mentioned in the letters (for the writers addressed their letters to up to a dozen men by name) were almost entirely Egyptian. Their letters provide snapshot notices of events at times, but mostly the soldiers were stationary, in garrisons at Ptolemais-Ake or at Pelusion or at Mendes in the Delta. There is no information on campaigns or battles. (This, of course, is typical of any group of mobilised soldiers, who spend most of their time waiting for something to happen, and usually being disappointed – or relieved – when nothing does, and are left in complete ignorance of reasons and other developments and movements.)

Strategically, Pelusion was the key to the whole situation, and the letters, being mostly from Pelusion, accurately reflect that situation. At Pelusion, Ptolemy Alexander took command. This was the citadel defending Egypt against attack from the east. This was more than a frontier fortress, it was a fortress surrounded by a range of smaller forts, which collectively prevented an invading army from reaching the Delta and freshwater supplies, and forced it to camp in the desert. (This was a defensive system originally developed by the later pharaohs, brought up to date by the men of the Saite dynasty as a defence against Assyrian or Persian attack, and kept in careful repair by the Ptolemies.) It was this defensive system that now foiled Ptolemy Soter. From Gaza he marched his army along the northern coast road of Sinai, but was halted at, or rather before, Pelusion, which by the time he reached it was fully manned by the Egyptian army, with Ptolemy Alexander in command – though he was not called on to do anything except be present. Ptolemy Soter could do nothing against the fortifications, and within days, his army would begin to die of thirst. He returned almost at once to Gaza.[43]

By this time – probably the autumn of 103 – the positions of the Ptolemaic forces had changed again. Ptolemy Soter was back in Gaza, Ptolemy Alexander was at Pelusion, or had probably gone back to Alexandria once Soter had retreated, and Kleopatra III's forces took over Ptolemais-Ake about the end of the year. Some of her people wondered aloud if they could reconstitute the old empire, but this would have involved fighting the newly independent cities, many of them well fortified in the latest manner, and fighting the Seleukid kings and the Jewish state in Judaea as well. Kleopatra had had two Jewish generals in her forces, Chelkias and Ananias, and Ananias made it clear that to invade and fight in Judaea would be extremely difficult.[44] His personal reason may well have been a Jewish loyalty, as he said, but he also had military experience on his side, since the Jews in Judaea reverted almost automatically to defending the forts and town, and harassing an invader by guerrilla tactics. It was also only a few years earlier that Antiochos Kyzikenos' army had been defeated and harried away from Samaria by John Hyrkanos' Jewish army, employing those same guerrilla tactics, and including at least some of the same men. Kleopatra may have been commanding an army, but she had no personal experience of commanding in war, and her achievements in Palestine were diplomatic; Ananias' warning was clearly well meant and well taken.[45]

The idea was dropped, probably as quickly as it was raised. But she moved into Ptolemais-Ake, taking up a position very like that of her sister Kleopatra Thea three decades before – a woman who had also ruled with a compliant king under her thumb. Kleopatra III must have been tempted to consider holding on to the city, if not undertaking the reconquest of Palestine; with a dominant navy, it would certainly have been possible to hold the city as an Egyptian outpost.

She met Alexander Iannai in the city. He arrived bearing gifts, the very model of a compliant ally. The meeting place she chose, however, was no doubt her way of rubbing home his failure to capture the city earlier. They made a treaty, or reinforced the earlier one, which probably compelled him to agree to leave the city alone in the future. Kleopatra then returned to Egypt, but left a garrison in Ptolemais-Ake for the rest of 102,[46] probably to ensure that Iannai kept the peace, and his word, and perhaps to prevent Ptolemy Soter from seizing the city, and perhaps even to ensure that it paid its dues for its rescue. This was also probably a strong hint for Ptolemy Soter to return to Cyprus in that he had no hope of repeating his campaign in Syria and Palestine, for if he had it would be against the forces of not just Alexander Iannai, but those of Kleopatra III and Ptolemy Alexander as well. Probably during early 102, he did return to Cyprus.[47]

This war had done more than block Ptolemy Soter's ambitions. (In fact it had not even done that, but it did prevent him from realising them, for the present.) It brought Kleopatra's determined exercise of power out into the open, but in such a way as to produce a defeat for her – for her aim had been to destroy Ptolemy Soter, and she had failed. It also enabled Ptolemy Alexander to exercise power by himself, both in Phoenicia and in Palestine. Soter had failed in his ambition, but survived. It seems likely that Ptolemy Alexander, having successfully defended Egypt, was now able to realise his own ambition.

During the late summer or autumn of 101, that is not long after Kleopatra III had returned to Egypt, she died. It was alleged that Ptolemy Alexander organised her murder, and this is widely accepted, though direct evidence is absent, and the alternative of a 'natural' death is possible – she was of a considerable age, after all.[48] It appears that the relationship between mother and son was as bad with Ptolemy Alexander as it had been between Kleopatra and Ptolemy Soter when he had escaped to Cyprus, and that in the year or so before the war in Syria began, Ptolemy Alexander had himself fled from the court for a time.[49] But he had to be used in the Syrian campaign, and the taste of independence and power during the year in Syria was probably so pleasing, and also so liberating, that he was determined that it should continue. Command of an army and a fleet will have provided him with the opportunity to develop a loyal following, men ambitious to achieve wealth and position who may have been blocked by those around Kleopatra. The story of Kleopatra's death is thus unclear, but there were plenty of people in the city of Alexandria after the war to support the notion that Ptolemy organised the murder of his mother.

Chapter 7

Royal Brothers: Dissension and Rebellion

Kleopatra III having died, or been murdered by Ptolemy X, he was now the sole Egyptian ruler. Ptolemy IX was back as king in Cyprus. And suddenly, Ptolemy Apion took over as ruler of Cyrenaica. The date of this is not certain, still less precise, but until about 100 BC, Ptolemy IX had been recorded on inscriptions as king in Cyrenaica,[1] and by 100, Ptolemy Apion is known to have been ruler there.[2] That Apion should suddenly at last inherit his kingdom just at the moment when Kleopatra III died, and the rest of the Ptolemaic territories were once again divided between Ptolemy IX and Ptolemy X, is not a coincidence.

We do not know how it happened, or precisely when, but at a guess, it was a contrivance of Ptolemy X, to deprive Ptolemy IX of part of his territories. Either that, or Kleopatra III had arranged that he take the kingdom in the midst of her conflict with Ptolemy IX in Palestine.[3] He or she could install Apion by force from Egypt while Ptolemy IX was in Gaza or travelling back to Cyprus, using Egyptian sea and land power. At the same time, if it was Ptolemy X, he could proclaim that he was righting an injustice perpetrated by his mother, citing the intention of Ptolemy VIII in his will that Apion should become king in Cyrene. In addition, Ptolemy X would thus be revealing an unexpected talent for clever political manoeuvring, and swift decision. Ptolemy seems more likely to be responsible, as against Kleopatra III, since it is difficult to see the queen surrendering control of any territory she had gained.

Ptolemy X then bolstered his position as king by marrying his niece Kleopatra Berenike III, who was the daughter of his rival Ptolemy IX and Kleopatra IV.[4] Berenike was by her ancestry now the prime Ptolemaic female, the daughter of a king and his sister, and in 100 she had just reached the marriageable age of fifteen or sixteen. This planning of incestuous marriages, however, was beginning to go awry. Ptolemy X had been married before, but the name of his first wife is not known, and probably she was not one of the Ptolemaic family, though they had a son. Ptolemy IX had been married twice, to Kleopatra IV and to Selene, and each time his wife had been taken from him by Kleopatra III, and married to someone else. He was now married for a third time, though who the wife was is not known. He had children by all his wives – Kleopatra Berenike III by Kleopatra IV, two sons by Kleopatra Selene, and two sons and a daughter by the third wife. It is not clear if the third wife was of the Ptolemaic family. Of the eight children of these two men, half were probably regarded as ineligible for the throne. It could therefore be that the brothers had both ended up married to women whose descent was either unsuitable, or that their relationship was unofficial. Ptolemy X's marriage to Berenike would be regarded as legitimate, though they only had a daughter. The succession was becoming very complex once more.

As an example of the future difficulties, Ptolemy Apion had been Ptolemy VIII's firstborn son, but because he was not formally married to Eirene, his courtesan, he was excluded from the Ptolemaic succession, except for Cyrenaica. It seems that this exclusion may well be applied to the children of Ptolemy IX and X as well. In addition, some of their children had been sent to Kos by Kleopatra II in 103, and were still there, along with her treasure. Neither Ptolemy IX nor Ptolemy X apparently made any attempt to recover them or the treasure.

Ptolemy X apparently established his sole rule fairly readily, although, of course, he had been king in name for several years already. The departure of Ptolemy IX to Cyprus, and the removal of the virago Kleopatra III, were no doubt reliefs to all. The generosity of planting Apion in Cyrenaica (and the consequent deposition from that position of Ptolemy IX) could well have been good publicity, as well as a clever political move. The royal marriage was no doubt an event for a public celebration, and in 99, the married couple went to Memphis, possibly for a coronation ceremony, though Ptolemy had gone through one already, and the record of the visit mainly consists in complaints about the treatment of a man called Petesis.[5] Berenike gave birth to a female child about this time, though her name is not known – one would suppose it was Kleopatra or Berenike; it appears that Berenike had no further children, and the girl child is not otherwise recorded. There is a degree of doubt over these several parentages, at least in modern accounts, although presumably not at the time.

Until this point, the imminence of Rome had not affected internal Ptolemaic politics in any serious way, but judging by the increased presence of Roman visitors noted in the last chapter, and probably Roman trade, in Alexandria and the *chora*, Roman knowledge of, and familiarity with, Egypt was increasing. It is quite possible that Roman officials kept an eye on Ptolemaic politics, though to go by the summaries of Livy's later books, it was only the atrocities – the murder of Ptolemy Memphites, Kleopatra Thea's killing of her son – which made their way into the exiguous record.[6]

In 102, a Roman naval expedition, commanded by the propraetor M. Antonius, who had been praetor in 103, campaigned in Kilikia against the pirates who were based there.[7] This was a warning for all neutral states in the eastern Mediterranean, for Kilikia was technically Seleukid territory, and yet Rome blithely operated militarily there. Rome had a reasonable excuse for this interference, in that none of the Seleukids, long preoccupied by their civil warfare, had made a serious attempt to suppress those pirates, whose targets were very largely ships of Roman origin or which were trading towards Italy. The reason for Seleukid inattention was largely due to the continuing civil war in Syria, but the problem in fact predated the time of the Roman campaign. Piracy was endemic in the Mediterranean, but became much more prevalent after about 150 BC.[8] As usual with such expeditions, Antonius could claim a victory, having killed some Kilikians, sunk some pirate ships, and destroyed some villages, and received a triumph and became consul in 99, on his return from the campaign. But the problem revived as soon as he withdrew, as the Kilikians continued their piracy as a means of recovering from the Roman onslaught.[9]

The campaign was followed, in 100, by a Roman law directed at suppressing piracy, the *lex de piratis*.[10] For the inhabitants of non-Roman territories, this contained provisions that were clearly threatening. One clause allowed Roman commanders to operate against pirates up to 75 miles inland. Since, by definition, piracy did not exist in Roman territory (they were probably called bandits or rebels), this was an indication to Roman commanders that they had Roman permission to encroach on neutral territory, which is what Antonius had done. It was, of course, all of a piece with Roman political and diplomatic theory, which made any state with which it had relations automatically subject to Roman authority – though most such states did not realise this, and would have rejected it if they had known. This was not usually acted upon, but was to be a useful theory, particularly in later justifications in Rome itself.

The piracy problem was, of course, partly the fault of the eastern kingdoms in the first place. The Kilikian pirates, for example, were usually described as having started operations in the Seleukid civil warfare in the 140s, when one or other of the competitors for the kingship enlisted the pirates (who, of course, already existed) as allies.[11] They acquired a taste for wider operations, and the later suppression of naval power in the Aegean opened the field for their activities much further. But the Cretan piracy problem could not be so easily blamed on the kings; it had been an issue for all Aegean states for centuries, and the dominant naval power in the sea had generally assumed responsibility for their suppression. This had been Athens for a time, then the Antipatrids in Macedon, and eventually the Ptolemies until their collapse, then the city of Rhodes, but after 150 or so, no power was capable of adopting such a position, largely because any power showing real strength and initiative would soon cross with Rome, which had become intensely suspicious of any such initiatives. The removal of Ptolemaic ships from their island posts in the Aegean in 145 no doubt also removed one piracy deterrent.

The creators of the Piracy Law seem to have appreciated this, and it contained exhortations to the kings – which meant the Ptolemies and the Seleukids in particular (there were many other kings, but none in 100 with the requisite naval strength) – that they should suppress pirates in their own lands and ports. For the Ptolemies, only Cyrenaica counted in this, but for the Seleukids the responsibility lay essentially with the Syrian cities that had become independent. And there was also a threat implicit in this 'law'. If they did not do as the Romans wished, the Romans would be able, by the terms of this law, to enter their territories and 'justly' act against the unsuppressed pirates. All in all, the Romans were providing themselves with a political theory and the self-justification that would enable them to invade any foreign state that they chose to attack, using the suppression of piracy as their excuse. The 'Piracy Law' was an exercise in imperialism, similar to the United States' modern pursuit of sanction busters.

The Roman anti-piracy campaign of Antonius in fact ended soon after the Piracy Law was adopted, though piracy, of course, continued. By this time, since the Seleukid kings had little in the form of naval strength, and the Ptolemies no longer concerned themselves with piracy, the responsibility for policing the seas lay with the Romans, but it was another generation before they properly accepted that responsibility. The pirates had to threaten Rome directly before effective Roman action was taken. It is not clear if the Piracy Law had any effect anywhere, although it was certainly publicised in Greece – inscribed copies have been found at Delphi and at Knidos in

Lykia,[12] and so others may be assumed to have been set up in other frequented or naval places.

Ptolemy Apion may have been cognisant of the provisions of the Piracy Law and understood the implications. But his only notable action was to adopt the device of his father, Ptolemy VIII, who had written a will back in 155 in which he bequeathed his kingdom, which at that time consisted of Cyrenaica only, to Rome. Apion had clearly been treated well by his father, considering his attitude to his wives and his other children, and no doubt, this subject had been discussed, since Ptolemy VIII could regard it as a clever device that warded off his enemies.

Making a will in Rome's favour was a defence against internal and external threats. Ptolemy VIII appears to have been the first to do so, then in the 130s, Attalos III had copied him, not necessarily in order to favour Rome, but more to be sure that his enemies at home did not attack him, since, if he was removed, they would not benefit. Rome was not necessarily expecting to benefit or take over the inheritance, and in some cases the city did not know of the will. It was pure luck (good for Rome, bad for Asia) that Rome was in need of Asian wealth at the time Attalos died, so the will was accepted and executed – though it resulted in a three-year war and the break-up of the kingdom.

Apion's will is not extant. There is no indication of his reasons, but political defensiveness is the most likely.[13] The key element in the situation was to publicise the will to those who needed to be deterred – Ptolemy VIII had had his inscribed and set up in public where it could be read and understood, though it seems that Attalos III kept his will quiet; perhaps only the family was his target. One would suppose that Apion used his father's method.[14]

Apion had been born in the 150s, and so was over fifty years old when he finally achieved the kingship in Cyrenaica, but the family was relatively long-lived and he could expect to last ten more years at least. He does not appear to have been married, nor to have had any children. His kingdom, if he had not made a will in favour of Rome, would have presumably reverted to one of his Ptolemy half-brothers, and perhaps this had been Kleopatra III's assumption, with Ptolemy X becoming the beneficiary. Ptolemy IX had a good claim as well. These two were both ruthless enough to eliminate him in pursuit of his territory – hence, perhaps, his will for Rome, which would no doubt deter them.

In the event, he was king for only four or five years, dying in 96.[15] Rome, as it had been with the Attalid inheritance, was choosy. The Cyrenaican kingdom was huge, geographically as large as Italy, 500 kilometres from east to west, and was bordered on the south by an open desert frontier. Such a country would need to be constantly garrisoned, patrolled and guarded. It was, however, productive of grain, and had supplied Greece for centuries. When needed, this could be purchased; it was not necessary to control the territory to benefit from its products. Probably the sheer size of the land was the main deterrent. There was no real sign that Rome was eager to acquire overseas territories at the time; the city had quite enough problems without having another gratuitously foisted on it. Yet the legacy was not refused. The cities were declared 'free',[16] which put them under effective, if distant, Roman protection. The royal estates were neverthelss retained in Roman ownership, with a view to profiting from them.

In effect, the political status of the country was put on hold. It was, however, a candidate for being annexed as a new Roman province, which would probably be activated at a time of Rome's choosing and convenience. The situation must have been deeply unsettling within Cyrenaica; its co-ordinating kingship had been removed, and each city – there were five or six of them – was now supposedly independent and existed on its own resources. For the moment, Rome couldn't be bothered to spend any money on it, or use troops to defend it, though Rome did collect a substantial quantity of silphium, the local drug, which was of considerable value.[17] The cities had their own militia, which was familiar with the problem of defending the country, and could be trusted to do the job.

The reaction of the Ptolemaic kings to this development is not known, but twenty years later, when later Ptolemies did attempt to claim the region, this only pushed Rome to finishing the process of annexation, and a governor was appointed.[18] It is reasonable to suppose that there was a good deal of resentment at Apion's action amongst the Ptolemies, and at Rome's lack of action, but perhaps not much surprise. No doubt, the people of Cyrene were also disquieted. But it was a clear reduction of the Ptolemaic Empire, as one of the three kingdoms that composed it was suddenly removed. From that point onwards, the threat of further Roman amputations hovered over the kingdom.

The crisis over Cyrenaica with the death of Ptolemy Apion came at the same time as a much greater problem in Syria, which could well have distracted the Ptolemaic kings from the Cyrenaican issue. The injection of Ptolemaic forces into the Seleukid civil war during the 'War of Sceptres' had kept that war going for a time. But in 96–95, it briefly came to an end. One of the commanders of Seleukid forces, Herakleon, seceded, and formed a military state centred on Beroia (Aleppo). His diagnosis was that both rival kings were incompetent, and he organised a plot to take out Antiochos Grypos, and killed him.[19] This did little good for his rival, Kyzikenos, who died in battle soon after, either a victim of Grypos' son Seleukos VI, or committing suicide to avoid capture.[20] The removal of these two only made matters worse, since their children inherited the fighting. The people of Syria, like Herakleon, were now quite prepared themselves to kill any claimant king who fell into their hands; this happened to Seleukos VI at the hands of the population of Mopsuestia in Kilikia, which he was in process of looting, and found himself burned to death in the palace.[21] The Seleukid kingdom disintegrated for the last time; most communities moved into independence, and the surviving kings held only small sections of Syria.

One of the notable survivors was Selene, who was soon on her fourth husband, having been forcibly separated from her brother Ptolemy IX, and later married to Antiochos Grypos. She became a widow once he was murdered; she then married his brother, Antiochos IX Kyzikenos, but he was killed within a year.[22] She was finally married to Antiochos X Eusebes ('faithful'), who was her stepson, the son of Antiochos Kyzikenos. He was king for five or more years, before he fell in battle against the Parthians, whose invasion came in 88.[23] Despite Selene being much older than her final husband, they had two children. She took up residence with her children in Ptolemais-Ake, which, in effect, thereby, once her husband died, became another independent monarchical city state.

Ptolemy IX in Cyprus had attempted to intervene by assisting Demetrios III, the son of Antiochos Grypos. With Ptolemy's help, he was able to set himself up as king in Damascus.[24] But by this time the Seleukids could be ignored in the power stakes. From the east, the Parthians were approaching steadily, and were a presence already in Mesopotamia by the early 80s. Meanwhile in the west, the Romans had been drawn into fighting Mithradates of Pontos, in a continuing crisis that lasted a generation. This concerned the Ptolemies because one of Mithradates' early successes in his war was the capture of Kos, where he annexed the treasure left there by Kleopatra III, and carried off the Ptolemaic children to be educated at his court, and of course to be hostages.[25]

The lack of reaction by the Ptolemaic kings to the rise of Mithradates may be explained, at least in part, by the preoccupation of Ptolemy IX in Cyprus with Mithradates' developments in Asia Minor, his neighbour, and Ptolemy X's preoccupation with a new rebellion that had broken out in the Thebaid.

This new rebellion in the south is known only from occasional notices in the papyri and a confused account in Pausanias. It appears to have developed in the upper Nile Valley south of Thebes in 91, although it is clear from various notices that trouble was endemic in the area.[26] The cause may be assumed to be peasant discontent, high taxation and governmental oppression – the usual causes, and it had no doubt then been based on strikes in the Egyptian style, where peasants desert their farms and move into the desert for a time, a process called *anachoresis*. Pathyris, the home of those military correspondents whose letters provide useful information about the war in Syria, and who had been conscripted several years before the rebellion, was defended effectively against the rebels in that year and again in 88.[27] Some of the leaders of the resistance to the rebels appear to have been priests from the local temple, so the rebellion is hardly a nationalist Egyptian protest.[28] Its neighbour, the Latopolite *nome*, was also involved, and it seems, from the confused notice in Pausanias, that Thebes joined the rebels,[29] no doubt still resentful at previous defeats by the ruling dynasty.

This condition of peasant rebellion, which will have affected those with estates in the area, had the effect of further undermining the position of Ptolemy X. He had already lost any control over Cyrenaica, which he might have expected to recover when Apion died, but which had gone for good in 96. And although he had acted decisively against Ptolemy IX in 102 at Pelusion, he had not actually conducted any military operations, and the army had been in the necessary defensive positions at that city well before he arrived, and was not called upon to campaign, not even to undertake any military operations.

It is worth reverting to the personnel whose names were recorded in the Pathyris correspondence.[30] Several of the letters were written in demotic Egyptian, so it is unsurprising that the writers and the addressees all had Egyptian names. Yet in most of the letters in Greek, the case is the same, with just one man, Philammon, who had a Greek name. No doubt other soldiers were Greek, whose letters, if they wrote them, have not survived. But these names do show that the conscripted (or volunteer) soldiers at Pathyris were keen to defeat the enemy at the king's behest, and that the officers were Egyptian as well as the other ranks. Philammon actually was from Krokodilopolis,[31] which was probably a cleruchic settlement with an original Greco-Macedonian population, but Pathyris was purely Egyptian. Of course, it is the fact that many Egyptians seem to have adopted Greek names as well as using their original Egyptian names, but that makes them all the more Egyptian, since few Greeks adopted Egyptian names. When the rebellion approached the town, the rebels were detested as coming from Hermonthis, some distance down the river from Pathyris, and were described as 'impious inhabitants'. In the same letter, Pates, the writer, who had the rank of *hegemon* in the force sent to Pelusion, addressed his correspondence to the '*philobasilistai*', a local club of soldiers with an obvious loyalist aura.[32]

It is, therefore, not too surprising to find that the town was vigorously defended against the rebel attack. The governor of the south at the time was the governor general of the Thebaid, Plato; he had been in office since 101 and served until the end of the rebellion in 88 – or until dismissed by Ptolemy IX.[33] He wrote to the fighters at Pathyris to encourage them, dating his letter to year 26, which is 88 BC, and in the reign of Ptolemy X, even though the king had left Egypt some months earlier.[34]

That is, the rebellion was still under way after three years. One reason for its longevity must be the lethargy of Ptolemy X. He is reported to have been a copy of his father, grossly overweight, lazy, self-indulgent and widely disliked among his subjects. He had rarely displayed much energy, and then only during the war in Syria, when Ptolemy IX threatened his position as king. Even there he is recorded as travelling mainly by ship. That he could display sudden energy on occasion (he was reported to have been a vigorous dancer, which must have been a horrible sight), as in Syria and after his expulsion from Egypt, only emphasises his neglect and lethargy most of the time.[35]

It was possibly the continuation of the rebellion over such a relatively long time that induced Ptolemy IX to arrive from Cyprus and take a hand in its suppression. He had a useful and large army in his island, which he had used in Syria, and detachments of which had assisted various Seleukid kings, queens and claimants. It was, that is, a rather more professional force than Ptolemy X had at his disposal in Egypt. Ptolemy IX's arrival was communicated to the Parthyrians by the *strategos* Plato in a letter dated 11

November 88, a few months after the earlier letter. Ptolemy IX had arrived at Memphis, he reported, and had appointed a general called Hierax to command a large army (the numbers are not actually quoted) with which he would 'subdue the Thebaid'.[36]

It appears that Ptolemy IX arrived uninvited, though Justin claims that he was asked to come by the citizens.[37] It also appears that Ptolemy X managed to return to the city after his original expulsion. But he was short of money, and had mercenaries to pay, so he is said to have appropriated the golden sarcophagus holding the embalmed body of Alexander the Great, and melted it down to coin more cash. This so annoyed the Alexandrians, or at least revived the original anger of part of the citizenry, that he was driven out again. No doubt, the mercenaries knew a loser when they were commanded by one, and having received their gold coin in payment, faded away.[38]

Ptolemy IX's arrival coincided roughly with Ptolemy X's departure, return, and departure again, and therefore with the uprising that occurred in Alexandria. One of the causes of the rising was said to be Ptolemy X's favouritism towards the Jews,[39] something he had probably inherited from his mother – presumably her court officials had transformed themselves into his court officials. We do not know the exact reason for the rising, other than it included complaints about the king's employment of Jews. This element, of course, resonates strongly with historians of the twentieth century and after, but there is no real reason to assume a general attitude of anti-Semitism because of it. The obverse of the preference for Jews is a failure to favour Greeks and Macedonians, and it would take no more than a few Jews – or Parthians or Galatians or Romans – in favour to raise resentment among those who felt they were entitled to preference in their place.

Court appointments were taken to be opportunities to get rich at public expense, which was normal behaviour, more a cause for envy than enmity. The public revenues, however, had been somewhat reduced of late by the secession of Cyrenaica, the inability to control or profit from Cyprus, and the rebellion in the Thebaid, which became the more obviously expensive the longer it lasted. So the annoyance at court extravagance would have been even more a cause for envy than usual, and when it was attached to a preference for part-alien groups, then this envy became enmity. The uprising was the result. The dispute expedited the expulsion of Ptolemy X, some of the rioters annoyed at his favouritism to the Jews, others at his melting down of the Alexander sarcophagus; this latter, of course, is a further sign of royal (relative) poverty.

The rising may possibly have been sparked off by the interference of Ptolemy IX. If he had arrived unexpectedly, with an efficient army, loudly proclaiming his willingness to suppress the rebellion, this could have set off the volatile population of Alexandria; alternatively, and more probably, the rising could have started first, and Ptolemy IX may have seized the opportunity to bring his forces to Egypt while his brother was expelled for the first time – 'expelled' means only that he was pushed out of Alexandria; he could still operate in the *chora*, if less effectively. His return perhaps did not last for very long. A loud claim to be able to sort things out would have been part of Ptolemy IX's programme – which would, of course, have included replacing Ptolemy X on the throne as well as suppressing the rebellion, through the agency of his general Hierax.

It certainly worked, whichever the sequence. It is worth noting, however, that Ptolemy IX's adventure was taking place at a fraught international moment. In 89, the year when Ptolemy X was first driven out, and Ptolemy IX moved into – one might say, invaded – Egypt with his army, Mithradates began his first great war with Rome, by which in a very speedy campaign during 89 and 88 he conquered Asia Minor and Greece. This included the capture of Kos, and with the island he seized the treasure left by Kleopatra III and a brace of Ptolemaic children, including the future Ptolemy XI. There must be a suspicion in this that actions were co-ordinated between the kings. Ptolemy X had been notably friendly towards Rome, no doubt for good defensive reasons – he was lazy, not stupid – not protesting at the Roman assumption of authority, if distant, in Cyrenaica, for example, although that had been part of Ptolemy IX's kingdom, and the consequent reduction of Ptolemy IX's strength was something Ptolemy X would be pleased to see. By contrast, Ptolemy IX was less than friendly to the Italian city, if not actually hostile. With Rome fully occupied with Mithradates, and its own internal civil conflict – if not actually heading for a complete collapse – this was clearly Ptolemy IX's opportunity to take action, probably doing so between his brother's first expulsion and his return. His presence in Egypt would then encourage Ptolemy X's domestic opponents to drive him away a second time.

According to Appian, the Bithynian King Nikomedes' envoy had warned the Romans before Mithradates began his war that he had been in contact with Ptolemy X, seeking his friendship and wanting to hire skilled sailors for his much-enlarged fleet.[40] Whether Ptolemy responded is not known, but skilled sailors could clearly have been hired privately, and by permission of Ptolemy. Ptolemy is in fact only referred to as 'the king of Egypt', which was a post Ptolemy IX also claimed, so the precise identity of Mithradates' correspondent is not certain. If it was Ptolemy X in Egypt he was negotiating with, this could mean that he was also seeking an alliance.

Ptolemy X in Egypt had had enough to preoccupy him without joining in the war between Rome and Pontos, on either side. He had made no progress against the rebels in the Thebaid since the rebellion began, and had lost control of Thebes itself (which follows from the later attack to recover it). The uprising in Alexandria took place late in 89 or early in 88, after the Roman–Pontic war had begun. Ptolemy IX's presence in Egypt can be dated to fairly early in 88, although Ptolemy X's reign was still being used for dating as late as November. The crisis in Egypt – the rising in Alexandria, the flight and return of Ptolemy X, the arrival of Ptolemy IX, the definitive expulsion of Ptolemy X, the final campaign in the south – all therefore happened during 88,[41] and must have been extremely confusing to those not actually involved. Whatever Mithradates' hopes for an alliance with one of the Ptolemies, he was clearly disappointed. He would, of course, be pleased to see the replacement of the pro-Roman Ptolemy X by the anti-Roman Ptolemy IX.

Ptolemy X, having fled from Egypt in the face of the Alexandrian rioters, went to gather a fleet of ships and mercenaries with the intention of recovering his throne. The source of his ships and troops seems to have been Syria, perhaps contributed by Selene, his sister, though this was the year of her husband's death in fighting the Parthians, and she may not have had many troops to spare.[42] This was probably being done in mid-88, and war was raging in the south of Asia Minor at the time. He gathered enough forces to form an armed fleet, probably from Syria, courtesy of his sister Selene, though what his intention was is unclear. The obvious target would be Cyprus, with Ptolemy IX away in Egypt, but Cyprus was a naval base and it was probably a fleet loyal to Ptolemy IX, which met and defeated Ptolemy X's ships.

Mithradates had come up against effective resistance in that region, where Rhodes rebuffed him, assisted by Termessos and other places, and Patala stood a siege. Termessos, inland, actually fought back.[43] That is, Mithradates' first rush of victory had spent itself, and treatment of his victims had stiffened the resistance of those he now attacked. Ptolemy X now aimed to recruit men in this region – Myra in Lykia is mentioned in this connection.[44] He cannot have been able to hire many men in this crisis, when the cities of Lykia and Pamphylia were intent on resisting the invader, and while the Syrian cities were threatened by the Parthians. He was, however, showing a determination and persistence in this crisis that he had not shown, it seems, in Egypt during the earlier period of this collection of problems. At Myra, he set about gathering another fleet and more soldiers. He contacted Romans to finance his new campaign, although exactly what Romans were involved is not known, and whether they were private contractors or officials of the city.[45] It is difficult to imagine any official being distracted from the greater war to assist a refugee Ptolemy, who had been driven out of his kingdom twice. Nevertheless, he certainly assembled a worthwhile fleet, but when he came out to campaign again in early 87, he was met again by the Cypriot fleet, which was evidently still loyal to Ptolemy IX, defeated and killed.[46]

So by this point, Ptolemy IX could celebrate a string of multiple successes: he had secured the kingship in Egypt, his competing brother was dead, his general Hierax had put down the rebellion in the Thebaid (in which he caused serious damage to Thebes itself),[47] and his fleet commanders in Cyprus had defeated the attempts by his brother to regain the Egyptian kingship. He had now reunited Cyprus and Egypt under one ruler. He cemented his rule by taking Ptolemy X's widow Berenike as his co-regent, though whether they were married is not certain. She, with her children, had accompanied Ptolemy X on his campaigns, but had survived. She returned to Egypt and married (possibly) Ptolemy IX. They travelled to Memphis for a new coronation ceremony, although Ptolemy had been crowned originally many years earlier. But the celebration was also to commemorate Ptolemy's thirtieth year as king, discontinuous though it was.[48] Berenike was, of course, his own daughter, one of the most extreme of the incestuous marriages in the dynasty.

An equally important success for Ptolemy IX may be counted as staying out of the war between Rome and Mithradates. Given his need to defeat the rebellion as a first priority, and the need to ensure his control of Egypt, and volatile Alexandria, keeping Egypt neutral between the combatants in the north cannot have been a difficult decision, nor can it have surprised anyone. For by this time, from his need to concentrate on internal matters, this was the default Ptolemaic attitude to all such wars. A sign of the general appreciation of Ptolemaic neutrality was when Mithradates' forces threatened Athens, and the members of the academy in the city evacuated, choosing Alexandria as their refuge, if only temporarily.[49] This of course could be construed as a pro-Roman gesture, or at least one hostile to Mithradates; it would be sensible by this time for Ptolemy to mend any fences with Rome that were broken.

Next year (86), L. Licinius Lucullus arrived in Alexandria in search of naval support for the campaign against Mithradates. He was acting on instructions from L. Cornelius Sulla, who commanded the Roman forces in Greece, but who was also under condemnation at Rome, where a coup had removed his supporters from power. On his journey to Alexandria, Lucullus had called at Crete and then at Cyrenaica, where he attended to a civic crisis at Cyrene (incidentally, therefore, applying Roman authority in the city, which had been declared 'free').[50] He then clashed with a pirate fleet, allied to Mithradates, and most of his own ships were lost. Despite this misadventure, when he arrived at Alexandria, he was met by Ptolemy IX, who had laid on an extravagant welcome, possibly deliberately elaborate to emphasise that he was comfortably in power, and was welcoming a defeated Roman. It could be construed as another pro-Roman gesture. Ptolemy, however, was facing an awkward decision.

Mithradates had custody of the Ptolemaic princes, children of his dead brother, who had been captured at Kos, while he was negotiating with an enemy force. Mithradates' enemy was now Sulla, but Sulla's whole political situation was ambiguous, to say the least. If Ptolemy supported Lucullus, and therefore Sulla, he might find himself on the receiving end of a Roman attack if the regime in the city won the civil war. Or he might suddenly face a new Ptolemaic anti-king produced as a rival by Mithradates – and the candidate was about twenty years old, an ideal age for inheriting a throne. If he supported Mithradates, both the Roman parties might turn on him, and, if they could not combine, the winner of the contest no doubt would. The only possible answer he could make to Lucullus' request for help was a refusal of assistance and a statement of neutrality.[51] This in fact fitted in well enough with his own earlier policy, since Ptolemy X had been notably friendly towards Rome, while Ptolemy IX had therefore been neutral or anti-Roman.

In the Roman civil war, this attitude was dangerous, even though he could claim to be following his own, and his dynasty's, now-traditional stance, and until late 88 he had been concerned to suppress his own rebellion. He did, however, provide a protected convoy to carry Lucullus on his way to Asia, in which they went only as far as Cyprus. Thus, Ptolemy conclusively demonstrated his possession of a useful naval force, providing a conspicuous diplomatic courtesy, and held to his neutrality in a Roman civil war (and did not extend himself beyond his own territories). Needless to say, neutrality did not suit Sulla, whose point of view had narrowed down to the need for as much support as he could find. A neutral, therefore, was all too easily seen as an enemy.

In fact, Ptolemy was in luck, for Sulla, having won his war against Mithradates, proceeded at once to wage war against his Roman enemies, but then had to spend the rest of his life holding down, or killing, those enemies in Italy. Mithradates was equally difficult for Rome to control, and Lucullus, whom Ptolemy had welcomed and assisted, was deployed to conduct the next campaign against the king. As a result, Sulla was too busy to make any move against Egypt, and Lucullus, also busy enough in Asia Minor, had no cause to.[52]

During his exile from Egypt, Ptolemy X is said to have made a will in favour of Rome. This, however, only happened – if it did, and one must have doubts – after his expulsion from Alexandria, so at the time he did not have a kingdom to bequeath. If Ptolemy X did write such a will, therefore, it had no legal effect, though had a Roman politician such as Sulla been able to take action on it, these paltry legal details would not have stopped him.[53] It could have been used in a Roman assault on Egypt.

Sulla, in fact, did have another arrow to his bow, for during negotiations with Mithradates in 84, Mithradates' hostage, who became Ptolemy XI, had either escaped from him into Roman protection, or had been handed over to Sulla by Mithradates, for whatever reason.[54] Sulla took him to Rome when he returned to the city – that is, he kept the boy a semi-prisoner while he was campaigning in Greece and Asia. Sulla, therefore, had in his custody a viable pretender to the Ptolemaic throne, who could be used at any moment against whoever was in power in Alexandria. As it happened, Sulla was unable to use this weapon against Ptolemy IX, probably because he did not have time to do so. Ptolemy IX was thus able to spend the rest of his life in relative comfort, mainly in Alexandria.

Ptolemy IX served as priest of Alexander and the Deified Ptolemies in 84, an isolated record of these priests, which is discontinuous at this point.[55]

It was no doubt recalled because he was king. But it was possibly noted also because this was the year his cousin escaped into Sulla's protection, and thus became even more dangerous, dynastically speaking, than before. Ptolemy as priest, a very public position, would be a useful way of reminding all who were concerned that he was in office and in power in Egypt; possibly, it was also a subtle message being sent to Rome. But both Ptolemy and Sulla were getting old.

He made one journey to the south of Egypt, visiting Thebes and Hermonthis, the latter in connection with the bull cult of the god Montu. But these two places also figured in the end of the southern revolt, which finally ceased in 88. Thebes was badly damaged in general Hierax's reconquest. The two cities Pathyris and Hermonthis had taken opposite sides, but had contrasting and ironic roles and fates. Pathyris, the loyal community, was destroyed, though by whom is not known; Hermonthis, apparently supporting the rebels, survived, possibly damaged, but it flourished as the centre of the cult of the god Montu, and as a metropolitan centre for the whole region. Presumably, Pathyris was destroyed during 88, no doubt by the rebels before Hierax descended on them; it never recovered, with the result that the letters its soldiers wrote home have survived to be read today.

Of the two potentates, Sulla and Ptolemy IX, Ptolemy died first, in March 80, of natural causes, as they say – that is, of old age; he was sixty-two years old, about average for his immediate family. Sulla lived on in to 79, but never had the opportunity to attend to Egypt, if indeed he ever intended to. Ptolemy IX's successor was his daughter/wife, Berenike, already installed as joint ruler with her father/husband, and now sole ruler.

Chapter 8

Ptolemy XII and his Competitors

For a man who had led a turbulent life, Ptolemy IX died remarkably peacefully – at least so far as we know. He had finally bested his awkward brother, Ptolemy X, and reunited his Cypriot kingdom with Egypt, and had ended up linked to his daughter, a liaison unspecified, but probably only political. But at his death, that daughter, Berenike III, who had added the dynastic name Kleopatra to her titles, became ruling queen.

For a generation that was unusually prolific in producing children, and whose women were so frequently married, there was an unfortunate dearth of male members of the dynasty who were capable of inheriting the kingship. Apart from Berenike III, there was only one male Ptolemy left, the son of Ptolemy X Alexander, who also had the surname of Alexander (II). The children of Ptolemy IX Soter and Selene appear not to have survived. There was, apart from Berenike, also Selene herself, who, after three husbands, was now married to her stepson, who died in this year, 88; she had established herself somewhere in Syria in independence, though the locations most of the time are unknown. A daughter of Ptolemy X Alexander and Berenike appears also not to have survived. Ptolemy X had had a liaison with a concubine, whose name is not known, but by whom he had three children, Kleopatra VI Tryphaina, and two Ptolemies; these were the boys held by Mithradates after being abducted from Kos. Their maternal descent, however, like that of Ptolemy Apion, was outside the Ptolemaic family, and this excluded them from the royal succession, even though they were the children of the king. One of them had been carried off to Rome by Sulla. No doubt, Rome would find a use for him.

As a result of all this, and in the absence of present male heirs, Berenike inherited the kingship of Egypt from her father on his death in 80. There is in this case no record of a will. She was said to have been popular with the Alexandrian crowd, an excitable and untrustworthy body, and had, of course, been consort queen since 88, but all this did not prevent opposition to her rule from developing.[1] One aspect of the demands of her opponents was that she should be partnered with a male Ptolemy. There was only one such person available, Ptolemy Alexander II, living in Rome as Sulla's prize. Sulla, now dictator of Rome, having extended the position from a brief office to oversee emergency elections into a lifetime position, responded to messages from Alexandria that Ptolemy Alexander was needed there.[2]

One can see here a part of the dispute between the parties in Alexandria. Clearly one group wanted Ptolemy Alexander as king; another party, however, feared that his accession would be to foist a Roman puppet on the Ptolemaic state, and could use his non-royal ancestry against him. No doubt, this possible Roman influence was also an aspect of Sulla's calculations. There were also some who felt repugnance to see a woman ruling.

It is likely that Berenike was having trouble imposing her authority – we have no idea of her effectiveness as a ruler – and it is clear that after only six months or so, her authority was to be supplemented, or superseded, by the arrival of Ptolemy Alexander II, who was at once married to her. He was in his early twenties, she was twice his age. Appian, the only source for this event, claims that it was the 'women of the royal house' who demanded a man as the ruler – if he means members of the royal family, the only one was Berenike herself, although he probably meant the women around Berenike. This suggests that Berenike's position was already somewhat shaky. The dynastic situation and the need for a reinforced royal authority pointed to the need for Ptolemy Alexander II, but whereas Berenike was a woman, and therefore unacceptable to many, Ptolemy Alexander was completely inexperienced in Ptolemaic politics and government, and was highly ignorant of Egypt and its systems; the only active model of political behaviour he was familiar with was that of Sulla, whose methods were hardly suitable for anywhere but Rome, and were disastrous there.

Given the apparent demand for his services, Alexander – now Ptolemy XI Alexander – having been recognised as king, clearly felt that he was in a very strong position, 'relying upon Sulla' – or perhaps because he was 'inspired' by Sulla. So much so that he turned on Berenike and murdered her, presumably so as to rule by himself; perhaps the best explanation would be that he wished to rule alone.[3] One may imagine instant disputes between the two over their roles and that Ptolemy Alexander was assuming an authority that would only diminish that of Berenike. He had been in power as king less than three weeks. His ignorance of the attitudes of the Alexandrians was now fatal to him. When the news emerged of Berenike's death at her husband's hands, the volatile crowd, which had only three weeks earlier agitated for him to be king, invaded the palace, dragged the new king out, and killed him in the gymnasium – a repetition of the killings of the family of Agathokles over a century before.[4]

A number of uncertain consequences followed. In Syria, Selene began considering a claim to the Egyptian kingship; she had two sons by Antiochos X, and their descent from her (and from Ptolemy VIII and Kleopatra III) gave them a claim to Egypt now that the direct legitimate line of Ptolemies had ended with the killing Ptolemy XI. In Rome, Ptolemy XI Alexander II had apparently raised a loan from a group of Roman moneylenders to finance his venture, promising that he would repay them in money gained from the Egyptian tax revenues. A variant of this is that he had deposited money at Tyre, presumably once he became king, which was to be used to extinguish the loan. A third variant is that Sulla had financed his venture on the assumption that he would extract repayment from Egypt, 'because he wanted to become rich'. A fourth element is that it was alleged that Ptolemy Alexander had composed a will, though the terms were only rumours; the obvious idea would be to make Rome his heir to Egypt. But the will is never quoted, and indeed may have been an invention of the Roman moneylenders to get control of the money in Tyre.[5]

The complexity of these various notices rather suggests that they were inventions based on rumours, or perhaps simply inventions. It is a fact that later Roman politicians did their best to extract money from Egypt, and this may have been attributed to Sulla by assumption. The will looks very like a Roman invention, for use only until the Tyrian money could be collected. If this ever existed, why would Ptolemy XI need a loan from the moneylenders when he had enough to deposit a repayment sum at Tyre? He had become king by Egyptian request; a loan was scarcely needed. And without a visible will, no claims needed be acknowledged, though the confusion in Egypt might produce promises from candidates for the kingship. The problem therefore landed in the lap of the new king.

Ptolemy's personal ancestry is disputed among modern historians. He was certainly the son of Ptolemy IX Soter, but his mother's name and ethnicity is what is in dispute. The closer one gets in the sources to the time when he was alive, the more certain the statements on the matter. Cicero, for example, was a contemporary, and called him *nothos*, that is, a bastard,[6] and Selene's claim for the kingship for her sons was an indirect indication, at some time after his accession, that she believed he had no claim. He had a younger brother, who was placed as king in Cyprus at about the same time as Ptolemy XII reached Alexandria. With Cyprus as an independent Ptolemaic kingdom this was regarded as a legitimate action.

From the Roman point of view – that is, in particular, Sulla's point of view – this was the placement of a Roman client on the throne of the richest kingdom in the Mediterranean. Ptolemy XI was beholden, particularly to Sulla, who could claim to have rescued him from Mithradates. None of this needed to be spelled out, but it is one of the elements that underlies the whole episode. Sulla probably assumed that Egypt as a whole was now, since Ptolemy was in post, a Roman client state.

The constitutional theory of the Alexandrian mob in establishing the two brothers as kings (if this is not too pretentious a term for something that was apparently decided in the heat of the moment) was that Macedonian kings were subject to such decisions by the army of the kingdom. This had been exploited in the past by such unscrupulous ministers as Sosibios in the late third century BC to legitimise their own (and Agathokles') barely legitimate power, but earlier there had always been a legitimate descendant of Ptolemy I available as king, and the practice had degenerated in the greater Hellenistic kingdoms to a post-accession shouted acclamation by the royal guard, or part of it, only a part of the army and a picked group with a strong self-interest in retaining their posts. The last time it had been used in Macedon, for example, was to bring the regent Antigonos III forward as king in 228 after winning victories. But as a theory of constitutional practice, it was clearly useful, and the Alexandrian mob was no doubt perfectly familiar with it, possibly as no more than a legend.

This practice had, of course, been used twice already in 80, first to confirm Berenike as a ruling queen, though she could be said to be already in such a position, and then to bring Ptolemy XI from Rome, in theory at popular request. Both royal installations had ended disastrously. The second regicide, of Ptolemy XI, could be argued to be the crowd exercising its right to remove a criminal king, the reverse of the acclamation process. It may also have been realised just what was involved in emplacing a man obligated to a distant Roman politician such as Sulla. There is no doubt that, whatever assumptions the Romans, or Sulla, had made in promoting Ptolemy XI's candidacy, they were dealt a serious blow by the actions of the Alexandrians.

It was no doubt also in the minds of some at least of the Alexandrians, that, by turning to Ptolemy XII, a man who was almost thirty years old, they were choosing one who was not beholden to a Roman politician or to Roman moneylenders in any way. Mithradates might have a claim to Egyptian gratitude, but he need hardly be considered. As their new candidate had been held hostage by Mithradates of Pontos for several years, and might have friendly feelings towards him, there may have been the added pleasure of administering a deliberate snub to Rome.

The new king, Ptolemy XII, adopted the surnames Theos and Philopator – 'god' and 'father-loving'. The absence of Philometor ('mother-loving') has been used to indicate his illegitimate birth, commemoration of his non-Ptolemaic mother being omitted,[7] but this seems more a desperate search for significance than a likely dynastic claim. There arrived with him from Mithradates' court his sister Kleopatra (VI) Tryphaina, and they were married at once, at which point Philadelphos ('sibling-loving') was added to his name.[8] Later, he also added Neos Dionysos to the set of names, harking back to Ptolemy III in particular, who had elevated that god to be a patron of the dynasty. He carried this elevation a stage further, however, by playing the flute (*aulos*) at the musical competitions that were a feature of the worship of Dionysos; the Alexandrians nicknamed him Auletes – the flute-player – as a result.[9] This is taken by many to be an insult (since flute players were usually slave girls who were hired to play at parties), but perhaps it does more suitably indicate the seriousness of the king's devotion to the god, and it would be best to be seen as an affectionate compliment.

Ptolemy Auletes had a helpful start to his reign in various ways. His selection by the Alexandrian crowd – in effect, his election by the Greek and Macedonian citizens of the capital city – was an action devoid of foreign influence, so he did not owe any obligation either to Rome or to Mithradates. His rapid marriage to his sister, which was something both must have expected to take place as soon as he became king, was a second legitimation, and an affirmation of their joint dynastic ancestry. And, to improve his position further, in the same year as this marriage, Sulla abdicated the dictatorship in Rome, and then soon died, which drove Roman political attention inwards, and reduced any pressure from Rome, at least for the moment.

On the other hand, Roman interest could not be assumed to be ended. Ptolemaic Egypt was the only Hellenistic state of any power still left now that Mithradates had been defeated and the Seleukid kingdom had vanished.

The lack of direct Roman attention also meant that the new king was not being formally recognised by the Roman Senate. This may not have bothered the Alexandrian mob, but it certainly concerned the more aware of the Alexandrian politicians, since by this time, 'recognition' – to use a modern diplomatic term that is not quite appropriate to the time – gave a degree of protection from Rome's erratic and dangerous politics, although it would emerge later that even this gave no real protection. A lack of Roman recognition, on the other hand, could be used by Roman politicians to exert pressure on Ptolemy, in any way from blackmail to conquest. It left the dynasty and the country in a precarious position, still subject to the vagaries of Roman politics.

Ptolemy XII was therefore living with the danger of a threat of Roman interference in Egyptian affairs, and probably Roman enmity, any permutation of which might emerge at any time. He had made the right political moves after his arrival, whether because he already knew what to do, or, more likely, because he was well advised, but these were internal to Egypt and the dynasty. (The failure of his two predecessors might have persuaded him to seek local advice.) And he had not yet gone through the ceremony of coronation, which was the local equivalent to Rome's lack of 'recognition'. Again, this was an act that was not wholly essential, but to be crowned at Memphis would be another mark of legitimisation. For a man who could be regarded as a usurper, was not wholly recognised by Rome, and was an illegitimate king, who might not be acceptable to a substantial part of the Egyptian population, as so not entitled to be king, the longer a coronation was delayed the more it would become necessary.

The coronation eventually took place in 76. As ever, various reasons for the delay have been produced. Generally, the influence – the malign influence – of Rome is adduced,[10] but there is no exact evidence for this, and, in the face of it, there seems no real reason why Rome should interfere in the Ptolemaic coronation process; recognition by Rome, or any other foreign body, was not a necessary element in that process, though having gone through it would certainly enhance his position at home. More useful is the information that the priest whose task, or honour, it was to conduct the coronation ceremony died earlier in that year. This was Pedubast II, who held the hereditary office of priest of Ptah at Memphis.

This office was of high prestige and had been held within the same family at least since the time of Alexander the Great, and probably before. The priest had charge of the large temple of Ptah in Memphis, and lived in a palace; in effect, he was of the highest of Egyptian nobility, the priests by this time being almost equivalent to the Ptolemies, and, with a direct descent for ten generations, they could be have claimed a greater legitimacy than the kings.[11]

Pedubast II was the current head of this distinguished Egyptian priestly family. His ancestors had officiated at coronation ceremonies and in other ways at Memphis and at other temples, at least since the reign of Ptolemy III, and for Alexander the Great. Pedubast lived from 121 to 76 BC, and had probably officiated at the coronations of Ptolemy IX, Ptolemy X and Berenike, and perhaps that of Kleopatra III. It appears, however, that he did not do so for Ptolemy XII. He would not have had time to crown Ptolemy XI, and may not have needed to do so for either Ptolemy IX in 88, when he simply returned to the kingship, or for Berenike earlier, for she was already queen when she took direct power. But Ptolemy XII, more than other Ptolemaic kings, needed the validation of a coronation, yet Pedubast did not carry through such a ceremony in the four years between the king's accession and the priest's death. It seems unlikely that he was deterred by the lack of recognition from Rome.

The method by which Ptolemy XII became king, however, will certainly have concerned him. First, there was the confusion in 80, with the deaths in various ways of three rulers within a few months, two by violence. Pedubast may not have felt the permanence of Ptolemy XII's regime to be sufficiently established to merit a coronation. In other words, it is possible that he was merely waiting for an opportune moment. But, second, there was also a more personal element in his failure to act: he may have felt that, since the direct legitimate Ptolemaic line had failed at the death of Ptolemy XI, he should have aimed to become king himself.

For Pedubast was the son of a Ptolemaic daughter, Berenike, who had married Pasherenptah II. Her exact ancestry is unclear, but she had been conjectured to have been a daughter of Ptolemy VIII and his concubine Eirene, and so the sister of Ptolemy Apion of Cyrenaica.[12] Her royal name is a clue, but it is also the fact that such royal names – Arsinoe was another – had become fairly popular in priestly circles in Egypt with the establishment of the cult of Ptolemaic queens, notably Arsinoe II.[13] Since Ptolemaic dynastic theory assumed that the right to be king was transmitted through both male and female children, the husband of a royal princess, even though he was not born of a king, gained a claim to the kingship through her. This had been the purpose of the repeated incestuous royal marriages back to Arsinoe II and Ptolemy II, aiming to keep the inheritance within the royal family, and the restriction of handing such princesses only to foreign kings, until relatively recently. The failure of the direct dynastic line in 80, and the election by the Alexandrian citizenry (or by a group speaking in their name) of Ptolemy XII, only drew attention to the existence of other descendants. These included the children of Selene, who were the sons of the Seleukid dynasty, and the current priest of Ptah at Memphis.

Pedubast II had been born in 121, the son of Pasherenptah II and Berenike. He was thus, if Berenike was of royal birth, the grandson of Ptolemy VIII. He was the priest of the dynastic cult and of Ptah at Memphis, and this ancestry, therefore, gave him a theoretical claim to be king, but one that clashed with the constitutional theory that kings of a Macedonian house should be installed by the decision of a meeting of the armed citizenry. (And it was highly unlikely that an Egyptian priest, even if he was the descendant of a royal princess, would be chosen at such a meeting.) But these conflicting sources of power could not efface the personal claimants, not that of Selene and her sons, nor that of Pedubast II in Memphis. And it was Pedubast who was charged with the validating coronation ceremony for his successful competitor, Ptolemy XII. This probable reluctance by the officiating priest seems to be a better reason for the delay in the coronation of the new king than any non-existent objections from Rome.

Pedubast II died in 76. Ptolemy XII now persuaded Pedubast's son, Pasherenptah III, who was only fourteen years old, to perform the coronation ceremony at last. No doubt, his youth was a factor in his agreement to carry out the ceremony. It was indeed fortunate that his father had died at that time. It may have been this event, which was a particularly visible royal performance, emphasising Ptolemy's royal status and position, which set off a series of disputes and decisions in the next year or so.

The reaction of Ptolemaic claimants to the coronation ceremony was to dispute Ptolemy's right to be king in Egypt – this was the argument of Selene and her two sons by Antiochos X – and a claim by two unnamed men to Cyrenaica, sons possibly of Apion, or of Auletes by a non-royal woman. The two Ptolemies could argue that Apion's bequest of Cyrenaica to Rome, not having been formally taken up by Rome, was no longer valid, and that Cyrenaica should therefore revert to Egypt's rule. It is not a strong argument, especially in the face of the ruthlessness of Rome, and the occasional activity of Roman magistrates such as Lucullus in Cyrenaica, but it was clearly worth a try.

Ptolemy Auletes' new status as a crowned monarch no doubt persuaded all involved that to expect any further change in Egypt was now highly unlikely; without a coronation he could be regarded as a mere temporary ruler. But now that he had gone through a coronation ceremony, the only recourse for those hoping to remove him was to appeal to Rome to accomplish the change. If it was Auletes and his brother claiming Cyrenaica, the same enhanced status for Auletes might persuade Rome to hand the region back to one or other of the two kings, or jointly. (Ptolemy of Cyprus was probably Auletes' heir at this point; Auletes had only one daughter so far.)

Any claim by Auletes would come up against Apion's will, of course, and there were also the disputed wills of Ptolemy X and Ptolemy XI, both of whom purported to bequeath Egypt to Rome. The former was no longer king when he made a will; the latter's will may have been a forgery – but in Roman hands both could be used as validating the seizure of Cyprus and Egypt, or both. Raising the issue of Cyrenaica, therefore, Ptolemy XII was also awakening dangers, probably unnecessarily; he did not get Cyrenaica.

Certainly, it was known that Cyrenaica was in need of some imperial governance. Ten years before, L. Licinius Lucullus had intervened at Cyrene city to sort out an internal quarrel, and this may have been unsuccessful, while other cities probably suffered the same problem of irreconcilable internal disputes.[14] The land had been under firm Ptolemaic rule for well over a century until Ptolemy Apion died, with some problems under Ptolemy VIII when he ruled it in the 160s. The removal of a strong and dictatorial government was likely to have upset the local balance, both within the cities and between them. Twice it had been willed to Rome by its kings, (Ptolemy VIII and Ptolemy Apion), neither of whom probably expected the bequest to be carried through, since they seem to have made the wills primarily to fend off predators. But Rome was becoming addicted to inheriting kingdoms – Attalid Asia, accepted in 133, but only secured in 129 after a war, was a very wealthy land, and its riches were now pouring into the pockets of Roman agents and moneylenders. Cyrenaica was rich in grain production, where the harvest was ready a month before that in Greece, so it could relieve the winter shortages (and charge high prices) and it had a profitable trade with interior Africa. The need to import food was a problem that Rome was now having to face, particularly as the city itself expanded, and it has been suggested that the threat from Cretan pirates against the grain trade between Cyrenaica and Italy was one of the reasons for increased attention by Rome to sea safety in the next years.[15]

So the results of the appeals to be assigned some or all of the Ptolemaic territories were not what the claimants wanted or expected. Cyrenaica having been brought to the Senate's attention, its reaction was to impose a measure of Roman government; yet the minimal importance of the region to Rome so far meant that it appointed a governor of only quaestorian status, the first being P. Cornelius Lentulus Marcellinus, who was assigned in 75, although the names of any successors are not known. It may be that Marcellinus was given the same task as Lucullus ten years earlier – to sort out local disputes; it is probable that the two men had the same quaestorian rank, not the usual qualification for a provincial governor, who were normally of praetorian or consular rank. The request by Selene on behalf of her sons for Egypt was refused by the Senate in an unsettlingly blunt and brusque, even insulting, fashion, no doubt in hopes that the request would not be repeated, but Selene had virtually no territorial base by this time, and therefore little or no power, so she could be effectively ignored.

The requests were therefore refused. And meanwhile, the teenage priest who had performed the coronation ceremony was rewarded by Auletes, not just by his appointment as priest of the dynastic cult at Memphis, but also as 'prophet of pharaoh' at Alexandria, while the king undertook more frequently than his predecessors to attend to the pharaonic duties at Memphis in person.[16]

This is therefore part of a general royal effort to bring the Egyptian priesthood round to support the new royal dignity. The priests may well have hesitated until the priest of Ptah actually conducted the coronation. At the same time he aimed to defuse the possible claim of Pasherenptah III to the throne; the fact that Pedubast's successor was a child helped. The issue of Cyrenaica, which the Ptolemaic government would appear to have felt was still in question since the apparently unwilling Roman near refusal of the bequest of Ptolemy Apion, was settled by the imposition of Roman provincial government, even if intermittent and minimal, and so in the most decisive fashion. Selene and her sons, snubbed by the Senate, were ignored also by Ptolemy XII, while Pasherenptah III's potential claim was smothered. But the new closeness of Roman power to Egypt could be a threat once Rome had emerged from its own problems at home – a new war with Mithradates in 72–69 helped to keep the Roman threat away. But Rome's other reaction, refusing Selene's request in so peremptory a fashion, could be assumed to be, in effect, the diplomatic recognition that Ptolemy may well have been hoping for, but delivered in a characteristically ambiguous Roman manner.

Ptolemy XII survived these challenges, mainly because of Roman actions and inactions – that is, Rome pursued its own interests, as one would expect, just as did Egypt and every other power. Rome was also much preoccupied with undoing Sulla's oligarchic reforms, and then solving disputes with Mithradates, which culminated in that war in 72–69, exactly at the time that Ptolemy XII had a succession crisis to overcome, and Selene was besieged and captured at Ptolemais-Ake by Tigranes and was then executed. Ptolemy continued to conciliate the Egyptian priesthood by enhancing the authority of temples at Ptolemais in the south, and at Theadelphia and Euhemeria, both in the Fayum. These were Egyptian-type institutions where Egyptian gods were worshipped – two temples of Isis, one of the crocodile gods and one of Ammon – but they were in heavily Greek-settled places. All of these temples received the right of asylum. He also founded the building of, or improvement of, or decoration of, other temples throughout the country; this included the completion, after a century and a half, of the temple at Edfu, started in the reign if Ptolemy III in the 230s.[17]

In 74/73, there is the first mention of a new official, 'the *epistratego*s and *strategos* of the Red and Indian Seas'.[18] This is the first official acknowledgement we have of such an office, since the voyages of Hippalos and Eudoxos. It is an indication that the Red Sea and Indian Ocean trade had become large enough to merit the government's full-time attention. It may also be an indication that an attempt was being made to exert an official control over the trade. It had been initiated originally under official initiative by decisions of Ptolemy VIII, and it may have languished since then in the face of official attention being directed at wars and succession problems, though it must be said that the *strategos* inscription of 74/73 is not necessarily contemporary with the origin of the office. There may have been individual sailings since Hippalos' voyage or voyages then but the innovation of a *strategos* for the seas would suggest that there had been an increase in official supervision and the institution of naval patrols, specifically for the Indian trade in addition to the naval anti-pirate patrols and escorts; no doubt, any increase in such a valuable trade would stimulate an increase in piracy. The title of the new official certainly suggests that it was a naval office. If it was under strict naval supervision, no doubt it was also to a degree restricted, even if protected.

Strabo suggests that there were only twenty ships sailing to India each year in the 40s or 30s BC, which might suggest an annual convoy, not individual sailings.[19] Of course, the geography of the Indian Ocean and the monsoon climate regime imposed restrictions of their own on the timing of sailings; this would make government control all the easier. One may note also that the Ptolemaic regime had normally ensured a state control over the whole series of individual trades or products, and to do so for the Indian trade would probably be an automatic royal and bureaucratic reaction. In addition, the regime had normally exercised a strict control over the export of metallic currency. This would explain why, whereas the discovery of Roman coins in India is relatively common and widespread, few Ptolemaic coins have been found. It is assumed that the Roman coins were in part the product of exporting Indian goods; the absence of Ptolemaic coins may imply a trade by barter, or only a small trade.

In 70 or 69, the problem of the succession re-emerged. Ptolemy XII had been married to Kleopatra Tryphaina, his sister, for ten years. They had produced one daughter, Berenike IV, but no other children. It may have been the lack of a male heir that led him to put Kleopatra Tryphaina aside. She is recorded officially in a document on 7 August 69, but not in another document dated 25 December 68, which therefore mark the time during which she was removed, though she was apparently not killed.[20] Instead, the king, or rather a new wife, began producing children – probably four of these – in the next ten years, beginning with Kleopatra, the future Egyptian ruler, who was born about the end of 70.

The birth date of Kleopatra, the future queen, indicates that the king had two wives simultaneously for at least two years before putting Berenike aside. (Any significant trawl through Ptolemaic history would produce other instances of this.) If the need for an heir was indeed the reason for this family development, as seems very likely, Ptolemy XII was evidently successful: his new wife produced two daughters, and then two sons. This second wife, despite her prolific childbearing, is an even more shadowy person than Tryphaina. Her name is not known, though she is thought to have been of noble Egyptian ancestry, specifically perhaps from the family of the boy priest who put the crown on the king's head back in 76.[21] There are certainly no alternative Ptolemaic women available for him to marry (other than his

Drachma coin from *c.*138 BC showing portrait of Ptolemy VIII.
(*American Numismatic Society via Wikimedia Commons*)

Probable bust of Ptolemy IX.
(*J. Paul Getty Museum via Wikimedia Commons*)

Bust of Ptolemy X Alexander. (*Wikimedia Commons*)

Tetradrachm coin of Ptolemy X Alexander, *c.*101 BC.

Bust of Ptolemy XII, who came to the throne after the murder of the last legitimate member of the family. His portrait, presumably more or less accurate, does show a strong Ptolemaic likeness. This was the father of Kleopatra, king of three decades, but a man who succumbed all too readily to Roman demands. (*Wikimedia Commons*)

Wall relief of Ptolemy XII (third from left) at the Temple of Sobek receiving the Breath of Life. (*Adobe Stock*)

Kleopatra VII – the classical view. This is the portrait that is usually accepted as a good likeness of the queen, though the nose has been 'restored', and it is not actually labelled anywhere as of her. What is perhaps the most convincing argument in favour of this as a portrait is that it is manifestly of a very plain face; her reputation for beauty clearly lies in her position rather than her looks. (*Wikimedia Commons*)

A possible coin portrait of Kleopatra VII. It bears little resemblance to any other portraits, but this only emphasises that few, if any, were actually taken from life. It is certainly of a queen, wearing the diadem, but Kleopatra was not the only queen of Egypt. (*PHGCOM via Wikimedia Commons/CC BY-SA 3.0*)

Kleopatra – the Egyptian view. (*Kevin Dinno via Wikimedia Commons/ CC BY-SA 3.0*)

The Roman Invaders

Julius Caesar, careworn and old.   Mark Antony.

Kleopatra and Antony. A fairly flattering view of the pair. (*CNG Coins*)

The Victors

Octavian, soon to be Augustus. (*Carole Raddato via Wikimedia Commons/CC BY-SA 2.0*)

M. Vipsanius Agrippa, the great commander. (*Marie-Lan Nguyen via Wikimedia Commons/ CC BY 2.5*)

The Victory

The field of victory – the remains of Nikopolis, the city founded as a monument to the victory at Actium. (*Mark Landon via Wikimedia Commons/CC BY 4.0*)

'Egypt taken'. A coin issued in Octavian's name to publicise and celebrate his victory. (*CNG Coins*)

infant daughter), but, if the priestly family did have a Ptolemaic woman (the Berenike noted earlier) in their ancestry, he was selecting his replacement wife from the rival semi-Ptolemaic family of priests of Memphis, the same family he had honoured, and which had crowned him. Nevertheless, the marriage was regarded, as so often in these late Ptolemaic years, as illegitimate. But, after the accession of Ptolemy XII, whose origin was very similar, it could be assumed that new rules in the royal succession now existed.

At the same time as the problem of Kleopatra Tryphaina was being summarily dealt with by Ptolemy XII, the problem of Kleopatra Selene was morphing into a new version. Selene had spent the last twenty years somewhere in Syria or Kilikia – she had to be expelled from Antioch in 83 by a popular rising – and by 69 she had been driven to take refuge finally in Ptolemais-Ake. She had been married four times but had been a widow since the death of Antiochos X at the hands of the Parthians in 88. It is not known exactly where she had been since then but she had made an attempt in 75 to persuade the Romans to set her and her two sons up as replacement rulers of Egypt, though the Romans had brushed her off summarily. This ploy had therefore not worked and by 72, her residence in Syria had been reduced to Ptolemais by the invasion of Syria by the King of Armenia, Tigranes.

Tigranes laid siege to the city where Selene had taken refuge, and she had persuaded the citizens to resist the attack. This ploy was as unsuccessful as all her earlier attempts at marriage or refuge or political claims. Tigranes captured the city. It seems likely that the citizens were less than enthusiastic, and Tigranes had proved himself to be a successful diplomat, so perhaps he was able to persuade them to accept his rule. The price they paid for an end to the siege was to surrender Selene to him. He took her into north Syria, where she was executed.[22]

No Ptolemaic attempt was made to interfere in this process; indeed, the death of another competitor for Ptolemy XII's throne would perhaps be welcome, despite Selene's consistent failure to have any effect. But if she was unsuccessful, she left two sons, Antiochos and (probably) Seleukos, who had as good a claim to the Ptolemaic throne as to the (recently extinguished) Seleukid. The removal of Selene had not therefore removed the threat of interference from Syria. And the threat from Rome was now developing once more.

Chapter 9

The Tribulations of Ptolemy XII

The existence of an Egyptian priestly branch of the Ptolemaic royal family was descended from the marriage of Berenike, probably a sister of Ptolemy Apion, and the chief priest of Ptah of Memphis, Pasherenptah II, as noted in the last chapter. This is mirrored by the emergence, a generation or two earlier, of Egyptians in high positions in the administration and the military. The army that Ptolemy X Alexander gathered and posted to Syria and to Pelusion to defend the country against Ptolemy IX's Cypriot army was composed in part, possibly in large part, of Egyptian troops, as the letters sent home from there to Pathyris show. Add to this the probability that Ptolemy XII's second wife, the mother of four of his children, including Kleopatra and two sons, was probably Egyptian, maybe from the same priestly family as that into which Berenike had married two generations earlier, and which had formed the dynastic link.

There was thus a visible process of intermarriage at the highest social level between Egyptians and royal Macedonians between the Ptolemaic royal family and the family of the priests of Ptah at Memphis, and there is evidence of the enlistment or conscription of Egyptians into the Ptolemaic army, and the possibility of Egyptians rising to the highest ranks. Also, there were Egyptians who rose through the bureaucratic ranks to the highest levels of the government apparatus, to governor general of the Thebaid, one of the most important posts in the bureaucracy. This was an erratic process, interrupted by the great revolts by Egyptians in the south.[1] It is clear therefore that the pressure of integration into one ethnicity was under way, if with difficulty, and at long last. It had, of course, been under way from the beginning of the Macedonian conquest, at the lower levels of the social situation, by the marriage of Greeks with Egyptian women. Of course, the great Egyptian revolts were also an aspect of such integration, in that they were protests at the existence of the general oppression of the native Egyptians. The new aspect of the integration process, at the official level and at the royal, existed mainly between the royal family and the Egyptian priestly class, not at that of the peasantry, for among the latter it had happened already.[2]

There is no doubt, nevertheless, that the majority of those in high social and administrative positions were still of Greek or other European descent in the first century BC. The royal family was also still essentially Macedonian in origin, and had, by its system of incestuous intermarriages managed to preserve intact its blood heritage as Macedonian for more than two centuries from the first Ptolemy to Ptolemy IX and X. The royal out-marriages that had taken place, however, since the marriage of Kleopatra Thea to Alexander Balas, and then to the Seleukid kings Demetrios II and Antiochos VII, had resulted in two developments: first, the export of Ptolemaic princesses in the next generation (Tryphaina, Kleopatra IV and Selene) whose quarrels and mutual murderousness encouraged the failings and divisions of the Seleukid family. This had certainly happened before, but the family had revived. Second, it led to the eventual arrival of Egyptian women into the royal family in Egypt itself. These two changes took place more or less simultaneously: the presumed Ptolemaic lady Berenike married Pasherenptah II at some time in the 120s (their son was born in 121), and the Ptolemaic princesses were married into the Seleukid family in the 110s. The effect of these out-marriages were profound.

The presence of Ptolemaic princesses within the Seleukid family was probably one of the main reasons for that family undergoing disintegration. The murders of two of these princesses not surprisingly soured relations within and between the families for the future, and the Seleukid family ceased to rule anything two generations before the Ptolemaic family itself failed. The presence and hapless inactivity of Selene, rocketing from husband to husband and in the end being expelled even from the Seleukid city of Antioch during the last decades of the family's struggles, was clearly a hindrance, if nothing worse.

The introduction of Egyptian blood into the Ptolemaic royal family in its last generation, as a result of the marriage of Ptolemy XII to an Egyptian woman, on the other hand, resulted in the genetic refreshment of the increasingly interbred family, and the production of a group of descendants of Ptolemy XII whose work to hold their inheritance together preserved the kingdom's existence for several decades in the face of Roman greed, interference and enmity; both Ptolemy XII and his daughter Kleopatra VII worked heroically, in their different ways, to save their kingdom.

The failure of the two imperial dynasties, however, happened in contradictory ways. The Seleukids quarrelled and conducted several serial wars between themselves over a period of thirty years, during which the kingdom broke up into principalities for various members of the family, while other parts of it detached themselves into independence – provinces turned into independent kingdoms, cities revived their long-held wishes to become independent city states, and external enemies approached. The final blow was perhaps the expulsion of Selene from Antioch, the Seleukid capital city, in 83, though the autonomy of Seleukeia-in-Pieria, the original royal city, in 109 was another obvious blow. Of the approaching enemies the most dangerous from the 120s onwards was the Parthian kingdom; there seems to have been minimal Roman interference in Syria during the disintegration process, and the first distinct interference by a Roman official only came in 70 BC.

For the Ptolemies, by contrast, there was a steadily rising threat emanating from Rome, beginning with the acceptance of the bequest of Cyrenaica to the city in 96. Compared with this, the dynastic quarrels and peasant uprisings within Egypt were of minimal importance. These quarrels and risings, on the other hand, though hardly serious in themselves, progressively weakened the kingdom in its resistance to Roman encroachment. The debility of the Ptolemaic kingdom was the result of these internal disputes as well as Rome's pressures, and yet the kingdom still had sufficient power and resources to make a good fight of it when the final battle approached. Kleopatra's conduct at the battle of Actium, when she pulled her forces out towards the end – 'desertion', said the Romans – was all of a piece with her aim of preserving her kingdom. To consider Actium a purely Roman battle is to ignore Kleopatra's own personal and political agenda – probably Mark Antony did so; Octavian, on the other hand, deliberately exaggerated her involvement, while ignoring her purposes, a distortion that has misled many historians.

The weakening of the dynasty, however, was a contributory factor of great importance in the general weakening of the state, and this was self-inflicted by the dynasty. For over a century, the Ptolemies had been building up a serious genetic problem for themselves by their practice of incestuous marriages. This practice was adopted, of course, in the interests of the dynasty's continuing hold on power, so it is ironic that it was one of the prime causes of its failure. The theory was that the capability of transmitting royal authority passed into all royal children, so that all the male children had the capability to become kings, and the female children could transmit this capability to their husbands. Two brutal consequences followed – surplus males tended to be culled, and females were kept unmarried, or culled. These issues originated even in the first generation of the dynasty, notably with the apparent sequestration of Philoteria, the daughter of Ptolemy I. The particular Ptolemaic refinement of incestuous marriage followed from this theory. It is not that uncommon a practice amongst ruling families, down to the European Habsburgs, though the claim that it was a practice inherited, or copied, from the previous pharaonic dynasties is not correct, at least not since the fifteenth century BC. The theory included a particular Ptolemaic refinement, which was the notorious practice of sibling marriage; the mistake was that although this seemed the best way to keep the dynasty safe and in power, it would work only for a time, and the history of the family indicated its flaw.

For this practice limits the genetic inheritance of the next generation, not at first, but by repetition, the limits become narrower. For several generations the Ptolemies had, probably unintentionally, succeeded in avoiding the major genetic damage that is caused by incest. The first generation that committed incest with the intent to produce offspring was that of Ptolemy IV (222–204). (The earlier case, the marriage of Ptolemy II and his sister Arsinoe II (between 274 and 270) was not fertile, whether or not the absence of children of the marriage was deliberate.) Ptolemy IV married his full sister Arsinoe III (their brothers and mother had been killed); they had one child, Ptolemy V, who married out, to Kleopatra Syra, the Seleukid princess. This rescued the dynasty for a time, and the next generation, with Ptolemy VI and VIII, was generally capable and efficient, as was their sister, Kleopatra II, and all three were long-lived as well. In that generation, however, the incest became embodied into the family's practices – Ptolemy VI and VIII both married their sister Kleopatra II (simultaneously), though while Ptolemy VI lived, only he fathered children – Ptolemy VIII had to wait his turn. And Ptolemy VIII also later married his niece Kleopatra III (his first wife's daughter by Ptolemy VI). All these marriages were fertile, but the sons of Ptolemy VI and the elder son of Ptolemy VIII died early (though not necessarily from the effects of incest – Ptolemy Memphites, for instance, was murdered – but this act was a part of the concentration on restricting the genetic inheritance). In the next generation, Ptolemy IX, the son and grandson of incestuous marriages, married two of his sisters, Kleopatra IV and Selene; the first marriage produced one daughter, Berenike III, the second two sons, who disappear from the record and probably died as children. His brother Ptolemy X married twice, first to an unknown and therefore probably non-Ptolemaic woman, with whom he fathered Ptolemy XI, and then to his niece Kleopatra Berenike III. The marriage with the non-Ptolemaic woman produced Ptolemy XI, who demonstrated some vigour, but was lynched by the Alexandrians after murdering his wife – the wrong sort of vigour perhaps. The second marriage, with his niece, produced a daughter only, who seems to have died as a child. Ptolemy IX married yet again, his third wife, or took a concubine, whose name is not known, but was therefore probably a non-Ptolemy. They produced three children, two sons and a daughter.

This, therefore, is the generation in which the cumulative genetic damage caused by repeated sibling marriages becomes clear. Between them, Ptolemy IX and X married two sisters and a niece, and produced two daughters, one of whom died young. They also married, between them, two non-Ptolemaic women, and had four children. These non-sibling unions had the same effect genetically as the marriage of Kleopatra Syra to Ptolemy V in enabling the production of healthily long-lived children.

But the practice of sibling marriage was now embedded in the family. Ptolemy XII, son of Ptolemy IX, married his sister Kleopatra Tryphaina; after ten years, they had produced only a daughter, Kleopatra Berenike IV, and no sons. One of the effects of the series of incestuous marriages would thus appear to have been the inability to produce children, or to produce children who did not live very long. Modern studies point to the increased likelihood of spontaneous abortion, and the probability of exaggerated unwelcome physical characteristics.[3] Another possible effect was that children that were conceived tended to be female, which rather defeated the object, which was mainly to produce sons to inherit the kingdom.

The conclusion to be reached is that the fertility of the Ptolemaic family was already failing in the generation of Ptolemy IX and X (only one surviving child from three marriages), and the kings were resorting to what in contemporary law would have been regarded as illegitimate liaisons – those with non-Ptolemaic women – to ensure the continuation of the dynasty. Even so, one of these illegitimate lines failed to reproduce (Ptolemy XI was murdered, having himself murdered his Ptolemaic wife). It was becoming clear that only by means of a marriage to a non-Ptolemaic woman would the products of repeated incestuous marriages be able to reproduce, though this was not the lesson learned. The obvious resort would have been marriage to a foreign royal woman, probably a Seleukid, the only family the Ptolemies seem to have recognised as socially equal, but by the time the problem had become clear, there were none left, and anyway, Seleukid children by this time were also of Ptolemaic descent. Or, of course, they could abandon this dynastic theory, but this evidently did not occur to them.

The difficulties of Ptolemy XII followed in part from his genetic inheritance. He was a son of King Ptolemy IX, but not of a Ptolemaic wife, which should have guaranteed a reduction in the genetic damage. But then his marriage to his sister produced only a daughter, Berenike III; his liaison with a new non-Ptolemaic wife (who is thought to have been a daughter of the Egyptian priestly family of Memphis) by contrast was immediately fertile, and eventually produced two daughters and two sons. He apparently married her well before Kleopatra Tryphaina was 'put aside', presumably in order to ensure that his new marriage was fertile. (Kleopatra VII was born before her stepmother was put aside.) To complete the story, in the next generation Kleopatra VII married her brother, which produced no children – indeed, she disdained him; it was probably a nominal marriage only. Her later liaisons with Julius Caesar and Mark Antony, brief and intermittent though they tended to be, were again immediately fertile; these were also illegitimate in the view of the legal practice of the time, not only in Roman law but in Greek – as well as not being acceptable in Ptolemaic dynasty theory. One may say, therefore, that by the time of Kleopatra VII, the Ptolemaic dynastic problem had become desperate; it had clearly been evident in the time of her father and grandfather also. Kleopatra VII could only produce children who were unacceptable in both law and dynastic theory; no doubt had she survived, however, the dynastic theory, not having worked, would have been jettisoned – but she did not have time to organise that.

The dynasty was therefore, in the generation of Ptolemy IX and X, heading for extinction by genetic suicide unless the practice of sibling marriage, and probably marriages between all close relatives, was abandoned. By their marriages to non-Ptolemaic women, the kings had clearly had some indication of the necessary solution. Perhaps Ptolemy Auletes, with his decision to 'put aside' Kleopatra VI Tryphaina, understood that probability when he chose as his second wife a woman with only a small element of Ptolemaic genetic inheritance. The lesson had presumably become clear earlier to those who could see, but it was disregarded when his daughter and son were married, and there is no real sign that it ever was understood in a genetic sense.

The dynasty had broken its own rules more than once in recent generations by its marriages with non-Ptolemaic women. This suggests a degree of desperation to ensure a male inheritance. It is also an element in the weakening of the royal authority. No king from the death of Ptolemy IX in 80 was born of a 'legal' marriage of siblings – legal in the dynastic sense, that is. After generations of insisting that this was the correct way of producing legitimate children, the abandonment of the practice undermined the family's own legitimacy.

That inheritance, however, included another fatal element that continued to work in the family. The lack of living children in the generation of Ptolemy XII at least located the practice of sibling marriage as part of the problem, but the antipathy of the times to obeying a ruling queen had been evident in the difficulties of Kleopatra II and III, Kleopatra Thea in Syria, and Selene, and it made Kleopatra VII, clearly the most able member of the family since Ptolemy VI, into a vengeful murderess. She eliminated her siblings in order to be able to rule alone, and extended her killing to any other apparent competitor. Incest reduced the production of living children, and misogyny restricted rule to males, despite the evident ability of many Ptolemaic females; add in the willingness, even necessity, to murder any other relatives, and there is a conspectus of conditions that were guaranteed to bring any dynasty to an end.

The Ptolemaic family and the priestly family at Memphis, being particularly exclusive, had been among the last to integrate with members of the other ethnic group, Greek with Egyptian, Egyptian with Greek. It was normal that Greeks, the majority of whom had migrated into Egypt, originally as soldiers, acquired wives from amongst the Egyptian population. Since they were generally wealthier than the Egyptians this was not too difficult, and must have been the custom from the arrival of Greeks and Macedonians in Egypt with Alexander.

Collections of papyri detailing the vicissitudes of families present examples of the process. The family of Dryton, a cavalry officer from the Macedonian *polis* of Ptolemais in Upper Egypt who lived from *c*.195 BC to *c*.113, left a set of documents from which the family history can be recovered in outline.[4] Ptolemais was in the south, a city clearly planted not too far from Thebes in order to be a government watchtower over the local Egyptian population.

Settlements of Greeks, either as cleruchs or as individuals, were fairly rare in the region, which is one reason why the area was prone to rebellions by Egyptians. The plantation of Greek-speaking colonists began to be more significant after the great revolt of the Thebaid between 207 and 185. In that time, Ptolemais was in the front line of the fighting that was going on when Dryton was born. As an adult he joined the army and quickly was promoted to an officer in a cavalry regiment; he was thus of a high social status, particularly in the south, where such officers were rare. He married about the time he joined the army, a factor that suggests that even as a recruit he was well paid, or had other resources.

Dryton's family had Greek names – Pamphilos, Dryton, Esthladas – which indicates that his ancestors were from the Dorian part of Greece, quite probably Crete. The family is only known from Pamphilos, Dryton's father, and from Theron, his wife's grandfather, but this carried the genealogy back to at least the 250s. Their ancestors had arrived in Egypt as mercenaries and so he was in a family with a tradition of military service. Dryton married Sarapias, the daughter of Esthladas (and granddaughter of Theron), probably about 175, when Dryton himself was about twenty years old. They had one child only, so far as can be discerned, or at least only one living child, and Sarapias vanished from the record soon after the child's birth, which appears to have occurred in 158 BC, after almost twenty years of marriage. It is assumed that she had died, possibly in childbirth. Dryton was transferred to Pathyris in the late 150s (after Sarapias' presumed death), and there he married again. His second wife was Sermouthis, also called Apollonia, who was one of four sisters, all of whom had names in both Egyptian and Greek like Apollonios/Senmonthis; others are Ammonios/Pakorbis, and Dionysios/Plenis, the Greek names having a distinct similarity to the Egyptian, at least when spoken; the Egyptian names are furnished with Greek endings. The women were, however, completely Egyptian in origin, and Pathyris was an Egyptian town in which much of the population spoke little or no Greek. It had been part of the great revolt half a century before, and Dryton had been posted there as part of a general strengthening of the military presence in the south; another revolt, led by a man called Harsiese, happened in 131–130.

Dryton and his wife produced five daughters, all recorded with the usual double names; this practice, however, ceased with the latest documents in the archive, by which time the women were being recorded only in their Egyptian names. By the time he died, it would seem that Dryton was fully immersed in the life of the Egyptian town. His wife had been busy for a quarter of a century in commercial dealings by which she had supplemented the family income considerably, above all in moneylending; Dryton himself had a considerable income as a cavalry officer and he had supplemented this by investing in land, including a vineyard. The family was one of the wealthiest in the town.

The family archive only documents their activities until about 100 BC; ten years later, the town of Pathyris became involved in the revolt that began in the area in 91, and by the end of 88 it had been destroyed by the rebels, in what was probably a final desperate offensive, for their centre, Thebes, was also badly damaged at this time in the governmental reconquest. Quite probably the Dryton family was also destroyed during the brutal reconquest, which was conducted by the general Hierax appointed by Ptolemy IX. Thebes itself also suffered heavy damage in the fighting; it was rebuilt, but Pathyris remained desolate and was never reconstituted as a community. (It is from this circumstance, and due to modern archaeological excavations, that we owe our knowledge of Dryton's family, from the discovery of their archive in the ruins, as with the letters sent home by the soldiers in Syria and Pelusion. The fact that these documents were left in the ruins is good evidence that if the bodies of the family had been found, then the family had been destroyed; no one had returned to find the documents, which were, in effect, the family archive.)

This family archive illuminates one aspect of the integration of Greeks and Egyptians, which is less than expected; the Greeks in the family became Egyptianised. Dryton, who married into an Egyptian family in an Egyptian town, probably had few Greeks as neighbours. The same sort of conclusion may be reached in the realm of religion. The new Greek city of Alexandria had temples of Greek gods, together with the Greco-Egyptian Serapis, but it remained a Greek city throughout its Greek and Roman history; in this case it was the Egyptians who were the immigrants, and who adapted to the Greek culture. Elsewhere in the country, the dynastic cult was fairly widespread, but it was almost the only intrusion of Greek religion into the Egyptian pantheon, and even this was less than wholly Greek. It could be said to have fitted into the divination of the Egyptian pharaohs in the past; significantly, the cult buildings of the dynasty were mainly in the north, with few in the rebellious and more strongly Egyptian south.

The Ptolemaic dynasty identified the priesthood as the key group who were to be conciliated in order to control the rest of the Egyptian population. This only worked intermittently. Egyptian priests, generally close to the peasant population, were usually involved in many of the Egyptian rebellions. It was an expensive matter in providing subsidies for the temples, for the construction of new temples, for the maintenance of them and the priests themselves, and even as outright bribes. Perhaps as effective was the pragmatic Greek acceptance of the need to honour the Egyptian gods, on the sensible grounds that they were the gods of the country, and therefore ought to receive their worship as new but permanent inhabitants. This was a major change from the guffawing incredulity of Herodotos in the fifth century BC when he discussed the Egyptian worship of animals; note also the attitude of Romans such as the senator Memmius, who regarded the crocodiles he saw in the Fayum as a playful tourist attraction.[5] Some Greeks became entangled in the Egyptian religion, and no doubt some Egyptians worshipped Greek gods, if it seemed useful,[6] but most Greeks simply behaved towards the Egyptian gods as they did towards the Greek gods they were more familiar with, and most Egyptians ignored the Greek gods as irrelevant to their lives.

Yet the societies of Greek and Egyptians were so different that integration was difficult, and it was certainly resisted by many on both sides. It could take place at the village level where Greek immigrants needed wives and servants, but they, like Dryton, because of their greater wealth, became socially and economically dominant; in addition, the Greeks had a strong tendency to live with other Greeks in the cities, or in cleruchic settlements, which were Greek villages and small towns. Their society was Greek, in which the people spoke Greek, and maybe had little contact with Egyptians other than as servants and slaves – and, of course, wives. Dryton lived both in the heavily Greek society in Ptolemais and then in an Egyptian town at Pathyris, surrounded by people speaking Egyptian. It is likely that he would be compelled to speak Egyptian, in Pathyris, even if he did not know it from growing up in Ptolemais. In Ptolemais, he was a Greek; in Pathyris he was a Greek who was slowly becoming an Egyptian. In Pathyris, the Egyptians continued to speak Egyptian, many with little or no Greek; Dryton, with an Egyptian wife, probably learnt some of the Egyptian language, indeed, he probably knew some before he arrived in the town. His wife certainly learned Greek, if the documents they left behind are any guide, and she was literate in both Greek and demotic Egyptian. The double names for the Egyptian women were apparently simply a formal Greek custom, as the later documents in the archive demonstrate that they were using their Egyptian names under normal circumstances; the Greek names could easily be discarded, as in the later documents they were.

The royal family and the Memphis priestly family were therefore only catching up with their subjects in the matter of integrating the two populations when Berenike married the chief priest of Memphis, and when Ptolemy XII, a long generation later, married his Egyptian second wife (as Dryton had a century earlier). The process of integration had therefore been slow – Dryton had a Greek life in a Greek polis for the first half of his long life. In part, this was no doubt due to a mutual antipathy between resentful Egyptian natives and arrogant Greek rulers, but, once the process of integration had reached the royal family, the Egyptians might come to regard that family as having become domesticated. One might argue, counterfactually, that at some time after the reign of Kleopatra VII – herself a perfect example of the results of intermarriage and Greek–Egyptian integration – the division between them might have faded away. But this process was halted and diverted by the arrival of the Romans as governors. They replaced the Greek rulers with an even more exclusive group of governing bureaucrats, living in Alexandria. Below government level the Greek–Egyptian integration did continue, but under Roman rule the exploitation of Egypt continued even more greedily than in the Ptolemaic time, and this will have hindered any integration process. The Emperor Tiberius rebuked one bureaucrat by insisting that he wanted his 'sheep' shorn, not scalped or skinned. Even 'only' shorn, would leave them only what they had hidden from the tax collector to live on. Eventually, the Roman army accepted Egyptian recruits, and the Ptolemies and Romans had always accepted Egyptian sailors for their navies, but the dominant rulers of the country remained exclusive and alien and excessively greedy (and this has remained the case until the mid-twentieth century AD).[7]

The condition of southern Egypt in the first century BC was apparently worse than it had been earlier, and worse than in the rest of Egypt. The destruction of Thebes in the suppression of the revolt in the area in 88 (and the destruction of Pathyris, which had been notably loyal to the dynasty) will have also destroyed a major market centre, and driven refugees out into the surrounding neighbourhood. Pathyris' detested neighbour Hermonthis became the new centre for the area, growing after the revolt, perhaps by receiving refugees from the damaged lands around. In other parts of the land, the peasant strikes called *anachoresis*, by which they moved out of their villages and failed to cultivate the land, thus rendering it untaxable, became more common. They are noted at Kerkeosiris in the Fayum,[8] and at Herakleopolis in 83/82.[9] From Herakleopolis most of the inhabitants had left, blaming both economic problems – which must mean lack of income, perhaps poor harvests – and oppressive taxation. They may have been enticed back, but twenty years later they had gone on strike again, and for much the same reasons.[10] These are the least disruptive form of these strikes, but by no means the only ones; the great revolts in the south had begun when peasants on strike turned to raiding other places for food, and perhaps to make their point. It would be safe to say that rural Egypt, not for the first time, was entering into a condition of widespread and long-lasting misery.

The complaints of oppressive taxation are indications that Ptolemy XII's government was in difficulties over its finances. The king had reduced his military forces in order to reduce his costs.[11] The increased expenditure on subsidies to temples was also in reaction to this problem, since heavy taxation was one of the main causes of the desertion of the land, which in turn reduced the production of food and so the availability of tax revenue; subsidising temples – and building of temples continued all through the first century BC, if on a reduced scale compared with the first Ptolemaic century – was possibly seen as a means of controlling the rebellious instincts of a population oppressed beyond bearing. For the next stage in peasant exasperation after *anachoresis* and raids was to rebel openly, a sequence undoubtedly clearly understood by both the peasantry and the government. Further, without a serious armed force at the government's disposal, such rebellions might well spread. We must envisage a continuing peasant crisis throughout the reign of Ptolemy XII, and an unusually helpless government.

For the king, other problems loomed from overseas. In Asia Minor, the Third Mithradatic War had resulted in the defeat of the Pontic king by 69, but had eventually ended with a Roman defeat at Zela when the commander against Mithradates, L. Licinius Lucullus, was defeated and retired westwards to rest his troops. Tigranes of Armenia thereupon campaigned south to take over northern Syria, which included the capture of Ptolemais-Ake and Selene in 69, followed by her execution. Ptolemy XII, as far as we know, did not react to this, even though she was almost the last Ptolemy alive, apart from himself, and she was his stepmother. His failure to intervene may not have been mere callous indifference, however, but a lack of power. Tigranes had defeated a successful Roman army; Ptolemy had only minimal armed forces. It would be hazardous to challenge Tigranes. Ptolemy's power had thus sunk to a general political and international impotence.

But Rome was now becoming determined to end the twin problems of trouble in Asia Minor – that is, Mithradates and Tigranes – and the pirate fleets which had extended their activities from the waters around Asia Minor and Greece into the western Mediterranean. These were increasingly threatening, and were particularly liable to interrupt the import of grain from Africa, Cyrenaica and Egypt into Italy. Several attempts to deal with the pirates by traditional means – assigning consuls and legions to specific problems – had had only temporary successes. It was time to try something new.[12]

This was Cn. Pompeius, called Magnus. He had been consul in 70, and had much military experience in Spain and Italy. He was not, however, adept at the intricacies of politics in the city of Rome, and had withdrawn somewhat from affairs after his consulship, referring to take up a consular command when something more to his taste was available.[13] The Senate's general, Lucullus, was finding difficulties controlling his troops, and the pirates of Crete, who had attempted to negotiate a peace agreement with the Senate, had been rebuffed. This had then brought a declaration of war on them from the Senate, which chose a new commander and gave him three legions to suppress the Cretans.[14]

By 69, piracy on a wider scale than Crete had become more threatening than ever, while Lucullus' command had been so constrained by his enemies in Rome that he was largely paralysed. A political ally of Pompeius, A. Gabinius, professed to solve these problems by an emergency law that would assign a fleet of 200 ships, troops to be recruited as required, and 15 legates to assist whoever it was given the command. No commander was named in the law, but Pompeius was the obvious man, and Gabinius was one of his associates.[15] After a turbulent popular debate, the *lex Gabinia* was passed, and then the resources allocated to it were more than doubled,[16] and both Asia Minor and the pirates were to be Pompeius' problems.

Within three months, he had cleared the seas of pirates in a superbly organised campaign. Further, he was generous to the pirates he had captured, providing many with land, settled as citizens in various places, notably in Kilikia, but also in Central Asia Minor and even in Cyrenaica; the Mithradatic Wars had left large areas of land devastated in Asia Minor, and this was available for resettlement. Settling the pirates into new homes was Pompeius' recognition that it was not love of piracy that had turned them into pirates but poverty and lack of land and opportunity.[17] But then, Mithradates and Tigranes were still active. By a new law, the *lex Manilia*, he was given the further command to deal with the former.

All this was happening rather distantly from Egypt, but had a tendency to be intermittently threatening. When Pompeius organised his sweep of the Mediterranean to eliminate the pirates by allocating sections of the sea and its coasts to individual legates, 'Egypt' was one of them,[18] but there seems to have been no overt interference in the Egyptian sea trade or in the Ptolemaic government. Ptolemy XII was, in effect, ignored; he and Egypt were not the problem. In the new war against the kings, Pompeius defeated Mithradates, but he escaped to the Cimmerian Bosporos, a subordinate kingdom of his. Tigranes was caught between Pompeius and his temporary ally the Parthian king, and chose to surrender. He was restored to his kingship, thus becoming a Roman client king, but was compelled to withdraw from his Syrian conquests. This removed one threat to Egypt, but it soon was replaced by another – Pompeius moved into northern Syria himself, annexing large parts of it to Rome. And within a year, Rome developed into an even more potent threat.

Chapter 10

The Menace and Greed of Rome

Ptolemy XII, a man unexpectedly placed as king in Egypt, had a reputation – 'Auletes' – as a dilettante, or, as Strabo put it, for his 'general licentiousness'. Despite this, or perhaps because of it, he had some success as king. His marriages had inflicted a further blow on the Ptolemaic practice of sibling marriage, which could have eventually become clearly dangerous. He had begun to organise the Indian trade. He had, as it proved, begun to accumulate a useful treasury, partly by reducing his costs (reducing the size of the army in particular), and partly by determined taxation collection. But his methods of recovery were costly in terms of power and authority, and a small army in a large and rich country could stimulate revolts and attract enemies. His marriage to a non-Ptolemaic woman, and his ancestry through a similar marriage, had, given the ideology of the dynasty, significantly further reduced his royal authority. And he had owed his throne, in effect, to popular election, and was therefore subject to popular approval, hence, no doubt, the flute, and the festivals in the palace.

He was no doubt very conscious of the developing threat from Rome, in part because of his time with Mithradates, who will not have failed to indoctrinate his 'guest' with his own hatred of the Italian menace. Pompeius was successful in suppressing the pirates in the early 60s, which will have benefited Egypt, since the export trade in grain to Italy was now free from threat, and insurance rates could be reduced. But Pompeius had then been commissioned to deal with the obstreperous kings of Pontos and Armenia, Mithradates and Tigranes. This he had done, driving the first to remove himself to his kingdom of the Cimmerian Bosporos,[1] and humiliating the second and compelling him to surrender several regions that were at once collected into the Roman Empire, including northern Syria, one of the richest and most vigorous regions in the Mediterranean.[2] But there were always other enemies and problems to be attended to. The last Seleukids were suppressed;[3] Judaea and Nabataea were now Roman victims; Judaea was dismantled into its constituent parts of the core Judaean kingdom and the conquered Greek cities, despite claiming to have been a longtime Roman ally;[4] the Nabataean kingdom was a more awkward victim, defended by its desert surroundings, and based in its distant desert city of Petra. Pompeius displayed a certain reluctance to tackle it, allowing himself to be distracted first by trouble in Judaea, which culminated in the three-month siege and capture of Jerusalem,[5] then by news of the death of Mithradates, at which point he withdrew, leaving M. Aemilius Scaurus to deal with the Nabataeans. Scaurus failed to reach Petra, for his soldiers were unable to march through the desert, so he then used the Judaean minister Antipater to negotiate a Nabataean submission, which in fact was simply a matter of payment for Scaurus to go away.[6]

This would, in Roman terms, however, count as a political submission, and the Nabataean kingdom would, from then on, be reckoned as part of the empire of the Romans, whether or not the victim realised this. This was not the practice of any other contemporary state, but it gave the Romans a justified pretext, at least in their own eyes, to interfere and annex more or less as they pleased. By this time, having had diplomatic relations with the Ptolemaic dynasty for two centuries, and having been diplomatically instrumental in apparently protecting the kingdom (as by Popillius Laenas in 166), Egypt was taken to be a Roman client, though the Ptolemaic kings may not have actually understood this, of course. To some Romans that meant it was available for exploitation and annexation; gradually, Ptolemy XII came to understand the situation, as he had more dealings with Rome.

In addition, there was the diplomatic stealth bomb that had been left by Ptolemy X in his supposed will, by which he was believed to have left his kingdom to Rome. The document did not exist, and no one could quote from it exactly, and it was in all probability an invention by the Roman moneylenders who had financed Ptolemy X's last attempt to recover his kingship. It was, however, something that was accepted in Rome as a detail available to be activated when required. This was the background to a curious episode in the Senate in 65, a census year at Rome. Pompeius was still active in the east, not far from Egypt, and was about to move into Syria. He was clearly a menace to the independent Ptolemaic kingdom. One of the censors was the ambitious M. Licinius Crassus, who had built up a huge fortune by various tricks and instruments and fancied himself as an imperial conqueror. One of the *curule aediles* of the year was C. Julius Caesar, a man who was perhaps, if that was possible, even more ambitious than Crassus. For the moment they could work together, which meant that Crassus financed Caesar's programme, and Caesar would return the favour when he achieved higher office.

Crassus had two major items on his agenda, though neither was the usual sort of measure with which a censor would concern himself. He wished to enrol the Transpadanes, those Roman citizens living in Cisalpine Gaul to the north of Italy, into the list of citizens in Italy, who were the men active in politics, or could be mobilised in an internal crisis. This would be an action that would have provided him with a very large clientele and boosted his political standing in Rome accordingly. And he wished to carry a law to annex Egypt.[7]

In the event, neither of these suggested measures was enacted. Crassus came up against his fellow censor, M. Lutatius Catulus, who refused to agree to his suggested measures, and so blocked them. In addition, many of the senators were hostile, and by attempting to use his authority as censor to put the measures through he was giving them a good reason to refuse them, in that he was overstepping the bounds of the traditional area of his office.[8] But it may be noted that Crassus was not wholly out of line: one task of the censors was to count the number of the citizens, and to enrol those not so far listed, and to bring the senatorial lists up to date by removing those who had died and enrolling those now qualified. (These tasks, Plutarch points out, were not done during this censorship.) The enrolment of the Transpadanes could be considered as only a small extension of the censor's task. And if the existence of Ptolemy X's will was accepted – and most Romans simply assumed its validity – annexation would simply be no more than an act of the Senate. Pompeius and his army in the east could then be instructed to accomplish the measure.

Neither of Crassus' suggested measures passed the Senate, but not altogether because they were outside the usual remit of a censor. The prospect of a large number of Transpadanes becoming active citizens and clients of Crassus was not something to the taste of any senator, whether friendly to Crassus or hostile. And the prospect of the annexation of Egypt was something of the same sort: the country was known to be, believed to be, the wealthiest in the Mediterranean, and if Crassus, as he clearly intended, was to be the instrument of the annexation, the wealth of the Ptolemaic government would fall into his hands. In effect, Crassus in his two measures, was aiming to become both the wealthiest man in Rome (even more so than he already was) and the man with the largest citizen clientele. He began to look like a new Sulla, coming from a different political direction.

The price of the involvement of Caesar in all this is somewhat obscure, apart from Crassus' financing of his career. He held the office of *curule aedile*, whose responsibility centred on the provision of games and entertainment for the citizens, and he laid on a spectacular display, financed, of course, by Crassus. In political terms, this was important but was hardly connected with the Transpadanes and Egypt. He appears to be have become an ally of Crassus partly in order to borrow money from him to finance lavish games during his term in office. A note in Suetonius, written a century and a half later, however, claims that Caesar proposed that the Egyptian measure be settled by a plebiscite;[9] this has been accepted by some historians, rejected by others, but it may really be Crassus' measure in a different guise, for it might evade the senatorial block. In the event, that ploy did not work either, because many senators did not wish Crassus to gain any more power, and accepting Caesar's proposal would simply be to assist a client of Crassus; Cicero made a notable speech supporting the senatorial Conservative opposition.[10] But one certain result was that Crassus and Caesar became allies, and both measures were now firmly on the Roman political agenda.

This was therefore the end of Ptolemy XII's easy period of kingship. From now on, he and Egypt would come under increasing Roman pressure; they were under notice that Rome aimed to annex the kingdom, sooner or later. There followed a curious contest in which Ptolemy used the wealth of Egypt to fend off Roman threats, and Roman officials used measures proposed in the Senate to threaten Egypt, and secure access in various ways to Egyptian wealth. Ptolemy evidently identified the political alignments in Rome accurately enough and set his sights on building his favour with Pompeius, who was busy in Asia and was somewhat detached from the politics of Rome as a result – but was building up a major reputation, enormous personal wealth, and a powerful set of clients. As the Roman conqueror advanced through Syria in 65–63, Ptolemy encouraged him and offered support. He could not offer military support, but he could offer money and materials. His first move was to send a golden crown to Pompeius when he advanced as far as Damascus.[11] A crown was the traditional offering by Greek cities and kings to a conqueror, but not signifying anything other than congratulations on his victory. (It is said that the value of the gold crown was 4,000 'pieces of gold',[12] which seems highly unlikely – unless this was a rumour put about by the Ptolemaic government while sending a crown of lesser value.)

When Pompeius advanced even further into southern Syria and became entangled in the Judaean War and his abortive attempt against the Nabataean kingdom, Ptolemy offered to finance 8,000 cavalry.[13] Such a force would be useful in both campaigns, since the siege of Jerusalem would occupy the Roman infantry, while the cavalry would be useful for controlling the countryside, and for gathering supplies. In a war against the Nabataeans also, it was cavalry that would be especially useful – the Roman infantry would be at a distinct disadvantage in the desert, and the Nabataean forces were themselves mainly cavalry. That is, Ptolemy accurately estimated Pompeius' needs, and offered to supply his deficiency.

The cost of this subsidy to the Roman conquerors was enough to compel Ptolemy to make his officials even more active and assiduous in extracting tax revenue from the Egyptian population – cavalry was very expensive. It is not clear if all the offers Ptolemy made to Pompeius were taken up – the subsidy to support 8,000 cavalry would be particularly costly, though the Nabataean campaign was delayed and then reduced. But the taxation pressure had stimulated at least one rebellion in Egypt.[14] Where exactly this was is not known – Herakleopolis suffered a new *anachoresis* in 61/60,[15] but this is the only local item that might be relevant – but the situation was serious enough for Ptolemy to request the loan of a Roman force to put it down. (This is one of the main items of evidence of the reduction of Ptolemaic armed forces at this period.) Pompeius refused to send any forces, though whether this was because he did not wish to become involved in Egypt, or could not spare the troops, or for some other reason, is not known; but it may be noted that Egypt was clearly outside the bounds of his *provincia*, unless he took literally the permission given him to operate 50 miles inland of the coast (an item prefigured in the Piracy Law). In terms of his task, as detailed by the Senate's commission, he had no need to operate in or against Egypt, which was not a sponsor of piracy, and he really had enough to do in Syria without adding another task.

Meanwhile, another subtle threat to the Ptolemaic state had emerged in Rome. The tribune P. Servilius Rullus proposed an agrarian law in the Senate that would establish a commission of ten men, two of whom were to be Caesar and Crassus, charged with establishing extensive settlements of retired soldiers and impoverished citizens on plots of land in Italy and the provinces. This, of course, was a traditional practice but one that had become entangled in Roman politics for the past two generations. Pompeius would certainly wish to reward his soldiers in this way when he had finished his campaigns in the east. He had settled ex-pirates on their own lands in the east; he could hardly do less for his own soldiers. The commission was to be provided with an extensive staff of guards, surveyors, clerks and so on, to have plenty of money to buy up land, and the power to allocate lands to those identified as worthy. It included provision for the settlement of Pompeius' soldiers from the east.[16]

This measure, like the earlier Caesarean measures for Egypt and Transpadana, was something that had been familiar to Romans over the previous sixty years, since the great crisis over similar measures proposed by the Gracchi in the 120s. The settlement of retired soldiers and impoverished urban plebs had happened in numerous places throughout Italy and in a few places overseas, but never on such a large scale. So once again the proposal was well within the normal bounds of Roman policy, although the ten-man commission was a particularly powerful version of the usual process and in itself would provide considerable patronage; and, once again, there were objections to it that had nothing to do with the proposal itself.

The same objection applied to this bill as pertained to the earlier attempts at the Transpadana and Egypt in that it would be obviously beneficial for some powerful individuals. Egypt, in fact, was regarded in the bill as being a land in which the commission would be able to buy up land and settle Romans, just as if it was any ordinary province. (The earlier Roman treatment of Cyrenaica was similar, but at least Cyrenaica had been formally annexed.) But this would, once again, create the same sort of extensive clientele for Caesar and Crassus (and Pompeius) as had been an objection in the earlier measures, and the Senate was no more inclined to accept the consequences. It did, however, provoke a serious argument, and stimulated enough support to produce an extensive senatorial debate. The new consuls for the year 63, M. Tullius Cicero and C. Antonius, took office in the midst of these discussions. Cicero made not less than four speeches against the measure, but perhaps the most telling objection was that Pompeius' soldiers were included in the bill, but Pompeius himself was not present. This could be criticised as government at a distance, and probably as an insult to the Senate. Another interpretation is that this was an insult to Pompeius; alternatively, it was at his request.[17] It is worth recalling that he commanded a large and successful army, with whose men he was very popular. More than one senator must have recalled the last time a popular commander in the east was thwarted by the Senate; Sulla's memory hovered over these events.

Pompeius scarcely needed the wealth of Egypt, having looted every treasury and blackmailed every king and kingdom he met with on his campaign. His focus, after 64, was on returning to Rome. He spent 16,000 talents in rewarding his soldiers,[18] and when he reached Rome in 62, he had to set about persuading the Senate to allocate lands for their resettlement. Rullus' bill had attempted to include Pompeius' soldiers in its provisions, but in this, it had failed. Pompeius had to make the request in person; this then encountered the same objection as the other measures of the previous two years, for the creation of a large clientele for one particular politician was clearly anathema to the Senate. Yet the demand was just, from the Roman point of view, and the threat from Pompeius and his soldiers was clearly dangerous.[19]

So one threat to Egypt and Ptolemy XII, of a sudden Roman annexation, faded away, and another, the unpleasant, threatening, presence of Pompeius' army in nearby Syria, had declined as he took most of the troops away, and dismissed his army when it landed in Italy, but then the alternative threat, the Rullus bill, had emerged, and then also faded in the face of senatorial opposition. The whole situation was a sequence of difficulties and threats, a very unsettling process. And there was no guarantee that the next Egyptian bill, or a bill with Egypt added as an appendix, or one disguised by something else, might not pass the Senate. The vagaries of the Roman political system were no secure foundation for a stable Ptolemaic regime.

It is worth recalling, in this connection, that the basic strength of the Ptolemaic regime in Egypt lay in precisely a result of this same colonising activity. For the Roman practice of settling ex-soldiers on purchased or confiscated lands was only a later version of the same process that had been part of the Ptolemaic governmental system since the time of Alexander the Great – retired soldiers could expect to be settled on lands as cleruchs, and even new recruits could be persuaded to join the Egyptian army on the promise of, or even the gift of, such lands. Ptolemy XII's main military support lay in these men and their descendants, just as it was assumed Crassus and Caesar and Pompeius were relying on their soldiers' votes in Roman politics. The irony may have struck Ptolemy; it did not apparently strike any Romans.

Ptolemy XII had survived the recent threats, but he now turned, as he had with Pompeius, to influence Crassus and Caesar in the only way they would be likely to accept his requirements – bribes, or perhaps he thought of them as subsidies. What Ptolemy wanted was formal recognition by the Roman Senate as king, which had not been specified in all the relations he had had with Rome, despite their regular connections, and he would also need the status of a friend and ally of the Roman people.

Ptolemy appears to have concluded that his salvation lay in this formal process of recognition and alliance by Rome: recognition of his kingship – which seems redundant after twenty years on the throne – and his enrolment as a friend and ally of the Roman people. The first should protect him from Roman intervention, but allow him to appeal to Rome for support, which he had been unable to secure from Pompeius; the second would protect him from international enemies, such as they were, and possibly against the threat of Roman annexation. To accomplish this he is said to have laid out considerable sums as bribes to Roman politicians, though it is noticeable that no names are ever mentioned;[20] in fact, he quickly located the man who was both in great need of money and in a position to effect the recognition Ptolemy felt he needed by passing through the Senate the necessary acts. This was Julius Caesar; there was really no need to bribe anyone else, though he coupled Pompeius with the offer to Caesar.

The fluctuations of Roman politics produced an alliance between Pompeius, who wanted a land settlement to be agreed for his troops, Caesar, who wanted to be consul, and Crassus, who was Caesar's long-time ally and financier. Caesar had his eyes on Gaul as his future proconsular province, as a place where he could gather wealth and glory and clients. This 'triumvirate' was finally organised in the spring of 59, after Caesar had been elected and installed as consul, partly financed by Crassus, at which time he was able to use his political skills and muscle to push through the measures he and his allies required. But they faced a determined opposition by a Senate group led by M. Porcius Cato, and it would need all their strength to produce enough political might to succeed in their measures.

Ptolemy XII correctly saw Caesar as the key man in all this and offered him a subsidy/bribe of 6,000 talents to secure the recognition as king and Roman ally that he apparently believed essential to his own security.[21] Roman recognition would eliminate the threat of the possibly non-existent will of his uncle thirty years before, which, in fact, is not heard of again. Caesar set his measures in the context of the assistance Ptolemy had given Pompeius in the fighting in Syria, though that was little enough.[22] The ease with which these measures went through the Senate suggests that Rome was basically uninterested in Egyptian matters, that such measures were of little note in Rome, and that Ptolemy himself had no political authority outside Egypt. Such measures would hardly count for much when or if annexation again became a Roman objective – that is, Ptolemy's apprehensions had not been calmed. Ptolemy deceived himself if he really believed these Roman measures were any support or protection.

Calculations, based on figures from the size of the 'bribes' and from Roman and Egyptian sources, have concluded that the 6,000 talents offered to Caesar (144,000,000 Roman *sesterces*) were equivalent to two-thirds of the Egyptian revenue for a year.[23] This may be so, although how accurate the various figures are is not known any more than is the real size of the bribe, which is attested only in secondary Roman sources. But whatever the size of the bribe, it was not actually paid from the Egyptian treasury; instead, Ptolemy had negotiated the cash as a loan from Roman moneylenders (or financiers), as no more than a potential sum. More than ten years later, Caesar was still complaining that he had not received his full share;[24] Pompeius, who was to receive another cut, was probably also short-changed. So, whatever the size of the bribe, it probably cost Ptolemy considerably less than '6,000' talents. No doubt, all involved were busy cheating each other, and the transactions were largely kept secret, so were deniable. After Caesar had secured Ptolemy's requirements, of course – the recognition and the status as ally – there was no requirement on the king to cough up the rest of the money.

Similarly, since Pompeius, using Caesar's political muscle again, had secured the passage of his land law for settling his soldiers, there was no need to dun Ptolemy for the rest, especially since Pompeius had emerged from the east an extremely rich man. The land law set up a twenty-man commission to arrange the settlement – that is, essentially the measure Rullus had been pressing for five years before, but adjusted somewhat so that the first priority was to reward the Pompeian veterans. There were in fact two land laws, one, the *lex Vatinia*, to settle Pompeius' veterans, and the second, which divided up a large part of Campania into 20,000 allotments for the Roman urban poor. Both measures were passed by the Senate in the first months of Caesar's consulship. Both Crassus and Pompeius were members of the commission, which was to last five years, and, of course, they had the spending of a large sum of public money; no doubt, he succeeded in diverting some into his own cash box.[25]

The result of Caesar's work, for Ptolemy XII, was partway satisfactory. He had his personal guarantees, although those guarantees may not have been as useful as he clearly believed; he also had considerable debts to service. He would now need to concentrate on internal security and tax collection; paying off the debts was one priority, though he could probably do so slowly. It clearly helped that both Pompeius and Caesar had expectations of future financial payments (assuming Pompeius was also kept short-changed). Ptolemy could now assume that the great men of Rome were on his side, and not merely for sentimental reasons.

But there was no reason for the Romans to feel they were on Ptolemy's side. After his term of office, Caesar departed from Rome into a strenuous and complex campaign in Gaul, for which he had been allotted a proconsulship of five years. Pompeius was satisfied with the land law; Crassus was busy with his own affairs – the 'triumvirate' had faded away during the latter part of Caesar's consulship. Other politicians emerged as men of power in the aftermath. A new and active politician, P. Clodius Pulcher, secured election as tribune in 58, and, like Crassus as censor seven years before, he exploited his office to indulge in foreign affairs. He restored a group of exiles to the city of Byzantion, made a Galatian into a king, appointed a priest to the great temple at Pessinus in Asia Minor, and organised proconsular commands for two of his Roman friends. In this collection of miscellaneous decisions for eastern territories was included Cyprus.

The island had been ruled by Ptolemy 'of Cyprus', a younger brother of Ptolemy XII, in peace and presumed contentment since 80. He had been placed there by the decision of the Alexandrian citizen crowd acting as a legislature at the same time as Ptolemy XII had been summoned to take up the kingship in Egypt. It followed from this that the island was still technically a Ptolemaic possession. There is no indication that Ptolemy of Cyprus had any heirs, so the island would probably revert to the Egyptian king when the Cypriot king died – as maybe Ptolemy of Cyprus would inherit Egypt in the absence of a male heir to Ptolemy XII. For once this division of the kingdom had not occasioned a fraternal civil war, though it was a not dissimilar situation to that between Ptolemy VI and VIII in the 150s, and a degree of uncertainty about the Egyptian succession clearly existed, and could cause more trouble.

None of this mattered to the Romans, and certainly not to Clodius, as he played games with the empire. It seems that in the past Clodius had once been captured by pirates, and had appealed to Ptolemy of Cyprus to finance his ransom. Ptolemy's offer of two talents was rejected as inadequate by the pirates, who presumably regarded it as merely an opening offer. Then, somewhat oddly, they released their prisoner without any payment at all. (It was not unknown for the pirates to do this because they had received a promise by their victim of future payment; if this was the case with Clodius, that detail is not recorded in the story.) Just as oddly, Clodius came away from the experience with a grievance – but against Ptolemy, not the pirates; he had got away without payment of any ransom, but he complained that Ptolemy had not offered enough. (If Clodius had made his own offer, his grievance could be that his appeal to Ptolemy had failed and that he would now really have to pay the money.) Now, in his office as tribune, Clodius had the power to seek revenge against Ptolemy, and that is how he used his power. He passed a law that decreed the annexation of Cyprus by the Roman Republic. The revenge motive is transparently flimsy for such an act, which had to be agreed by the Senate, where such a motive was sure to be criticised, even ridiculed. Ptolemy of Cyprus was roundly abused in Rome as greedy, dissolute and tyrannical, though since this is all Roman comment – fake news – it was probably invented to justify the annexation.

Other motives have been suggested to replace or supplement the revenge idea: the annexation of the treasure accumulated by the king (6,000 talents was eventually forwarded to the Roman treasury) became finance for the dole in Rome because the treasury had been emptied by much expenditure in the past few years (but Pompeius had deposited 40,000 talents in the treasury from the loot collected in the east). In the annexation law, M. Porcius Cato was named as the executor of the annexation, with the rank of proquaestor with propraetorian authority. He did it all well enough in a few months, and then enriched the Roman treasury with the 6,000 talents that arrived in Rome two years later. But the appointment of Cato did remove him from Rome and from Roman politics for a couple of years, and entangled him in the dispute in Rome over extraordinary commands, for Cyprus was one of these, and this too has been thought to be one of the motives for the action. None of these motives was any more convincing than the flimsy revenge motive.[26]

Geopolitically, however, if one may believe that the rather shallow Clodius was capable of thinking that way, Cyprus was in a very important position, close to the new Roman provinces of Syria and Kilikia – once annexed it was attached to the Kilikian province – wealthy, probably well-armed with plenty of soldiers and ships, as it had been in the earlier Ptolemaic time fifteen years before. It was a very useful acquisition, both for the value of its own resources, for the royal treasury, and for removing it as a threat now that the south Asian and Syrian coasts were Roman. Possibly the fact that it was technically Ptolemaic when taken did have an effect; some would note that, just as with Cyrenaica, also technically Ptolemaic, the home country, Egypt itself, was now obviously vulnerable to the same treatment.

It did not take long for the reaction to develop in Egypt. Ptolemy XII failed to protest, even when his brother committed suicide when Cato, based at Rhodes, insisted on taking over the island. No doubt Ptolemy XII could see that any protest would be futile, and if he urged his brother to resist the Roman takeover, he and Egypt would become involved as well, which would certainly end in a Roman invasion, and probably conquest, of Egypt. In the circumstances, he could do nothing. Ptolemy of Cyprus' suicide was the result of betrayal by both Rome and his brother. This was not the view of the Alexandrian crowd, however, or the members of his court, since the affair was seen as yet another fault of the king; they drove Ptolemy XII out of the palace and out of the city.[27]

Cato had so far operated from Rhodes, sending messages and demands to Cyprus without risking his person – evidently, the Romans did not know whether or not Ptolemy of Cyprus or the Cypriots (or indeed the Egyptians) would react peacefully or violently. (If the Ptolemaic regime in Cyprus ran true to form, the island was well-armed.) He sent his nephew M. Iunius Brutus to see to the details, but only after the news of the suicide of the king arrived, and so the possibility of armed resistance was over.[28] Ptolemy XII went to Cato in Rhodes after his expulsion. He was not greeted as a king, although he was received with sympathy – a personal attitude of the republican Cato. But he could get no material support – Cato had no military force to speak of with him, hence his own diplomatic campaign to take the island. (He had been allocated only two clerks by the *lex Clodia*, though clearly he was accompanied by personal staff.) Ptolemy therefore went on to Rome; Cato had explained to him the corruption of the Roman aristocracy, possibly hinting that the best way to get support for Ptolemy's restoration would be to promise an extravagant payment, but the displaced king hardly needed such information. He was given hospitality by Pompeius in his villa outside the city.[29]

In Alexandria, while Ptolemy XII was seeking Roman help, a decision had to be made about the succession. There were now only two adult candidates available, neither of them male. (If Ptolemy of Cyprus had simply left Cyprus to take refuge with his brother instead of taking poison, he would have been the third candidate, and indeed probably the primary one.) Both of the surviving candidates were women, Kleopatra VI Tryphaina, Ptolemy XII's abandoned wife and sister, whom he had put aside some ten years earlier, and their daughter Berenike IV, the only child of Ptolemy's who was adult; his four other children were apparently left in Egypt, but were not yet adults. Since they included two boys, these were genealogically valuable and no doubt were protected. The Alexandrian decision, taken probably by members of the court, but with some input from the citizen crowd, was to make Kleopatra VI and Berenike IV joint rulers, no doubt on a near-temporary basis until the boys were old enough to rule, which could be a dozen years or more.[30]

This joint regime lasted less than a year, until Kleopatra VI died.[31] There was some confusion in Egypt over who was in power; some papyri referred to the 'second year of Berenike and the 25th year of Ptolemy XII', as the news of Ptolemy's flight and exiled position had not reached the scribe – or perhaps he was not regarded as having been deposed. Then there was a farcical scramble for the selection of a husband for Berenike IV, preferably a man with military skills and some personal resolution. There were, so it was claimed, not least by the competitors themselves, several suitable husbands amongst the surviving members of the Seleukid family. The last Seleukid kings, Antiochos XIII and Philip II, who had been fighting each other as usual, had been removed by Pompeius in 64, and their territory had been converted into the Roman province of Syria.[32] These two survived, and there were also three landless Seleukid princes available as potential husbands. One of these died, a second was blocked from reaching Egypt by the Roman governor of Syria, A. Gabinius.

The third prince, called Seleukos, managed to get through to Egypt, which demonstrated a certain competence, and as far as the lady's bed, but she detested him, claimed he smelt badly, and she did not like his personal habits; he was nicknamed *kybiosaktes*, 'saltfish-trader', presumably from the scent he exuded. She had him strangled after a marriage and a reign lasting only a few days.[33] Then there appeared Archelaus, claiming to be a son of Mithradates of Pontos, who by this time was conveniently dead and could not gainsay him. He at least was satisfactory as a husband, but he had lied about his ancestry, actually being the son of one of Mithradates' military commanders, not of the king himself.[34]

None of this enhanced the reputation of the Ptolemaic family, or of Berenike IV, even as it provided entertainment for the Alexandrians, nor did it conduce to any sort of efficient rule from Alexandria. In Rome, Ptolemy XII had gained the support of Pompeius, but there were a number of other interested parties, above all Ptolemy's creditors, the moneylenders who had financed his earlier campaign to gain recognition as king, who were as keen to see him restored as was Pompeius. These were still owed, or claimed to be owed, a substantial amount of money and were prepared to invest more. This was no doubt understood in Alexandria, where there was anger at Ptolemy's profligacy; a large delegation, a hundred strong, went to Rome to try to prevent Ptolemy gaining enough support for his return.[35]

Ptolemy appears to have had advance notice of the arrival of this delegation. They landed at Puteoli, the usual port for ships from Alexandria, including the grain ships. Ptolemy had meanwhile hired a set of assassins to intercept them, and a number were killed even as they arrived. The survivors, perhaps made the more determined by such a reception, got to Rome, but more were killed there, and the leader of the group, a philosopher called Dion, died after eating a poisoned meal in the house where he had been given hospitality. Those still alive were intimidated into silence, or bribed with the same result.[36] The delegation could be said to have failed, since their purpose was to prevent Ptolemy from gaining support in Rome, and the whole affair was kept quiet and a Senate investigation went nowhere. So many Romans were involved in supporting Ptolemy that these interests were able to exercise the muffling process, but the very existence of the delegation will have warned the Romans that Ptolemy faced serious opposition in Egypt in his attempt to get home again.

The Senate was keen to return Ptolemy to his vacated throne, and gave the task of doing so to the governor of Kilikia, Cornelius Lentulus Spinther.[37] (Thus, at last, Ptolemy saw some advantage in his earlier recognition as king by the Senate.) The arrangements in Rome took time – which in Egypt was the time spent by Berenike in finding a suitable husband. Ptolemy meanwhile arranged for financial support for his returning expedition, a task that again took time. This meant intriguing in Roman politics to replace Spinther with Pompeius. Pompeius, however, was no more keen to lead an expedition than was Spinther, and the Senate had been annoyed at Ptolemy's actions, both the open bribery and the murders of the Alexandrian delegation. It is said that his bribes and the restoration were to cost 10,000 talents, although, as usual, this large, round, figure looks very suspicious, and anyway was not the actual sum that Ptolemy needed, but only a standby credit for use as necessary. His hopes were temporarily diverted when, after a lightning strike on a statue of Jupiter and a consultation with the Sibylline Books by the tribune M. Porcius Cato, a forbidding item was found and the idea of any military expedition against Egypt could be abandoned.[38]

Ptolemy sailed off to Ephesos, where he was at the end of 57, which was also when Kleopatra VI Tryphaina died. This was surely no coincidence; it is possible that Kleopatra had been a prime mover in the agitation that drove him out of Egypt in the first place; moving to Asia took him also Rome, where his presence had become an embarrassment, even to his supporters. Kleopatra VI had, of course, been 'put aside' as his wife a dozen years earlier and her return to power was a clear indication that Ptolemy's expulsion from Egypt had been not merely the spontaneous actions of the city's crowd and court, but a popular decision; it may also indicate that it had been a conspiracy.

It was also in 57 that Spinther had been instructed by the Senate to mount an expedition to return the king. Spinther did not like the assignment and kept well clear of it – but here is another reason for Ptolemy to be at Ephesos. Spinther was perhaps able to use the lightning strike as an excuse for not moving, just as did the Senate. The matter continued without a firm resolution through 56, but in the elections for consul for 55, the two successful candidates were Crassus and Pompeius, and their joint interests succeeded in compelling a decision.

Chapter 11

The Emergence of Kleopatra VII

In 55, Ptolemy XII managed to organise a restoration expedition, to be commanded by A. Gabinius, using forces he controlled as governor of Syria. Gabinius was doing this illegally. The Senate in Rome had repeatedly debated whether to send such an expedition, but there were sufficient votes in opposition – as well as the Sybilline Books – to prevent agreement.[1] The usual fear was that the country's wealth was too great a temptation to allow it to be acquired by one man. Lentulus Spinther in Kilikia was originally tasked by the Senate to undertake it,[2] but he delayed and eventually did nothing, deterred by all the obstacles he encountered, senatorial, military and religious. It was only when, in 55, Pompeius and Crassus took office as consuls that any sufficient authority existed to ignore these obstacles and mount an expedition. Even then the shadow of illegality continued.

Pompeius, as consul, wrote to Gabinius in Syria ordering him to march on Egypt to restore Ptolemy;[3] this was probably the only way to break the senatorial deadlock. Gabinius had had several projects under consideration during his time in Syria (57–55), against the Nabataeans, then against the Parthians when a refugee Parthian prince arrived in Syria, and he had intervened in Judaea. It would seem therefore that he was rather easily persuaded, but still needed a strong push to make him begin; it is also clear that he was quite prepared to ignore the injunction against moving out of his province, no doubt citing consul Pompeius' orders in mitigation. He had already begun to campaign into Parthia, and had crossed the Euphrates into Mesopotamia,[4] when Ptolemy arranged a large bribe for him, and, encouraged by Pompeius' letter of apparent instructions, Gabinius abandoned the Nabataeans and Parthia, and switched to undertaking to war with Egypt, a much more immediately profitable prospect, even discounting the huge bribe he had been promised.

He must have known that he was doing this in obedience to illegal instructions. He was leaving his province (and leaving it effectively undefended into the bargain), and a letter from a consul was not sufficient authority in view of the lack of decision by the Senate. Yet it was really no greater a violation of the Roman legal and political condition than, say, Caesar's disregard of his consular colleague's attempt to block his deeds as consul by 'examining the skies'. And the apparent prohibition by the notice in the Sybilline Books, was, like Bibulus' examination of the skies, no more than a political ploy; the expedition was, if not illegal, dishonourable and a clear breach of the political rules. (The Books had in fact stated that any expedition would require a large army, and he could argue that such was what he commanded.) In the event, when he returned to Rome after his stint in Syria, he was able to put up a good defence of his actions, assisted by Pompeius' backing and Cicero's forensic skills, though he was convicted nevertheless. The fine was equal to Ptolemy's bribe; he went into exile, unable, and no doubt unwilling, to pay it.[5]

So, yet again, Ptolemaic Egypt was invaded from Syria.[6] The commander of the Ptolemaic defence force was King Archelaus, Berenike IV's husband. Gabinius was commanding the Roman force in the name of Ptolemy XII, who accompanied the expedition. It was at this point that Ptolemy reaped a benefit from his reduction in the Ptolemaic armed forces while he had been king, for they could not resist Gabinius' attack for long. Details are few and no more than general but it does seem that the campaign was not altogether easy. Gabinius combined the Egyptian expedition with a march through Judaea, where he captured Aristobulus, who had been deposed by Pompeius earlier and sent to Rome. He had escaped and gathered support in an attempt to restore himself.[7] The high priest Hyrkanos II, perhaps in gratitude for this relief, helped by supplying money and equipment, as did the Idumaean Antipater[8] (already used by Scaurus against the Nabataeans). Gabinius was thus aiming to restore a deposed monarch and was prevented another, also deposed, from restoring himself.

Plutarch says that there were 'a whole series of hard-fought battles',[9] and Dio, while referring to Mark Antony, mentions two battles 'at the river ... and also on land',[10] but only two places are noted as being captured. Mark Antony, who had been recruited by Gabinius and put in command of the Roman cavalry, proved himself an inspiring leader. He captured Pelusion after a dangerous march along the Sinai coast road, thanks in part to the intrigues of Antipater, who was able to command the allegiance of the Jews who lived in the city and let the Romans in. He then prevented Ptolemy from slaughtering the captured garrison, and perhaps also the civilian population[11]

– this is the first sign that the restoration of the Egyptian king would be a nasty business. Alexandria was captured after a battle near the city, in which King Archelaus was killed.[12]

Ptolemy was thereby returned to his kingship in Egypt. He wanted his revenge. His daughter and supplanter, Berenike, was executed. An unknown number of the wealthiest Alexandrians were killed, 'because he had need of the money',[13] which presumably means that the victims were singled out for their wealth as much as for their politics, and that their possessions were confiscated. He installed his greatest creditor, C. Rabirius Postumus, as *dioiketes*, in which office he directed the tax collection regime[14] (and no doubt profited from the confiscations). He was so effective and ruthless at this that Ptolemy eventually heeded the cries of pain from his subjects, and put Rabirius into protective custody; he did not stay there long, but was soon allowed to escape and go back to Italy.[15]

Gabinius returned to Syria to find it in insurrectionary mood. He had to fight a Jewish army, and then campaign against brigands and pirates, who had taken advantage of his and his army's absence in Egypt.[16] He was then superseded by Crassus as proconsul, whose plans included taking up Gabinius' abandoned Parthian aims. In Rome, to which he returned early in 54, Gabinius faced several charges. He had not reported his achievement in Egypt, allowing it to be become known through others, a method that indicated clearly that he was expecting trouble; similarly when Rabirius returned to Rome late in the year, he also faced charges. Cicero was the defence attorney for both men; for Gabinius this was under pressure from Pompeius, who in fact was equally guilty with Gabinius.[17]

None of this seriously concerned the Egyptians or Ptolemy, other than that the former might wish that the two men could have been punished in Egypt. Gabinius had left a force of Roman soldiers in Egypt as guard for the king. It was clearly understood between them that Ptolemy would be in constant danger of rebellion or assassination after the conquest and after the brutal taxation that had been overseen by Rabirius. These soldiers were the Gabiniani, several thousand strong, composed in part of Gallic and German cavalry. They were freely used by Ptolemy to suppress uprisings, particularly amongst the native Egyptians, who had, no doubt, borne the brunt of Rabirius' taxation campaign.[18]

The Gabiniani, together with such troops as Ptolemy could command from the defeated Egyptian army, kept the restored king in power for the next four years. During that time, he had the problem of maintaining control, which his army managed to do, but also he faced a decision on the identity of his successor. Having killed his eldest child, Queen Berenike, he had the choice of one or two of his children by his second wife. Of these, only one, Kleopatra, was near adulthood, being eighteen years old in 52. The others were Ptolemy (XIII), who was about nine, Ptolemy (XIV), who was perhaps seven years old, and Arsinoe, apparently born last, but exactly when is not known. By 52, Ptolemy XII had made a decision and made Kleopatra his co-ruler; he gave all four of the children the title of *theoi neoi philadelphoi*, perhaps in an attempt to head off the likely disputes between them once he had died.[19]

Since Ptolemy died early in 51, the succession arrangements were clearly made during 52 because he was presumed to be dying. He also produced a will in which, in Caesar's summary, 'the older of his two sons and the older of his two daughters' were made his heirs.[20] This, it may be noted, placed the elder of the boys as king (Ptolemy XIII), and ahead of Kleopatra. Caesar's formulation, which appears to be a quotation from the will, would probably be correct, given the general difficulties of the time, but it contradicted what Ptolemy XII appears to have actually intended, for he had made Kleopatra his co-ruler already.

The will was actually directed at Rome as much as to the Egyptians. He invoked the gods, and appealed to the treaties he had made with Rome, to see that the terms of the will were executed as he had intended. A copy was sent to Rome, where it was held by Pompeius, the treasury not apparently being deemed safe enough – no doubt there were memories of the confusion over the supposed will of Ptolemy X – but the original was kept in Alexandria. Ptolemy was certainly doing his best to secure his kingdom for his family, but the contradiction he had embodied in his last dispositions and in his will, and the fact that he was leaving his position to a young woman and a set of children, resulted in a situation that was highly poisonous.

Ptolemy XII died early in 51, only months after making his will and making Kleopatra his co-ruler. The arrangements detailed in his will lasted about as long, only a few months. In March 51, Kleopatra visited the Bucheon at Hermonthis in the Thebaid. The inscription recording the burial of the recently deceased bull notes her presence as 'a female ruler ... and the goddess Philopator', Kleopatra's chosen *cognomen*; the king is mentioned, but not named.[21] This all implies that Kleopatra had already asserted herself as the sole ruler, and that Ptolemy XIII may have been recognised as her co-ruler, but had certainly been sidelined. Probably the pairing had been intended by their father, as no doubt was their marriage, although it had probably not taken place.[22] Other documents are dated to year 30 of Ptolemy XII and her first year,[23] emphasising that she had been co-ruler with her father, and deliberately omitting Ptolemy XIII, her brother and possible husband.

The economic situation in the country had become very difficult in the last year of Ptolemy XII, and this continued in and beyond Kleopatra's first year. In Alexandria, food ran short, leading to riots, and the administration issued an order to farmers in Middle Egypt to send their products to Alexandria, threatening them with punishment up to a death sentence if they failed to comply. The brutal taxation instituted by Rabirius had not ceased with his departure, and as a result of this, and of the stringent order, which in effect sought to transfer the starvation from the city to the farmers, *anachoresis* had become even more prominent than before. A number of villages had become completely deserted; temples housed only a few priests. The deserted areas were the prey of thieves and bandits. A series of low Niles both caused and aggravated the general situation.[24]

In Alexandria, a group of men around Ptolemy XIII formed a cabal, which had developed into an opposition to Kleopatra. It has been suggested that her visit to the Bucheon resulted in a political attachment of the south to her, and that the south continued to be loyal to her even beyond death.[25] It is certainly curious that it was only Middle Egypt that was instructed to send its food to Alexandria; this may be a sign that the government in Alexandria did not wish to provoke the south too obviously. (On the other hand, it may have simply been that Middle Egypt was closer and so the requisitioned food could reach Alexandria more quickly.) The south was also the region more prone to rebellion than any other part of Egypt, most recently in 91–88, yet it did remain quiet under Kleopatra's rule.

The boy king Ptolemy XIII was in Alexandria, and the group around him assumed the royal authority, which he was too young to exercise for himself. Three men in particular were prominent. The eunuch Potheinos had been the boy's *nutritus*, his nurse, and moved into the post of the *dioiketes*, perhaps just by being able to operate the system. He and Achillas, an Egyptian soldier, who was the military commander, were the boy's official guardians. (They had presumably been appointed by Ptolemy XII, possibly in his will, with instruction to co-operate with Kleopatra.) They were joined by one of his tutors, Theodotos of Chios.²⁶ This group, using Ptolemy's position and ancestry, gradually excluded Kleopatra from power until in late 50 BC the name of Ptolemy XIII was being used alone in the dating formula of documents. Since Kleopatra appears to have travelled outside the city – certainly she was in the south in 51, and possibly went elsewhere, a journey probably taking a couple of months at least, the journey of a new ruler through her kingdom – this may have given the cabal the opportunity to seize the reins of power in Alexandria. No doubt, the cabal, which will have included others besides the three who are named in the sources, was in part interested in the well-being of the kingdom, not least because unrest threatened their own positions, but we may also suspect that they were avid for power for its own sake, and for the wealth available to men in their position. Hence their careful exclusion of Kleopatra from power.

In the year or so during which she had political power, Kleopatra had, besides alienating the cabal, accomplished two significant activities. In her year 3 (50/49), and probably after her ouster from power in Alexandria, the Apis Bull at Memphis died, aged twenty-three. She is recorded as contributing a sum of money for the burial rite expenses,²⁷ which fits with her attitude to the Buchis bull at Hermonthis. This had also died just before she visited the south; it was the equivalent of the Apis bull in the Thebaid. She was, in political terms, emphasising her devotion to, or at least her interest in, the native Egyptian religion.

In Syria, since Gabinius was succeeded as governor by Crassus in 54, the security position had seriously deteriorated. Crassus had attacked the Parthians and had been defeated and killed at Karrhai, with the loss of thousands of Roman soldiers' lives. His successor, after a two-year hiatus in which Crassus' quaestor, C. Cassius Longinus, was temporary governor in Syria, was M. Calpurnius Bibulus.²⁸ This had been the man who was Caesar's consular colleague in 59, during which he had ineffectively tried to prevent Caesar passing legislation. He arrived in Syria in 51, and almost at once sent his two sons to Egypt, possibly to order some or all of the Gabiniani to rejoin the Roman army under his father, who was certainly short of troops after Crassus' defeat. Most of these men did not wish to go, having settled down in Egypt, some with wives and property, and others were enjoying their power to become thieves and criminals.²⁹

The two sons of Bibulus arrived in Alexandria, but failed to persuade either the court or the Gabiniani to send some or all of the latter to assist their father. This request may well have widened the split between Kleopatra and the cabal around Ptolemy XIII. It would seem that Kleopatra was apparently seeking the support of the native Egyptian population, while the cabal relied on the Alexandrians and the Gabiniani. But the Gabiniani, who had no wish to join in fighting the Parthians under a barely competent Bibulus, perhaps felt that the request was tending towards a decision in favour of Bibulus. A group of them decided to take matters into their own hands, and seized, tortured and murdered the two young men.

This atrocity no doubt brought all negotiations in Alexandria to a swift halt. Kleopatra, showing a decisiveness that characterised her whole reign, had the murderers arrested and sent them in chains to Bibulus for punishment, clearly expecting that he would execute them, in accordance with Roman law and custom – no Roman would blame him if that is what he did. But Bibulus, arguing perhaps that the crime had taken place in Egypt, returned the murderers to Alexandria.[30]

This was disastrous for Kleopatra. She had angered the Gabiniani by arresting the murderers in the first place, and now the culprits had been restored (and presumably released). Her own life was now clearly liable to be ended by another group of Gabiniani, and she could not rely on the cabal around her brother for protection. The cabal could see clearly that her authority had been weakened. The Alexandrians were subject to the arrogance of the Gabiniani, which could only grow as their sense of restraint declined, and the citizens could blame her for their new plight. Her independence of action was seen to be mistaken. The dating formula for documents now began the formula 'year 1 and year 3', putting Ptolemy XIII ahead of his sister.[31]

In the wider Mediterranean, in January 49, Caesar invaded Italy from his province of Cisalpine Gaul ('crossing the Rubicon') and drove his senatorial enemies out of the peninsula to take refuge and recoup in Greece. There they constituted themselves as the legal government of the empire and appointed Pompeius as their military commander. He set about gathering his forces from all the eastern provinces and client kingdoms. He sent his son Gnaeus to Alexandria seeking troops, and the cabal delivered 500 of the Gallic and Germanic *auxilia* of the Gabiniani to him, plus fifty ships, quadriremes and quinqueremes, and their crews.[32] (This is a sign that Ptolemy XII had not been so avid to save money by reducing his forces as might be thought, for this was about half of the Egyptian fleet, and so a major force; he evidently considered a navy more useful than a large army. Some of those ships no doubt came from the Red Sea fleet commanded by the *strategos* of the Red and Indian seas.)

It is noticeable that none of the troops Gnaeus Pompeius took with him to Greece were Roman soldiers – the Gabiniani who were Italians were staying out of the Roman civil war, and no doubt the cabal were similarly leery of surrendering their main military supporters to the war overseas – 500 men were a drop in the ocean when Pompeius had an army of 40,000 men in the great battle.

By this time, Kleopatra had left Alexandria and was in occupation of the Thebaid in the south.[33] The cabal were in fear of the possibility of an Egyptian civil war as well as having to contemplate the Roman fighting and calculate their response to it.

Exactly when she left is not certain, but it was probably after Gnaeus Pompeius had visited Alexandria and taken his troops with him. Plutarch suggested that he and she had had a 'liaison',[34] but this is widely doubted; it seems, on the other hand, that she would be unable to resist using her undoubted charms and attractiveness to fish for his political and personal support. Her father had been associated with Pompeius himself for a decade and a half, and it would have been natural for her to assume that she could look to him for support, just as he would have expected her to support him. This is also the explanation for the willingness of the cabal to send troops to Pompeius, for they would have known of his interest in Egypt, while the Gabiniani had been part of a force commanded by Pompeius' loyal supporter, Gabinius himself.

What Kleopatra's intentions were in undertaking this journey to the Thebaid are unknown, but several possibilities can be suggested. The first is that she had by this time been effectively removed from any authority at Alexandria.[35] In the south, also, with the support of the local population, she might be content to exist quietly in the Thebaid, which had been exempted from the attentions of the Gabiniani and exempted from the forced seizure of local food supplies for Alexandria. The local propensity for seeking and seizing independence might appeal to her, if not another attempt at direct secession, then at least local autonomy. The *strategos* of the south, Kallimachos, was a supporter,[36] and kept his position until 39. But this resignation into peace and quiet was not her way, and it seems more likely that her intention was to use the south as a base from which to recover her position as ruling queen, and this time at the expense of her brother and of the cabal. It seems she had undertaken this *hejira* along with her young sister Arsinoe; removing her from Alexandria was presumably to prevent her being used to legitimise Ptolemy XIII as king by marrying her.

It was either impossible to mount her return to power from the south, or the cabal and Ptolemy XIII succeeded in exerting enough pressure to force them out, but the next time we hear of Kleopatra and Arsinoe is a comment by Strabo that 'she set sail with her sister to Syria'.[37] He clearly was thinking of them sailing from Alexandria, but being in the Thebaid it will have been by ship from one of the Red Sea ports, either Berenike or Myos Hormos. It does seem unlikely that they would have been able to travel through Egypt at this time, when the cabal was clearly hostile.

In 'Syria', by which Strabo must mean Palestine, Kleopatra attempted to gather an armed force.[38] Again, the sources give no indication of where the soldiers came from, or indeed where she went. We know that the city of Ashkelon, a traditionally neutral city in the wars in Palestine, was the site of a mint that produced coinage in her name.[39] She clearly had some resources, such as the silver that was being minted into these coins, and this would allow her to recruit soldiers from the mercenary market in the region. There is no indication that the Romans – the Roman governor in Syria, Q. Caecilius Metellus Pius Scipio Nasica, had been drawn into Greece to reinforce Pompeius[40] – or any of the local kings and cities, helped her, at least not openly. But by the early months of 48, she had a sufficient force to menace the fortress of Pelusion, which was defended by the forces of Ptolemy XIII. This must have taken up a large part of the available forces in Egypt, but it sufficed to prevent Kleopatra's forces from invading the country; she established an armed camp menacing Pelusion.[41] Meanwhile, as a reward for his contribution to Pompeius' forces, Ptolemy XIII was recognised as the legitimate king by the Senate.[42]

This stalemate could only be broken by an intervention from outside. The Egyptian fleet sent to Pompeius was busy in the Adriatic during 48,[43] but Caesar nevertheless managed to get his army across the sea, evading the Pompeian blockade (which was commanded by Bibulus, as ineffective as ever). After the siege of Dyrrhachium and Pompeius' escape from that trap, Caesar's army marched into Thessaly to confront Pompeius' main army. In August at Pharsalos, the two armies fought. Caesar's army, much smaller in number than Pompeius', won decisively. As the news spread, the surviving

Pompeians scattered; many went to Africa to join Cato the Younger, and the Egyptian fleet sailed back to Egypt.[44]

This was also decisive for the Egyptian situation.[45] The victory of Caesar changed the politics of royalty in Egypt, though not immediately. Ptolemy XIII and the cabal were now on the losing side; their enemy Kleopatra was, quite inadvertently, now on Caesar's side, therefore. The arrival of Pompeius at Pelusion was thus a shock to both sides.[46] He asked for asylum, but it was obvious that he would be gathering support from amongst his defeated troops, as soon as he felt he was safe. Egypt would be the refuge for some, some at least of the defeated army, and some of the Roman ships. The Ptolemaic fleet had fought very effectively on Pompeius' side, and it may well have been vociferous in his support.

The cabal and Ptolemy XIII had to decide whether to accept him as a refugee, and whether to continue to support him politically. They were in a difficult position. If Pompeius was received and helped, Egypt was liable to be invaded by Caesar's victorious army; Pompeius' forces were scattered and it would take time for them to be collected, if, in fact, many of them could actually reach Egypt. If the cabal refused to receive him, they implicitly took the side of Caesar, and he might well not be pleased at their earlier support for his enemy, and he might take the opportunity to 'solve the Egyptian problem' once and for all by annexing the country.

They took two decisions, to receive Pompeius, and in doing so to assassinate him. They were thus assuming that this would put them in good stead with Caesar. But this would also leave them open to criticism as oath-breakers and as untrustworthy politicians. In all this there is no sign at all that Kleopatra did anything but stay quiet. This in itself is a testimony to her political sense, for she was thus permitting the cabal to dig their own graves, and very carefully she did not take sides in the Roman quarrel, despite the fact that she was the daughter of Ptolemy XII, Pompeius' associate, and her actions so far had in fact put her on Caesar's side, if only by the chance of events. Even if Caesar was pleased that Pompeius was dead, there was no possibility that he could trust the cabal.[47]

The murder was carried out by an old associate of Pompeius', L. Septimius, who had fought under him in the pirate campaign, and had since taken service with the Ptolemaic government. He and the Egyptian army commander, Achillas, went aboard Pompeius' ship and invited him to go ashore to meet the king, who was sitting on a throne in full view, and in full royal robes.

Pompeius rather dubiously agreed, and they all sailed to shore in the Egyptian rowboat, at which point Septimius stabbed Pompeius to death; Achillas and another man joined in. Egyptian ships set out to capture the ship he had arrived in, but it got away. The idea presumably was to keep the killing quiet for some time. If so, it was the first part of the plan that went wrong; other parts followed.

That they were pleased with the obvious treachery was shown when, four days later, Caesar sailed into Alexandria harbour with a small fleet of ships and 4,000 soldiers. Theodotos of Chios went on board Caesar ship and presented him with Pompeius' severed and pickled head and his signet ring. He presumably expected to be congratulated, but Caesar was a seasoned politician, and affected horror at the site – it must have indeed been a horrible sight, and a nasty surprise – and pointed out that he was the son-in-law to Pompeius, which perhaps the Egyptians had not remembered. His display of horror was also in part calculated to have its effect on his men, who may well have included soldiers who had fought with Pompeius in the past. But there was also the possibility that Caesar had gone out of his way, accompanied by only a relatively small guard, to go to Egypt in pursuit of Pompeius in order to attempt to persuade him to make peace. Pompeius was the key man on the enemy side, and if he agreed to a peace – and he was known to have been made commander with reluctance, the Roman civil war would have been over.

Caesar landed with his consular guard carrying the *fasces* marching ahead of him, to the annoyance of the Alexandrian crowd, who took it as an insult to their king, and reacted with anger. They were driven back, and Caesar took up residence in the royal palace.[48] He played the moderator between Ptolemy XIII and Kleopatra, inviting them to a meeting to sort out the situation.[49] In his account of all this he quotes the will of Ptolemy XII,[50] and so his authority for the summons was that Rome had been nominated as guardian of the royal family in the king's will. It is unlikely that he felt very friendly towards Ptolemy XIII, who had been the beneficiary of the rival Senate, and had supervised the killing of Pompeius. He, however, knew little of Kleopatra except that she had conjured up an army out of nowhere in an attempt to enforce a royal claim. It must have been clear to Ptolemy and his cabal that the intentions of Caesar would be less than beneficial to Ptolemy. Caesar's inclusion of Kleopatra in the summons had raised her from a refugee princess to the equal with her ruling brother, and was an implicit demotion of the cabal.

Caesar's arrival, however, remained unpopular with the Alexandrians, and any Roman soldiers who went into the city alone did so in peril of their lives. Caesar now played the tourist, visiting the tomb of Alexander the Great (and thus also those of the Ptolemies, which were in the same area), and taking part in discussions with the local philosophers.[51] He had added to the summons to the king and queen the requirement that they disband their armies first. As the weaker party, Kleopatra was quite agreeable, but Ptolemy's advisers, while agreeing that he should meet Caesar, insisted that his army remain mobilised and Potheinos ordered it forward to occupy Alexandria. Caesar could hardly have expected otherwise. Meanwhile, Kleopatra had sailed from her camp outside Pelusion to Alexandria, and went into the palace. There she presented herself to Caesar, who proved to be highly susceptible. She had prepared for the meeting by asking that it take place in secret and she ensured that she arrived in the night dressed in her best and yet exhibiting a woebegone appearance of deprivation. (The story of her arrival rolled in a 'carpet' or in a 'bed-sack' is highly unlikely in a queen always insistent on her personal dignity.)[52]

Caesar was, as Dio puts it, 'a love-sated man already past his prime', and Kleopatra had no trouble seducing him – or perhaps she permitted him to seduce her – and when Ptolemy arrived as instructed he saw at once that 'he was betrayed', and that the meeting would be one in which the mediator would be taking the side of his enemy sister. He rushed out of the palace in anger, and the crowd outside threatened to storm the building. Either that or it was Potheinos who perceived the new relationship, and arranged the demonstration.[53]

The Egyptian army in Alexandria besieged Caesar in the palace along with the king, the queen, her sister, and her brother – in effect, he had the whole royal family hostage. He had already sent messages around the eastern Mediterranean to summon help after he had perceived the basic hostility of the Alexandrian population, but this help was very slow to arrive during the winter. He had only his 4,000 men and his ships, and faced five times that in Ptolemy's army under Achillas, and double the number of ships in the Egyptian navy. He did attempt to scotch the danger by securing the persons of the king and Potheinus, and by reading aloud the terms of Ptolemy XII's will to show that he was, despite his relationship with the queen, intending to arbitrate fairly. Achillas, however, escaped the net.

There followed a complex period of fighting, which lasted nearly six months, on or off, until the spring of 47. In the process, Caesar's military abilities were tested to the full. At one point Arsinoe escaped from the palace with her eunuch Ganymedes. Potheinos intrigued to encourage Achillas, but Caesar discovered this and had Potheinos killed; Arsinoe, clearly as capable and determined as her elder sister, despite her youth (she cannot have been more than twelve years old) disagreed with Achillas over the command of their army, and had Ganymedes kill him. She appears to have taken command herself.[54] There were battles in the harbour, in the palace, in the city,[55] but it was all indecisive. Kleopatra was not to forget Arsinoe's enmity.

A relief army commanded by Mithradates of Pergamon and Antipater of Idumaea approached from Syria in the spring of 47, and, passing Pelusion easily because that fortress was no longer guarded, approached Alexandria along the Canopus branch of the Delta. Caesar was then able to break out of his palace-fortress. In a battle south of Alexandria the relief force, joined by Caesar and most of its forces out of Alexandria, defeated Ptolemy XIII (another child commander) and his army; Ptolemy died in the fight.[56] This ended the fighting, which had involved Ptolemy XIII and Arsinoe, but not Kleopatra or her youngest brother Ptolemy XIV, as he now became.

This had taken all the winter of 48/47, during which time Caesar's scattered Roman enemies recovered in the various parts of the empire they had fled to; as a result of his long immurement in Alexandria, Caesar now had to spend the next two years campaigning all over the empire, from Armenia to Spain, to suppress his enemies. Even so, he spent two more months after his victory in Egypt on a Nile cruise with Kleopatra before leaving.[57] This was the Roman price of the murder of Pompeius and the semi-imprisonment of Caesar at Alexandria. When he left, Caesar stationed three legions in Egypt as a garrison-cum-occupation force.[58] (They in effect replaced the disintegrated Gabiniani.) By then he had come to appreciate the queen's political abilities and he knew that she was dangerous; hence the substantial garrison – to protect her, of course, but it is unlikely she was fooled by such a protestation for more than a minute. As a sign of the danger she posed, the son she bore in June was named Caesarion.

When he made his judgment, his decision was made easier by Ptolemy XIII's death, and the fact that Arsinoe had technically been in command of the

Egyptian army after Achillas' death meant that she could be safely imprisoned, while thereby being a threat to Kleopatra.[59] All the indications are that Caesar did not trust the Egyptian queen under any circumstances.

And yet Kleopatra had succeeded in the aim she had pursued ever since her father died, to be the executive queen of Egypt, married, to be sure, to her younger brother, Ptolemy XIV, who became king – all part of Caesar's judgment – though since he was only about half her age, he was not an obstacle to her rule. Her ambitious and capable younger sister was carried off to Rome to be exhibited in Caesar's triumph and then sent into exile in Ephesos, a near visible possible Roman replacement. Kleopatra had achieved her goal, and now she had to keep it.

Chapter 12

The Reign of Kleopatra VII

Kleopatra had been, or had claimed to be, the ruler of Egypt since the death of her father in 51; not until 47, however, could she exercise that office with any pretence of freedom. In the previous four years she had either been attached to her brother, whose cabal of 'advisors' had been overbearing, or exiled by that cabal and impotently attempting to return at the head of an army. When she did return, she was subject to Roman control, in the person of Julius Caesar. Caesar left Egypt in mid-47, and only from then on did Kleopatra rule as a sovereign queen.

Yet there were still constraints on her power. She had learned that a woman on her own was not acceptable to the inhabitants of Hellenistic Egypt. She may have noted earlier queens who had certainly wielded considerable power, but none of them had ruled without the cover of a son or husband who had been the actual king. Kleopatra I had been regent for her son; Kleopatra II and III had been wives of Ptolemy VIII, or ruling as a mother; Berenike III had lasted only a few days as a ruling widow or wife; Berenike IV only lasted two years as queen and wife. It was thus necessary that the latest Kleopatra be attached to her father (as in 52/51) or to her brother, Ptolemy XIII, who died in the fight beside the Nile in 47; she was then married to her other brother, Ptolemy XIV. These 'husbands' were children, and were regarded in different ways, but then she promoted her half-Roman son. For the moment, after Ptolemy XIII died she was the wife of her other brother, who in the year of her marriage was only about eleven years old. Thus, the Ptolemaic dynastic system continued to operate, perhaps with some fairly desperate expedients.

Rather more serious was the restriction imposed by the presence of a three-legion Roman army left in the country by Caesar when he went off to fight more wars. There were probably auxiliary units left in Egypt as well. The stations of the forces are not known, though it seems probable that the later legionary and *auxilia* bases may well have existed in Kleopatra's time – under Augustus, the two legions stationed in the country were placed close to Alexandria, at a place called Nikopolis, developed as a legionary garrison to overawe the city;[1] the numerous *auxilia* units were spread throughout the rest of the country, and into the upper Nile region. Detachments from the legions were also placed in the south. The object of these dispositions is that they were stations suitable to a force used as a garrison that was holding the province. It was not really a supporting force bolstering the Ptolemaic regime on its last legs, though that was the effect of its presence. Rather, these forces were liable to be withdrawn if an imperial emergency developed. In fact, they were all sent away in 42, and their successors were used as reinforcements for Antony's campaign. They were in that sense a reserve for the Roman forces in Syria and Asia Minor. The legions were, as Caesar noted, very much under strength; he quoted 3,200 as the manpower of the legions he brought to Egypt, as their total joint strength;[2] so that two Augustan legions would be certainly well superior in strength to their Caesarian predecessors.

In addition, there is the issue of the presence of the Ptolemaic army, which still existed, even if not notably loyal to Kleopatra, and was clearly overshadowed by the Roman military presence. Its traditional stations were main garrisons in Alexandria and Pelusion, and detachments distributed along the Nile, with a certain concentration on the southern frontier, and more groups in the oases to the west and the Red Sea ports to the east. So the two forces, Roman and Ptolemaic, were presumably intermingled and tended to duplicate each other's positions, which would be a major problem if the two militaries did not get along. The fact that such disagreements are not heard of is no guarantee that they did not arise. Roman soldiers had a tendency to despise other forces – at least until they were defeated by them.

Kleopatra in 47 took control of a country that had undergone a decade of troubles since the expulsion of Ptolemy XII in 58. There had been six different kings and queens in that time, two of them having been expelled and then returned (Ptolemy XII and Kleopatra VII), two had been killed, and one had been carried off to Rome as a prisoner. Only one of these successive royal regimes had lasted for any length of time – Ptolemy XII's second reign had lasted four years; the rest had lasted no more than a year or so each. In addition, the country had been invaded from the sea and from Syria (twice), and a low Nile in 48 brought shortages of food, which produced food riots in Alexandria. These were to be relieved by requisitioning food from Middle

Egypt, not a popular decision in that area. It was clearly time for a rest from the troubles of the kingdom.

Of course, the whole monarchic situation had been aggravated by the shortages and the low Niles. Indeed, it could well have been that the shortages were one of the main causes of the monarchic problems since such events tended to be blamed on the government. A low Nile produced general shortages throughout the country, such was the subsistence level of supplies for the general population. Two and more low Niles in succession produced starvation. The loss of the overseas territories subject to the Ptolemies meant that there was no chance of requisitioning and importing supplies from, say, Cyrenaica, especially since Rome was greedily hoovering up supplies from that country, and from Egypt itself; for a time also there was a legion stationed in Cyrenaica that would have first claim to any local supplies, as did, no doubt, the legions stationed in Egypt.

The administration Kleopatra supervised was that which had been developed over the centuries of Ptolemaic rule (and which remained in use for a time under the Romans). The men in command of the various departments are usually anonymous, and it seems that the system continued to operate at its usual level of conservatism and partial efficiency,[3] that is, resources were leaked at all levels by corruption and greased by bribes. Strabo claims that Ptolemy XII had an annual revenue of 12,500 talents, although this seems optimistic.[4] But the best evidence for the relatively calm continuation of the administration is that Kleopatra could go off to Rome twice in three years for extended visits, only a year after taking over, without a rebellion calling her back. The presence of the legions no doubt helped here. She would seem to have accepted the traditional administration, so that the bureaucracy was on her side.

Her purpose in going to Rome was primarily political and diplomatic, but also personal. She needed the same political recognition by the Senate as her father and brother had received, and Caesar could probably provide that. She will have known by the time she went to the city that Caesar, despite his incessant womanising – 'love-sated', according to Cassius Dio[5] – had no children, though he had been married four times and had fathered one child, a daughter who had married Pompeius, but she had died in 56. But now he had a son, Caesarion, so another aim for the queen in her visit was the registration of her son as Caesar's heir. But this came up against the same problem that had bedevilled the Ptolemies since the direct dynastic line had ended with Ptolemy X and XI – it would take an act of the Senate at least to legitimise the boy; the son of a Roman and a foreign woman was illegitimate.[6] And Caesar showed no inclination to press for that legitimation. She had gained recognition as queen, and, along with her brother-husband (she had brought Ptolemy XIV with her to Rome), she and he were counted as 'kings who are allies and friends of the Roman people'.[7]

Ptolemy XIV, of course, was brought to Rome so as to ensure he did not become the focus for a new usurpation in Alexandria. Her sister Arsinoe was also in the city and featured in Caesar's triumph over Egypt, no doubt a teeth-grinding moment of humiliation for Kleopatra as much as for Arsinoe, though it may be that she arrived after the triumph had taken place.[8] She may also have had to watch triumphs over Pontos, Gaul and Mauretania. She and her brother-husband were in Rome as invited guests;[9] the gross display of Roman power and victories was not put on for their benefit, but essentially for Caesar's, and yet the display no doubt also had that intended demoralising effect. It would also have an effect on Roman politics, for it was always to be remembered that Egypt, with its army and its very effective fleet, was the only power left in the Mediterranean with a military capability of some size – except for the Parthian kingdom, of course.

The visit to Rome ended a month or so after the murder of Caesar on 15 March 44 – or perhaps it would be more chronologically accurate to date the return after the dictator's will had been published. Kleopatra had been in the city for over two years, and had observed the evolution of the consul into a dictator and into a dictator for life and, even if she did not witness it, she will have known of the offer of a kingship to him.[10] This may have been what she had hoped for personally, since a king would need a queen, and she was the obvious choice. Yet Caesar refused the offer in the end, though he seemingly knew of it in advance, and had been tempted. Then he was killed, and his heir, apart from the Roman people, turned out to be his adopted son – adopted post-mortem – C. Octavian, a student of eighteen years of age (and his grandnephew). Kleopatra left soon after the funeral, when the will's terms had become known. Her son had not been included in the will, nor was he to be acknowledged as Caesar's son, still less as his heir.[11]

The timing is tight but convincing. The assassination was on 15 March, and next day Mark Antony made his masterly speech in the Senate, which cooled matters in the city and drove the assassins into flight. Next day, or a day later, Caesar's will – the most recent redraft – was handed over by the

Vestal Virgins, to whom he had given it for safekeeping, and the contents were published. He had left three-quarters of his wealth – his enormous wealth – to Octavian, his grandnephew and now his adopted son, with the rest divided between two other men. There was no mention of his son Caesarion or Kleopatra or Mark Antony, who had assumed that he would be his successor in some way. Kleopatra then remained in the city for three or four weeks, but in mid-April, she left, along with Ptolemy XIV.

Kleopatra in Rome was, of course, in even more danger once Caesar was dead. She had been unpopular in Rome, particularly with those who opposed Caesar and had killed him. Assassinating her and her brother – and her son – would eliminate the whole Ptolemaic family, and open Egypt to annexation. And this was a country with a Roman garrison already in place. Leaving Rome a month after Caesar's death provided a space for publicly mourning the man, but not going so quickly as to exhibit fear.

Returning to Alexandria (by June 44), however, simply produced another problem. She travelled along with her husband, Ptolemy XIV, who was now fourteen years old, and so of an age when he could be made an active king; he must have had visions of becoming such, and possibly sole king. It was not difficult for Kleopatra's Egyptian enemies to see this obvious possibility. She could see it also, and she had a useful ruthless card to play. She organised, or ordered, the killing of Ptolemy XIV not long after they reached Alexandria. He was still cited in a document dating 26 July, but not later.[12] And, after a short interval, she played her card; her son Ptolemy XV Caesar was proclaimed as king and her royal partner.[13] The message to her enemies was that they were in clear danger of death if they persisted in opposing her, and anyway, there was not a single member of the Ptolemaic family left in Egypt – except Caesarion.

The aftermath of Caesar's assassination was a new Roman civil war, between the conspirators/assassins, referred to as 'Republicans', and the 'Caesarians', who were led by Mark Antony and Octavian, a fractious partnership. Kleopatra would certainly have watched events carefully, but there are strong indications that her grip on her kingdom was now somewhat uncertain, no doubt in part due to Caesar's killing, for he had been one of her main supporters, but also due to her long absence in Italy. She had twice returned from Italy to Egypt for a time, but she had been in Italy more in those two years than in Egypt – which, it could be argued, was neglect.

An indication of the general slackening situation may be seen in the south, where the *strategos* Kallimachos, who had earlier supported Kleopatra in her refugee status, was now not only *strategos* and *epistrategos* (governor of the Thebaid) but also *strategos* of the Red and Indian seas. He dedicated a new temple to Isis at Ptolemais – Isis might be considered to personify Kleopatra – but a civil decree in Kallimachos' honour referred to him as *soter* ('saviour'), normally a royal epithet.[14] He was a governor in office for decades, and it looks as though he had become impossible to remove. One wonders how many other such governors had so comfortably entrenched themselves.

At the other end of the state, Kleopatra had regained Cyprus. This had occurred in a notably roundabout way. Caesar, while fighting in Alexandria, had assigned the island to Ptolemy XIV and Arsinoe jointly, for their upkeep.[15] Then the latter had escaped from the palace and from Caesar and Kleopatra, and then became the leader of the insurrectionary army against him. Having been captured, or recaptured, she was bundled off to Rome to appear in his triumph; she could hardly be the lady of Cyprus after that. Then Ptolemy XIII was killed in the battle along the Nile, and his brother became Kleopatra's next husband, so Cyprus fell to Kleopatra's government, and she appointed a new *strategos*, Serapion, to govern the island.

Across the sea from Cyprus, the province of Syria was the scene of one branch of the Roman civil war, where there was fighting between P. Cornelius Dolabella for the Caesarians, and the assassin C. Cassius Longinus for the Republicans. The two men both looked to Kleopatra for help. Dolabella publicly recognised her status as queen, and, perhaps in return, she sent to Cyprus the legions that Caesar had left in Egypt, no doubt pleased to get rid of them, for they had become mutinous since Caesar's death.[16] Cassius, however, also appealed directly to Serapion, who in turn had no instructions from Kleopatra, so he agreed to hand over the legions and the naval force stationed in Cyprus to Cassius, who went to visit the island, clearly treating it as a Roman province.[17]

Dolabella was defeated and committed suicide; his legions then joined Cassius. Dolabella had stood a long siege in Laodikeia-ad-Mare, but then Cassius took his forces into Macedonia and was also defeated and killed in the battles around Philippi in October and November. It might be claimed that Kleopatra had hedged her bets over the Roman conflict, but it was hardly a serious or deliberate decision by her, for she did not control the legions in Egypt, and Serapion clearly was acting on his own initiative, just as Kallimachos was virtually an independent viceroy in the south. (Their similar attitude may well show a contempt for rule by a woman, a normal Greek and Roman misogyny.) It is noticeable that Caesar's Egyptian legions ended up on the losing side. Both Kallimachos and Serapion (who was seized and executed later by Mark Antony) were clearly out of control of the government in Alexandria.

While the Romans fought it out in their civil war, Egypt suffered a major disaster. The Nile flood had failed in 48,[18] but the next years allowed something of a recovery. Then in 43 and 42, the flood failed completely.[19] The consequence was not only famine, but widespread sickness as well.[20] Kleopatra opened the government grain stores to help relieve the distress. This is essentially what they were for, so it was not a matter of royal generosity, and it is doubtful if this was more than a brief help.[21] Since there had been emergency measures in 48, it is unlikely that the rations five years later were even adequate, and only citizens – not Egyptians or Jews, or even Romans, one supposes – were eligible to receive these handouts. It is possible for his work at this time that Kallimachos in the Thebaid was called 'soter'.

There were dangers in all directions. An over-mighty subject in the south, such as Kallimachos, might develop his local power into another secession of the Thebaid, which Queen Kleopatra would have considerable difficulty in suppressing; the Roman forces left by Caesar had vanished, and meanwhile the Ptolemaic army was less than supportive, as were the Ptolemaic aristocracy and the Alexandrian population. It is not surprising that the only indication we have of Kleopatra's political activity in these years is her apparent generosity with food, distributed to appease discontent amongst the citizens, for the Alexandrian population was liable to riot. The main force at her disposal by 42 was the fleet that was based at Alexandria. She began a voyage to assist the Caesarians in the civil war, perhaps as a means of counteracting the impression given by the diversion of the legions and the Cypriot fleet to support the assassin Cassius in Syria. The ships sailed west along the coast of Cyrenaica, evidently heading for either the Adriatic or Greece. But the gesture failed when the fleet was struck by a storm of the Cyrenaican coast and had to turn back; Kleopatra was on board but became ill.[22] Nevertheless, the gesture had been made and publicised, and no doubt, it made a useful impression.

Mark Antony, architect of the victory at Philippi, moved eastwards to clear out the remaining enemies, while Octavian tended to Italy and the west, and their third colleague in the triumvirate, M. Aemilius Lepidus, went to govern Africa. Antony summoned the Egyptian ruler to meet him in Kilikia, with the aim of securing her support for the war he was intending to wage against Parthia; she was reluctant to go, partly because Egypt was in a famine condition and leaving would create a bad impression, and partly because she rather resented, as a queen, being summoned anywhere, even by a Roman consul-and-triumvir. In addition, she would have to justify her conduct during the recent conflict, putting her in a dangerous situation. Once she finally agreed to go, after a long series of letters sent by Antony, and a visit by Q. Dellius, one of Antony's officers,[23] she put on a show, exaggerated by Plutarch and dramatised by Shakespeare, and in the process displaying some of the wealth of Egypt, even in its distress. Antony was susceptible to her charm and wit, just as Caesar had been, but his susceptibility was not the basis of his political decisions.[24]

Kleopatra, according to Appian, did justify her conduct, only slightly editing the truth; Antony accepted her account, though he must have known she was not wholly honest about it. But they were politicians, and did not need to be explicit about everything. They seduced each other, and made a bargain. Kleopatra would provide supplies for Antony's war in Parthia; Antony would remove Arsinoe from the possibility of being used to undermine her position in Egypt; Serapion, who had removed himself to the autonomous city of Tyre, was extradited. Like Arsinoe, he was executed.[25] The queen had now no rival of the Ptolemaic family, and her disobedient governor had paid for his conduct with his life – others should beware.

Antony spent the winter of 41/40 in Alexandria with Kleopatra, who by this time was pregnant with his twins. Both spent that time in a legendary round of parties and celebrations, no doubt justifying their actions to themselves – in the midst of an Egyptian famine – by reference to the hard work they had been doing. But there must have been more to their life of pleasure than that. For example, he assigned Kilikia to the Ptolemaic Empire, where it was linked with Cyprus into a single province, and, despite having apparently assigned the joint province to Kleopatra, it was Antony who appointed the governor, a freedman of Caesar's called Demetrios.[26] It is a curious transfer, of a territory that had never been more than marginally Ptolemaic in the past, and which was a crucial passageway between Asia Minor and Syria – Demetrios' appointment suggests that Antony was fully aware of these circumstances. The island and Kilikia were also both major centres for shipbuilding, and their food production could be made available to relieve the distress in Egypt. Possibly Antony had in mind the vigorous piratical communities that had existed along the coast of Rough Kilikia before Pompeius' campaign; no doubt he was hoping that Kleopatra would take the responsibility for keeping those pirates under control.

Their personal relationship was disturbed later in 40, when Antony returned to Italy to negotiate with Octavian. One item in their treaty (agreed in a meeting at Brundisium) was that Antony should marry Octavia, Octavian's sister, a highly capable woman very much of the Kleopatra stamp, if less flamboyant. She operated as a continuing diplomatic contact point between her brother and her husband, and certainly helped to prevent more civil conflict between them, for a time.

Antony required a treaty of peace with Octavian because his entire position in the east collapsed in 40 after a Parthian invasion of Syria. (This was also one of the reasons for the elimination by Octavian of a number of Antony's supporters in the west, exploiting Antony's weakness.) Antony sent off P. Ventidius into Asia Minor with reinforcements in 39, with spectacular results, when by his unusual military skill he drove the Parthians out of much of their Asia Minor conquests. They at one point had also penetrated into southern Palestine, and if Ventidius had been unsuccessful in the north, it is likely that Egypt would also have been invaded. Antony had to face east, to counter the Parthians, south to watch Egypt. He must have taken thought to Kleopatra's reaction to the approach of the Parthians; she might well have decided to join them, and their promises would very likely be generous – even extravagant – in order to detach her from Rome. He also had to face west to beware of the insidiously assertive Octavian. Finally, he was able, in 37, to make a new agreement with Octavian, by which Antony would govern the eastern part of the empire, from the Adriatic to the Euphrates, and Octavian the western part, basically Italy, Gaul and Spain – although next year he removed both the younger Pompeius, who held Sicily, and M. Aemilius Lepidus (the third of the triumvirate) from Africa.[27] The empire was now divided into two more or less equal parts, the Latin West and the Greek East.

By 37, the year before Octavian took over Lepidus' share of the empire (and Lepidus stayed alive because he was *pontifex maximus*), the war in the east between the Romans and the Parthians seemed to have reached a turning point. In that year, the Parthians and their collaborators were largely driven out of the territories claimed by Rome[28] and Mark Antony began to make serious preparations to take the offensive against Parthia.

This was another aspect of Caesar's legacy. In his last year or so as dictator, he had been making preparations to march against Parthia. It was, in a sense, to be a Roman revenge for the destruction of Crassus' army back in 53 at Karrhai in Mesopotamia, though in all likelihood he would have undertaken the campaign even if Crassus had never been defeated.[29] The intervening Parthian invasion of the eastern provinces, however, had emphasised that the project of a Parthian war was something that would need a lot more preparation than Caesar seems to have given it. The terrain, mountains and deserts, was extremely difficult, the enemy forces, mainly cavalry, cataphracts and archers, was not the type of force the Romans were accustomed to fight against, the distances were very great – the Parthian Empire was much the same size as the Roman. Antony clearly took note of all this, and spent several years gathering resources and soldiers.

One result of the Parthian invasion of Syria had been the emergence in Palestine of Herod, the son of Antipater, as ruler of the Jewish kingdom.[30] It had taken some time to reconstitute the kingdom from the fragmentation imposed on it by Pompeius, and recovering the territory from the Parthian invaders – they had been welcomed by the current king, Antigonos – had also involved a Jewish civil war. Herod had a keen eye for power and ability, and had quickly identified Antony as the man to ally with.

Antony had followed up the work of Ventidius in Asia Minor, and the similar work of C. Sosius in Syria, by imposing his authority on a whole series of small kingdoms that lay beyond the Roman provinces. This included mounting an unsuccessful siege of the great fortress of Samosata, which he was involved in during 37, and where he was assisted by Herod and a contingent from the Judaean army.[31] His work in the eastern provinces was essentially a continuation and refinement of that of Pompeius, but the various kingdoms had often ended on the 'wrong' side of the Roman wars – as had that of King Antigonos in Judaea – and had to be punished, or encouraged, or reinvented to ensure their loyalty to Rome in the coming war. Herod, for example, was accepted as king of the Jews in large part because the preceding Maccabee king, the usurper Antigonos, had in effect been installed by the Parthians during their invasion and brief occupation.[32] The failure to capture Samosata resulted in the acceptance of the resisting Kommagenean king's submission, even though he had, like Antigonos, taken the Parthian side earlier, and had resisted Antony at Samosata successfully.[33] Of course, many of these princes had little choice if they were to retain their thrones; but the Romans usually had no compunction about removing them even when they submitted in the most grovelling fashion.

The result of Antony's work in the years between 40 and 37 was therefore the organisation of the Roman east as a mixture of Roman provinces, and local kingdoms, many of the latter of considerable antiquity and stability, but all now obedient clients. Into this imperial system Egypt fitted well enough. To the Romans, it was simply yet another client kingdom, and had been for several decades, at least in Roman eyes, but even to the Egyptians by now. It was larger and richer perhaps than most such principalities but was part of the Roman Empire nonetheless. Kleopatra was a particularly glamorous and interesting client king, but never by any means wholly independent. She had acquired recognition and direct military assistance from Rome to hold her position, and her successor, if there was one, would require the same Roman recognition – and such recognition could be refused or revoked. For the Romans, it was probably advantageous that the ruler of Egypt was a woman, wielding very little power, not at least in any military sense. If it became necessary, removing her would produce little or no controversy – simply because she was a woman.

For Kleopatra, on the other hand, who probably had a better understanding of the Roman situation than most of the Greeks in the east, the position was extremely difficult and dangerous. She had to locate the most powerful man in Rome and ally herself to him. For her father, this had been Pompeius; for her, it had first been Caesar, and now it was Antony. Of these three successive choices the latter two had been useful; Caesar had secured her final recognition as ruler, and Antony was to prove briefly successful, but in the end a failure. Octavian, on the other hand, proved to be impervious. She therefore spent the decade between 40 and 30 scheming to ensure that Antony remained in power and on her side. This took a good deal of hard work, much generosity with Egyptian materials and resources, and, of course, plenty of personal humiliation. It may be that her relationship with Antony was amorous, though he was happily married to Octavia for several years while seducing Kleopatra, but on both sides, their relationship was essentially political; if pleasure came into it this was an added bonus. Both were essentially political animals more than anything else.

Chapter 13

Kleopatra and Antony

The overall purpose and policy of Kleopatra VII would seem to have been to ensure the continuation of the Ptolemaic dynasty, which in turn would ensure the continued independence of Egypt, and her own personal safety and survival. By the end, however, this programme had been refined down to personal survival. But she had worked hard, in her own way, to secure the kingship that she clearly felt was hers by right, and once securely in office, or relatively so, her principal aims seem to have grown from personal to dynastic size. She certainly aimed to be succeeded by one of her children, particularly the eldest child Ptolemy Caesar (Caesarion).[1]

For this, the instrument was to be Mark Antony. But Antony had his own agenda, and by the early 30s BC his personal and political aims were to fight and defeat Parthia, which would be a route to personal glory and to predominant power in the Roman Empire. To do this he spent his considerable energies in reorganising once more the system of local kingdoms and provinces in the eastern half of the empire, of which Egypt under Kleopatra was one; he transferred territories, installed kings, and enforced loyalties, and here Kleopatra could profit.[2] She was loyal to Antony, but she had no alternative she could turn to for protection, and Antony knew it. He could therefore award her territories that would gratify her ambition, and in return, this would require her to support his political aims; primarily, he needed her to deliver supplies for his campaign against the Parthians.

But to transfer territory in Syria to her would be to alienate those rulers and people who became her new subjects. Her aim seems to have been to reconstitute some approximation to the old Ptolemaic Empire in Syria, stretching north as far as the Eleutheros River valley, and most of that area had been a mosaic of small independent states for several decades, and subjection to Egypt would not necessarily be welcome. In particular, the Palestinian region was now under the rule of Herod, an ostentatiously Antonian friend and ally, the Nabataeans Arabs who were notoriously difficult to fight, and various autonomous cities and princes, while the former Seleukid part of Syria was now the Roman province of Syria. Herod especially had to be treated very carefully; he had secured control of Judaea and other places in Palestine with great difficulty, displaying energy, brutality and military ability,[3] and to undermine him or remove him would hand to the Romans the problem of controlling the Jewish kingdom – not a prospect to be attempted. This, if Kleopatra was blamed, would sour Egyptian–Roman relations. Here Kleopatra was more hindrance than help for she and Herod disagreed and quarrelled; she aimed to reacquire rule of Palestine, and Herod had his own agenda in that matter; it was a clash of rival imperialisms.

The defeat of the Parthians by Ventidius, first in Asia Minor, then, decisively, in Syria in 38, led to their expulsion from the Syrian region, and had been completed by 37; Herod had temporarily settled Judaea by that time also, though he required the assistance of a Roman army under C. Sosius to capture Jerusalem. So Antony, with Syria and Asia Minor under Roman control, could now make active preparations for his counter-attack on the Parthians. For this, it was vital that he could draw on the resources of Egypt, and this gave Kleopatra leverage. The recent fighting in Syria, Asia Minor and Greece had caused much damage in those countries, and had impoverished many of the cities; Egypt was the one region that had seen little fighting, although it had suffered the effects of several low Niles. It could, however, supply both money and resources to Antony's forces. A meeting at Antioch, the city used by Antony as his eastern capital, was arranged for the winter of 37/36; this time, Antony's invitation to Kleopatra was perhaps less than a summons, and more an arranged conference, for the meeting entailed a bargain rather than a Roman requisition. Kleopatra persuaded him to deliver several territories to her, which would feed her ambition, and he provided her with a series of personal assurances as well – recognition and favours to their children. In exchange, she generously supported his campaign.[4]

She may have made a series of fairly extravagant territorial demands, but Antony was very selective and careful in what he agreed to hand over to her. In Syria, whatever she had asked for was pared down to some smaller areas, but all of them were politically and/or economically useful to her, and so to him. The most spectacular was the grant of some balsam groves in the Jericho area, technically part of Herod's kingdom, which by Antony's arrangement he had to rent back from Kleopatra at a cost of 1,200 talents. It was a large sum, which incidentally demonstrates the wealth Herod had already derived from the groves (and no doubt, the rent was hardly the whole product of the plantation). It is, furthermore, unlikely that the rent Herod paid went into the Ptolemaic coffers for very long, since it was clearly aimed at subsidising Antony's Parthian campaign. Also handed to Kleopatra was a stretch of the Arabian coast, taken from the Nabataean king. This area had been the base for Nabataean pirates who had raided Ptolemaic sea traffic in the Red Sea, notably the Ptolemaic ships returning from India with rich cargoes.[5] These ships were now much safer and the profits – the ships were organised into supervised convoys – would pour into Kleopatra's treasury once more readily and bountifully.

The grants of Cyprus and part of Kilikia that had earlier been made by Caesar were confirmed, and again this was clearly a matter of getting the Ptolemaic kingdom to work for the benefit of Rome. Antony had handed over a large part of his fleet – 150 ships – to Octavian to help him fight Sextus Pompeius, and the shipyards of Cyprus and Kilikia were put to work replacing that loss, as were several cities of Palestine and the northern Phoenician coasts, also granted to Kleopatra – Byblos, Ptolemais-Ake and Gaza. And probably more; all of these places and areas used wood cut from the local forests for shipbuilding. Such a fleet was of little use against Parthia, nor would the new ships be allowed to increase the Egyptian fleet too much, and so it was obvious that these new ships were aimed at countering Octavian's growing seapower.

Many land grants transferred to Kleopatra were thus designed to send financial resources into the Egyptian treasury and there to be used to build resources for Kleopatra, or, more likely, to be handed straight on to Roman officials for their own military and naval use. Other grants were evidently aimed partly at satisfying Kleopatra's territorial ambitions, and at filling her treasury, which was a source from which Antony would be able to draw: the Ituraean kingdom in Syria, which Antony handed over to her after its local king died,[6] was another leaseback contrivance of Antony's. Along with the kingdom of Chalkis in the upper Bekaa valley, this gave Kleopatra possession of the old Ptolemaic defensive structures, the *'limes* of Chalkis', although Chalkis at least was not her direct possession, since the heir to the dead king could rent it back from her. One might suppose that here again Antony was being exceptionally careful; he must have known the use to which the Ptolemaic Empire had put the *limes* of Chalkis against attack from the north and he probably did not wish Egypt to be too militarily adept in the area.

The city of Cyrene was transferred to her, perhaps as an earnest of a promise to return Cyrenaica to Ptolemaic rule, though such a concession might have angered the rest of the Cyrenaica cities, and it was an important strategic area in the developing contest between Antony and Octavian. An estate in Crete was similarly transferred; it is not specified exactly where the estate was but it is possible that it included the former Ptolemaic naval base at Itanos, useful if the newly enlarged Ptolemaic navy was to be employed in European waters. These tracts of land and cities may also have been part of Antony's aim to hold on to such areas without allocating troops to them, that is, again, handing the responsibility over to Kleopatra to free up his own troops for the campaign.

These transactions may appear to be generous gifts to Kleopatra when listed as a set, and his apparent generosity could be used against him in hostile propaganda sallies. However, examination of them suggests that not only were they carefully chosen, and limited, they were given to her in order that they should increase the Egyptian revenues, which in turn would be available to the Roman war effort, and more than one was rented back to its original owner – a measure quite easy to cancel, as were all these grants. Antony was not really diminishing the Roman Empire; instead, he was meshing the Egyptian kingdom with the Roman provinces. Kleopatra also extracted some personal favours from Antony, but again, examination of them implies that politics was at the basis of them all. It is not altogether clear if any changes were imposed in these territories. In all likelihood, the former administration was retained, and the former personnel, some of whom will have been Romans; the transfer may have been considered only provisional, to be returned when Kleopatra died, or when the Roman government changed its mind, but was less than complete. Roman officials would no doubt look to Antony for their orders, even if they were delivering the tax product to Alexandria.

It is, in all, quite clear that both Antony and Kleopatra saw the Ptolemaic kingdom now as a part of the Roman Empire, and Egypt as a subjected and client kingdom, more important perhaps than the kingdoms of Asia Minor – Cappadocia, Paphlagonia, Galatia, and so on – but essentially at the same political level. Herod's Judaea was another of these, and so was, in Roman eyes at least, the Nabataean kingdom, which no Roman forces had yet reached.

Kleopatra celebrated this revival of the former Ptolemaic Empire by starting a new dating system, with 37/36 as her New Year 1, to run alongside her own date of rule, beginning in 51.[7] At the end of 36, she gave birth to another child, a son, called inevitably Ptolemy; he was given the surname Philadelphos, with the dual reference to Ptolemy II and to the fact that he had three siblings.

By this time, Antony had undertaken his long-planned Parthian expedition. He and his army set off on the Parthian campaign in the spring of 36, shortly after his meeting with Kleopatra at Antioch. He had been attempting to get under way for several years, but crises in other parts of the empire regularly distracted him. Even now, he was not altogether confident that his restructuring of the provinces and the client kingdoms in the east would hold while he was on campaign – a properly justified apprehension. Too many of the kings who had now submitted to him had been pro-Parthian in their campaigns in Syria in the last five years, and he had not always been able to control or regulate them. He did not have enough troops both for the campaign and to install garrisons in unreliable areas and he had to rely on Kleopatra's governors and forces in too many areas – Cyprus, Cyrenaica, Kilikia, Phoenicia – and on Herod in Palestine. He was also short of troops because Octavian had failed to honour a promise to send him 20,000 soldiers, in exchange for the ships he had sent west for the campaign against Sextus Pompeius.

Even so, Antony had a huge army. He commanded a basic force of 16 legions, perhaps 60,000 men, plus 10,000 cavalry recruited from Gaul and Spain; allied contingents collected from the local client kingdoms amounted to another 30,000 men, largely Armenians from the country recently conquered by Canidius Crassus.[8] He was undoubtedly energised by an upheaval in the Parthian court during 37, in which the kingship fell to Phraates IV, and which in turn resulted in the flight of many aristocrats from the court.[9] One of these was Monaeses, who came to Antony and suggested he act as guide for the army; similarly, King Artavasdes of Armenia recommended a route along the Upper Euphrates, through the mountains, and into Media Atropatene. The alternative was the desert/steppe route through Mesopotamia, which had been Crassus' choice twenty years before – and his doom. Antony was relying too much on these voluntary guides, neither of whom could be relied on to continue to be loyal, and both of whom resumed their loyalties to Parthia in the middle of the campaign. He clearly was short of reliable intelligence on the route and on the conditions; this was partly due to Parthian deceit and misdirection – an intelligent defensive tactic – and partly due to Roman ignorance.

Kleopatra had been apprehensive about the campaign from the start. She had travelled with him as far as the Euphrates, crossing at Seleukeia-Zeugma when the army set off. When he set off she was pregnant again, and the new child was born later in the year. Antony will have heard during his journey that his wife Octavia had also had a daughter; his marital affairs (he had already divorced three wives, all of whom had children by him) were clearly in some disarray. Going on campaign into distant regions may well have been a helpful distraction.

The distance involved in this campaign was a major cause of Antony's defeat. His army moved more slowly through the mountains than anticipated and became stretched out as the heavy baggage lagged behind; he had to leave two legions with that baggage as guards. He pushed on ahead of the main force to attack the city of Phraaspa in Media Atropatene, where he became locked into a siege, relying at first on cavalry and light-armed troops, who were not sufficient to take the city. Then, in a classic campaign to relieve the siege, the Parthians attacked his forage patrols, so reducing both his supplies and his forces. They raided the slow-moving siege train, and in a decisive battle, killed the men of the two legions; the siege equipment was destroyed, along with the men.[10]

The siege was abandoned, and the retreat was as difficult and costly as could be expected. But the retreat brought out the best in Antony as a commander, though it was close to a complete disaster even so. The Parthians attacked the Roman army daily for over three weeks, constantly inflicting casualties, while the Roman army marched steadily westwards. The last part of the march took place in the Armenian mountains during winter, in which the cold killed off at least 8,000 soldiers.[11] When the survivors finally reached Syria, they were met by Kleopatra with supplies of winter clothing and food. Antony had also wanted money, but she did not bring any, and he had to pay out a donative from his own and his friends' resources.[12] Quite possibly, Kleopatra was therefore using his dependence on her to make a strong point. He had lost a third of the army, and many of the allied contingents had deserted (and therefore mainly survived); he had now to rely even more than before on Egyptian resources.

Antony rebuilt his damaged army, which included recruiting five legions from non-citizens, Greeks and others, in the eastern provinces – promising them Roman citizenship on enlistment. How much of a draw this particular point was is doubtful, but maybe the prospect of regular pay for a year or two, and the chance of collecting some loot, was sufficiently attractive. His plan for the next campaign was to gain control of Armenia as a preliminary base before another attack on Parthia; he had already secured an alliance with the king of Media Atropatene. This, of course, would have been a better plan than aiming for Parthia's centre from the beginning.

He was ready to march again in 35. By this time, Lepidus in Africa had been eliminated and put into retirement by Octavian;[13] Sextus Pompeius had escaped from Octavian's campaign against Sicily to take refuge in western Asia Minor, where he raised a small army, and attempted to enlist Parthia on his side, but was then quickly defeated, captured and executed by Antony's forces under M. Titius.[14] The ease with which Antony's forces dealt with Sextus contrasted strongly with the lengthy campaign and intermittent defeats when Octavian had fought him.

The Roman world was now divided between two men and their armies. Antony had become more dependent on Kleopatra and her kingdom's resources, although, as noted, the various gifts and concessions he had surrendered to her were largely phony, yet they could be used against him. His relationship with her was a fertile source for hostile propaganda, and Octavian succeeded in portraying him as dependent on a wily seductress. This is not altogether inaccurate, of course, which made the propaganda sting all the more, since she was providing substantial supplies, and giving birth to his children.

Antony's marital history now interfered with his campaign plans in 35. (Kleopatra never did interfere in this way, always leaving military affairs to him, though she had some experience of war, and considerable knowledge of the affairs of the Near East.) His current Roman wife, Octavia, arrived in Athens while Antony was on the march against Armenia, bringing a force of 2,000 soldiers and 70 ships sent by Octavian, supposedly a contribution to the campaign.[15] In fact, Antony was owed 20,000 soldiers by Octavian, which he had promised but never delivered, and the ships were of no use in the mountains of Armenia. Surrendering the ships was no hardship to Octavian, who had acquired Pompeius' fleet, and by getting rid of the seventy that he sent east, he was easing his financial problems as well. But when Antony heard of Octavia's arrival at Athens he halted his campaign and returned to Egypt and Kleopatra.

This has provided Plutarch with the opportunity for another purple passage, depicting Kleopatra, whom he portrayed as present in Syria as the campaign began, as a simpering, wounded lover, which is supposed to have compelled Antony to turn back.[16] This is most likely a version of the Octavianist propaganda, which was getting into gear at this time to brand Antony as a traitor to Roman values. Antony accepted the forces she brought, and then sent Octavia back to her brother – which gave the hostile propagandists the opportunity to depict her as the mistreated and abandoned wife. The wider results of the episode was to delay Antony's campaign by a year, which his wife's brother was able to develop as Antony delaying because of his entanglement with Kleopatra, in the anti-Antony propaganda campaign he was mounting in Italy.

The apparent attempt by Octavia, with her visit to Athens and her 'present' of soldiers and ships and supplies for Antony's campaign in 35, may have been her personal initiative. Her aim would have been to engineer a reconciliation between her brother and her husband, which would have necessarily involved a rejection of Kleopatra, and one between herself and her husband, but it had failed. The marriage that Antony made with Kleopatra in Alexandria soon after he sent Octavia back to her brother was his public answer. The ploy, whether it was Octavia's notion or Octavian's, had little chance of success when he was in the middle of his campaign, which relied on logistical support from Kleopatra. (Even if it really was Octavia's idea, no doubt Octavian had approved it, with a view to exploiting it; it is exactly the sort of thing he contrived.) It is from this series of events that the dispute between the two men became deadly and the break between them, in effect, complete. Neither of them did anything obvious or immediate to prepare for the future conflict right away, but both did so after Antony's return from Armenia.

It was not, however, because of Kleopatra's ambition, or because of the insult to Octavia, that the breach had occurred. This had been developing ever since Caesar's assassination had brought Antony and Octavian together in an awkward alliance. It had been disguised by the number of aspirants for his position, and by such matters as the Parthian war and the need to locate and hunt down and punish the assassins. For Antony, the rise to power of Octavian was the emergence of a man who gradually became a threat to his own pre-eminence as Caesar's successor. For Octavian it was a matter of personal survival – he would not have survived defeat – but also a driving ambition. The propaganda conflict was not for nothing centred on the behaviour of both men – Antony's licentiousness and drunkenness, Octavian's cold cruelty. In this deadly dispute the two women stood as proxies, Kleopatra, portrayed as luxury-loving seductress, stood in place of Antony, Octavia seen as a modest Roman matron, standing in for her brother – and both portraits were, of course, inaccurate, but as with the men, defeat would mean death.

There was one other detail that riled Octavian. Antony acknowledged Caesarion, also known as Ptolemy Caesar, as Caesar's son, in fact his only son. This may or may not have been a deliberate blow at Octavian's status as Caesar's adopted son, but it is impossible to believe that Antony had not taken that into his consideration in announcing the acknowledgement of the adoption – and if he missed it, there was Kleopatra there to remind him, no doubt forcibly. Had Antony won the subsequent war, no doubt Octavian would have been condemned as a usurper and as the thief of the child's inheritance. It was another reason for Octavian's ire, but it remained a distinct issue worth airing – and Octavian's angry response indicated that the shot hit home; it was always possible, if Octavian died (he had been wounded in the fighting in Sicily) that Ptolemy Caesar would come into his imperial inheritance.

We know much less of Antony's propaganda exploits than Octavian's. The latter underlies much of the later literary accounts of the conflict produced in the centuries following, most particularly that of Plutarch, but that by Cassius Dio as well. There is no reason to believe that Antony's propaganda machine was any the less active and effective, and well directed – the controversy over Ptolemy Caesar is one indication of this.

Propaganda is, of course, not decisive in such contests, and is usually recognised as what it was by those involved, and is therefore easily discounted; its effects are always only short-term. What really counted was military power and generalship. In this matter of military strength, the balance was about equal, though Octavian's forces were slightly superior – and yet Caesar had demonstrated throughout his military career that it was rarely superior numbers that was decisive in battles.

Antony's new campaign in 34 succeeded in its object. He marched his army – thirty legions – into Armenia, captured King Artavasdes, who had deserted him in 36 at a crucial moment, and annexed the country, making it a new Roman province.[17] He had to fight Artavasdes' son to make the annexation stick, but he succeeded in doing so. In strategic terms, this was a most useful imperial acquisition, giving Rome an important base from which to dominate the approach to Parthia, overseeing that through Mesopotamia. He had been helped by the alliance he had made with the king of Media Atropatene, who had quarrelled with King Phraates over the loot captured from Antony's army in the first expedition. Controlling Armenia gave the Romans a base for invading Parthia if required, or a garrison situation that would prevent the Parthians invading Syria with any ease. But this depended upon the installation of a major Roman garrison in Armenia, and on the acquiescence of the Armenian population to Roman rule. The first had to be withdrawn when the war with Octavian began, and the second was never achieved. Armenia without a Roman garrison to oversee it at once slipped out of Roman control, and slid easily into full independence as soon as most of that garrison was withdrawn – those who remained were defeated and massacred by a joint Armenian–Parthian force.[18] At least the Armenians achieved what they wished, which was independence.

For the moment, however, Antony was victorious, and he returned to Egypt to celebrate his victory with a grand parade, dubbed a mock triumph by the historians. As part of the celebrations, he and Kleopatra went through the marriage ceremony,[19] which was also the answer to Octavia's attempt at reconciliation. His children by Kleopatra were given dynastic names; who chose the names is not obvious, but they were clearly Ptolemaic. The twins were Alexander and Kleopatra. They were thus named after the last two Ptolemaic kings (not necessarily Alexander the Great, as is generally assumed) who were of the direct descent of Ptolemy I – Ptolemy X Alexander I and his son the brief King Ptolemy XI Alexander II. The girl was given the name of the long series of Kleopatras, which name had become the automatic dynastic name for girls in the dynasty just as Ptolemy was for boys. They also received surnames, as did earlier members of the Ptolemaic family, in these cases Helios and Selene, 'sun', and 'moon', an indication perhaps of Kleopatra's ambitions for them, but this was also in the direct tradition of divine epithets. Indeed, Selene had been the name of one of the Kleopatras, and boys had taken such epithets as Dionysos in the past; the child born in late 36, a boy, became Ptolemy Philadelphos, even more obviously part of the Ptolemaic dynasty, but also indicating his relation to the family. One may conclude that it was Kleopatra, the mother, who chose these names rather than the father. Yet it was also clear that Antony had made his marital choice, and that he was linked maritally as well as politically decisively with Kleopatra.

Whether the marriage was legal or mainly a pretence is unclear. Antony was married to Octavia, and did not divorce her until 32; multiple wives in Hellenistic dynasties had not been common, but it was not unknown. If Kleopatra thought that this marriage entitled her to become Queen of Rome when Antony had overcome Octavian and become its king (as was clearly on the cards for the future by this time), she would need to compete with the large set of Antony's former wives and their children – he had been married three times before Octavia, and had perhaps ten children, apart from those with Kleopatra. It seems that she had entertained this political fantasy with Caesar, only to be disappointed by his failure to respond, and now Antony was her candidate. There is no doubt he enjoyed her presence, and her wit and behaviour, but, as the territorial negotiations showed, his head was hard, and was not turned by her when he discussed politic matters. He was taking from her far more than he was delivering, and all those land grants could easily be revoked, as many of the Near Eastern kings and princes had already discovered.

His children by Kleopatra were awarded mock kingdoms – Alexander Helios over Armenia, Media and Parthia (an enormous territory, none of which was in Antony's possession to bestow), Kleopatra Selene over Cyrene and Libya, and Ptolemy Philadelphos over Phoenicia, Syria and Kilikia (which at least were in Roman hands) – but none of these were anything but fantasy kingdoms. Kleopatra became 'queen of kings' as a result of the 'promotion' of her children; and Ptolemy Caesar became, as her royal partner, the 'King of Kings', but this was all still more of a fantasy, not to be taken at all seriously.[20] Of course, this all made no difference on the ground, for all the Ptolemaic territories awarded to the children were still directly or indirectly controlled by Roman, not Ptolemaic, officials, or not by either in some cases.

The union of the Roman general and the Egyptian queen was publicised within the east in the Ptolemaic coinage. Mints throughout the region produced coins with Antony's head on one side and Kleopatra's on the other; in some areas they were depicted together on the same side, Antony behind Kleopatra.[21] The marriage was thus made public, though Antony was not described as king to Kleopatra's queen. This in fact should have been his title in Ptolemaic terms, just as Archelaus was king to Kleopatra Berenike's queen twenty years earlier, but perhaps Antony had foregone such a title, either because he valued his Roman titles of triumvir and consul over that of a king, or more likely because he did not wish to provide even more fuel for Octavian's propaganda machine; he had attempted to persuade Caesar to take that title, and it had been refused because the Romans had a curiously visceral dislike of it – he could scarcely do less.

Antony's success in Armenia was his only conquest. By the time he had returned to Egypt and indulged in the great celebrations in Alexandria, it had become clear that his next conflict would be with Octavian; it must also have been clear that the future of Kleopatra, her children, and her kingdom, rested on the outcome of the approaching war. And if Antony won he would inevitably move to Rome, and spend his time in the city deep in Roman politics, or campaigning to suppress rebels and enemies, or to extend the empire; if Octavian won, Egypt would likely be annexed, and Kleopatra deposed at the least, murdered more likely, and their sons would be also likely to be killed.

Of the choice of evils in Kleopatra's future, staying with Antony offered the least worst chance of survival, both as queen and in some sort of independence. But even that would put the Ptolemaic state under direct Roman control, even more than it was during Kleopatra's reign, and the ultimate result would probably be annexation after Kleopatra's death. Kleopatra's aim of independent rule was as much a fantasy as the airy kingdoms invented by Antony for her children in their celebratory excitement. As an indication of what would be the result, it is extremely difficult to locate any source that gives any information about Kleopatra's actions and activities between Antony's return from Armenia in 34, and the beginning of the new Roman civil war in 32. Whatever she was doing has been smothered beneath the propaganda produced by her enemies.

This civil war had been heralded by the personal and political break resulting from Octavia's failure in her attempts to reconcile her husband and her brother. A year later, in 34, when Antony returned from Armenia victorious and confident, that civil war had become certain. For the next four years, the two warlords inched towards each other with their enormous armies and massive fleets, full knowing, as did everyone from Gades to Seleukeia-Zeugma, that the future of the Roman Empire depended on the result.

Chapter 14

Actium, and After

The decisive break with Octavian, which was precipitated by Octavia's failed attempt at a reconciliation and then by the victory of Antony in Armenia, which greatly increased his military confidence, was driven home by the marriage of Kleopatra and Antony in late 34. This provided yet another avenue by which Octavian could attack his rival. The fact that he was reacting to personal threats – Octavia was Antony's wife by Roman law, Caesarion was the only surviving, but hardly legitimate, child of Julius – may have inclined some to sympathy, but it may also have annoyed some who could see that the problem of the Roman Empire was much greater than Octavian's *amour propre*. But by this time anything Antony did was liable to bring Octavian's scorn and criticism, including the transfer of rolls of papyrus from the Attalid library in Pergamon to Alexandria, reported in Plutarch's words as the whole of the Pergamene library.[1] This is one of a string of minor annoyances he details that were perceived as such in Rome, but which under less stressful political conditions would have been ignored, seen as jokes, or even applauded.

Again, it was not this personal emnity that was the real issue but, by now, which of these two men should control the Roman Empire. In this, Kleopatra, Caesarion and Octavia were of secondary importance, except that Kleopatra was contributing money, men, ships and materials in great quantity to Antony's forces.[2]

Both warlords began serious military preparations about the end of 34, after Antony had returned from Armenia and held his Alexandrian celebrations. Octavian's reply to this display of success was a whole series of formal Roman triumphs, two of them over Spain, and a major display of games. His associate M. Vipsanius Agrippa took the nearly defunct office of *aedile* for 33, repairing the aqueducts of Rome, with full publicity,[3] accompanied by a barrage of insulting propaganda directed at Antony and Kleopatra – to which Antony's men replied in kind. More to the point, both men gathered and marshalled their military and naval forces.

Antony, with Kleopatra, spent the winter of 33/32 in Asia Minor, at Ephesos.[4] He had spent much of 33 summoning his supporters and his forces. Canidius, for example, brought from Armenia sixteen legions (though next year, Armenia slipped into independence as a result of the withdrawal of his forces, assisted by a Parthian army). Seven legions were called up from Macedonia, and recruiting continued actively; the many client kings in the east had to provide their own forces, usually auxiliaries to the legions.[5] The legionaries were mostly Italians; the client kings' forces and the new recruits were mainly from his eastern tributaries and provinces, so that Antony's army was more or less half-and-half western and eastern. As a representative of the Roman Empire's population, this force was a better fit than Octavian's forces. He also gathered a huge fleet of 800 ships, which included perhaps 500 warships, and of which Kleopatra contributed a quarter – at least 30,000 sailors and marines. Antony was still having more ships built throughout his territories in the last years before the battle, and many of his new ships were large – nines and tens. Kleopatra also brought, as her main contribution, a treasury of 20,000 talents with which to pay the troops and secure supplies.

Octavian, no more short of money than Antony, though he had to face down riots in Rome, provoked by his heavy taxation demands,[6] had a rather less varied army. His primary land force was his legions, perhaps 75,000 men in them, plus 15,000 auxiliaries. Both sides had about 12,000 cavalry, and Antony's 500 warships were a slightly larger naval force than Octavian's, which is said to have consisted of 230 major warships together with 140 lighter liburnians.[7] In 32, the two armies were separated by the intervening Aegean Sea, Greece and the Adriatic. This separation gradually narrowed.

Ephesos was Antony's headquarters at the beginning of 32, and there Kleopatra came with her ships and her treasure. But she was a problem. Some of Antony's colleagues were appreciative of her contribution – a much larger individual contribution than any other single territory except Italy's contribution to Octavian's forces. But she used the political weight this gave her to intervene in Antony's plans, such as they were.

When Antony called up troops from his client kings, Kleopatra objected to the summoning of the troops of Herod of Judaea, with whom her quarrel had become more and more poisonous. Many of these clients came along with their forces, and Herod and Kleopatra in the same camp would be explosive. He was sent instead into Arabia to campaign against the Nabataeans.[8]

Kleopatra had therefore, probably without intending it, produced a three-sided engagement in which all three kingdoms were in conflict with the other two. The Nabataeans resented having to surrender coastal territories to Kleopatra, and this anyway does not seem to have stopped their piracy. Herod and Kleopatra, if not actually at war with each other, were often close to it, and Herod undoubtedly resented having, like the Nabataeans, to hand over Palestinian territories to her; Herod and the Nabataeans had bickered on and off over border locations – a conflict initiated by the earlier Maccabean kings. No doubt these complications were not the only ones among Antony's clients, notably those in Asia Minor, where he had been shuffling territories more than once for the last decade, creating winners and losers, with the latter nursing resentments. These conflicts were muted in his camp, but could easily require Antony's attention, draining his energy and distracting him. In that sense, Kleopatra's refusal to accept Herod's presence in the camp may well have been a help.

Herod's diversion into Arabia probably made no difference to the outcome of the war, except that Herod was able to point out to Octavian after the battle, rather brazenly, that he had not joined Antony in the war, and so he survived in power, whereas Kleopatra was crushed. But such interventions by Kleopatra, and her power and presence, had a serious effect among Antony's colleagues, and gave Octavian yet another handle for his campaign of criticism. Her influence on Antony was probably less then it seemed to his colleagues, but it did exist, and it promoted division amongst them. As a woman, even a queen, she probably had to fight her corner every day. Ahenobarbus, for example, consistently refused to address her as queen.[9]

On the last day of December 33, the triumvirate agreement made five years before expired, and, although Antony suggested a renewal, Octavian refused. Then, on 1 January 32, Octavian was faced with two new consuls being installed in Rome, both of whom were Antony's supporters, C. Sosius and Cn. Domitius Ahenobarbus. Both of them, the emollient Sosius in January, and the blunt but cautious Ahenobarbus in February, launched verbal attacks on Octavian in the Senate where they met with a degree of agreement among many of the senators. So this concatenation of changes and counter-charges spelled danger for Octavian. In reply, he simply withdrew from the Senate and Rome so that he would not have to get into a bickering argument with the consuls. By mid-February, he had come to the conclusion that to do nothing would be to have his personal authority whittled away. He therefore reacted eventually by what amounted to a *coup d'état*.

The attacks in the Senate by Sosius had been blocked by a tribune loyal to Octavian, but the end of the triumvirate had also left him without a command, and so without legal protection. In mid-February, when Ahenobarbus was mounting another attack on him in the Senate, he collected a group of friends and guards, all armed, and went to the Senate to finally make his defence of his conduct; surrounded by his armed guard, he gave his reply to his critics' accusations, without any danger of contradiction or argument. In the face of his guard, no opponents spoke up. But as soon as they could, after he had finished and left the Senate, those opponents fled from Rome to join Antony, in total, some 300 or 400 senators, a little less than half the Senate.[10] This, of course, left the Senate in Rome consisting of Octavian's supporters exclusively, supposedly some 700 of them, though many were actually neutral or even indifferent, and this is probably an exaggerated number. The Senate, however, could now pass whatever measures Octavian wanted.

This also brought a large group of Antony's senatorial supporters to his headquarters, and many of them had not encountered Kleopatra so far; many of these men were annoyed to find how influential she was. The result was that Antony's party divided into his supporters and his critics – or rather, perhaps, her critics.[11]

The influence of Antony's two final wives was curiously different. Kleopatra was a source of both disunity and strength amongst his followers. He was persuaded to order her back to Alexandria, but she would not go, and he could not insist, for he depended on her and her naval and monetary contributions.[12] In Rome, Octavia remained loyal to Antony, living in his house, caring for her children by him and those born to Fulvia, his third wife, who had died in 40. Octavia's modest and loyal demeanour (probably exaggerated by her brother's propaganda machine) was rather in contrast to that of her brother and her husband, and brought admiration and sympathy,[13] though this was not as materially advantageous to Octavian as Kleopatra's to Antony. On the other hand, Octavia was not a source of division.

The senators on either side were hardly united in their attitudes or loyalties. Probably the majority, in Rome and in Ephesos, were in hopes of peace between the warlords, or at least some sort of a truce, and a sharing of power, but did not have the power to impose their wishes on the warlords with their huge armies and navies. Both men had become intent on establishing their own supremacy; there was no reason for equality between them, and reconciliation was out of the question. So Antony began moving his army through Macedonia, and his navy around Greece and into the Adriatic. He and Kleopatra went first to Samos, probably not by coincidence an old Ptolemaic naval base, and then to Athens.[14]

The two wives had a further part to play, as victims rather than direct players in events; from Athens, Antony announced that he intended to divorce Octavia, an unpopular decision with some of his people.[15] Two of them, L. Munatius Plancus and M. Titius, the former an adept at survival by his timely changing of sides, the latter the capable victor against Sextus Pompeius, used this to leave Antony and transfer to Octavian. M. Titius had apparently learned some details of Antony's will, which he passed on to Octavian; it had been deposited with the Vestal Virgins in Rome.

Octavian thereupon indulged in yet another illegality, raiding the Vestal Virgins' residence to seize their copy of that will, selected sections of which he publicised, though the whole remained in his possession. He followed this up with an attempt to bind all Italy to him by a general oath of support,[16] and finished with a declaration of war, not against Antony, who was nevertheless decried as a traitor, but on Kleopatra, as though she, as queen of Egypt, was a serious threat to the Roman Empire.[17]

The year 32/31 was therefore marked in Italy by Octavian's series of illegal acts – the armed intervention in the Senate, the illegal raid on the archives of the Vestals, and finally the pathetic declaration of war on, of all people, the queen of Egypt. Yet despite all this set of illegal actions, he was able to bind much of Italy (though not by any means all of it) to his support by a general oath.[18] Opposition existed, but was cowed into irrelevance.

Meanwhile, Antony's army marched through Macedonia to his chosen station for the war – and for his navy also – the sheltered and capacious Gulf of Ambrakia, large enough to hold his whole fleet, and still with room enough for the ships to exercise and practice manoeuvres. The army camped at the entrance to the Gulf, at Actium.

Antony's fleet had sailed round Greece to get to the Gulf, and he had planted garrisons at two of the Peloponnesian peninsulas, Tainaron and Methoni, to ensure the passage remained available. From the Gulf of Ambrakia his fleet patrolled as far north as Corcyra, and as far south as Zakynthos, hoping perhaps to intercept Octavian's forces, or at least to locate them, but Agrippa, placed in overall command by Octavian, had other plans.

Kleopatra spent much of the years 33–31 out of Egypt, and took with her many of the ships of the Ptolemaic navy. There appears to be little indication of any trouble in her kingdom during her absence. The distress connected with the disputed succession in 51–48, the low Niles, and the plague that followed, died away after 41, presumably due to the return of the usual annual Nile floods and the return to their homes of those villagers who had deserted them to avoid paying taxes. Kleopatra at one point did intervene to stop the tax collectors doing their jobs with excessive brutality, but that only meant that their normal brutality was accepted.[19] The Ptolemaic government was fully capable of providing extensive succour to Antony's army when it returned to Egypt in defeat in 36,[20] and she was able to contribute 20,000 talents to Antony's war chest in 32–31, plus ships and sailors.[21] No matter how the Egyptian peasantry was enduring poverty, the government, the court, and the aristocracy were coping very well; the remains of that treasure were enough to decisively enrich Rome when it was distributed and spent.

The preparations and movements that occupied 33–31 had brought the rival forces close to each other, but it was only in the spring of 31 that they finally clashed. Antony had the advantage in numbers, both in soldiers and at sea, and in the variety of types of soldiers in his army, if he could make use of their particular skills. On the other hand, Octavian's army was more homogeneous, with fewer of the auxiliary non-Roman soldiers that Antony had.[22] Also, Octavian's command system was centred on the person of Agrippa, certainly the most creative and capable commander on either side – apart from Antony – but the fight here was at sea and on board ship, not his natural element; had the battle been on land the outcome would probably have been different – that only emphasises Agrippa's skill at command. Octavian, in effect, ceded the command to Agrippa, which was an intelligent decision; he had usually made a mess of generalship himself when he undertook it. Antony, by contrast, had to take account of the opinions of his varied collections of colleagues, of Kleopatra, of his former colleagues in the eastern campaigns, and of the mass of refugee senators. His command system was, to say the least, less well organised than that of Octavian.

Antony was usually a good strategist, and the Roman army was all too familiar with the layout of the Ionian Sea coasts and northern Greece after the earlier civil wars, which had seen battles and campaigns in Sicily and Macedonia. Coming from the east, Antony was able to secure a string of bases that would guard the approaches to his strategic base in Egypt, and establish close subsidiary bases to guard the supply line from his main base. To prevent any attempt by Octavian's army in North Africa threatening Egypt, he had four legions in Cyrenaica. To guard his southern flank and his supply line from the east he had forces in Crete, at Capes Tainaron and Methoni in the Peloponnese, and ships patrolling and occupying the Ionian Islands from Zakynthos to Corcyra. Behind this guard, his army and fleet occupied the Gulf of Ambrakia and its shores, the army camping south of the entrance to the Gulf, at Actium, the fleet within the Gulf with patrols outside.[23]

This is self-evidently a defensive scheme, but it was spread over a wide area, and it left a number of Antony's detachments rather isolated and essentially useless, notably the Cyrenaican and Syrian legions, but also the Cretan and Peloponnesian garrisons. And in Agrippa, Antony faced an even better strategist than he was. Agrippa's first move was to seize control of the fortified post at Cape Methoni. The garrison, commanded by the Moorish king Bogud, fought hard but was defeated, and Bogud was killed. Antony had posted a strong garrison there, but Agrippa had brought a stronger one. Methoni now became a post that interrupted Antony's maritime supply line, so that he had to transport his supplies overland through Greece, or risk them being captured by the ships left by Agrippa at Methoni.[24]

Agrippa's force left a garrison in place of the enemy's in the castle at Methoni, and also left ships to attack any of Antony's vessels that attempted to pass the Cape. Then he sailed north along the west Greek coast, forcing the weaker Antonian patrols to retire into the Gulf of Ambrakia; the patrol at Corcyra retired also.[25] He ignored several other garrisons, such as that at Tainaron and Patras, which simply absorbed enemy manpower without contributing to his security.

The withdrawing of Antony's patrols into the Gulf left the passage from Brundisium in Italy across to Epeiros clear, and Octavian brought across his army to land well to the north of Antony's forces at Oricum and Panormus nearby.[26] He then marched his whole force south along the coast road, unmolested, to take up a position on the north side of the Gulf's entrance, facing Antony's army across the strait, which was camped at the Cape Actium; Agrippa seized control of Corcyra on the way.[27] Agrippa's squadron's cruise had effectively blocked up Antony's fleet in the Gulf, and by interrupting his supply line, he had begun a distant siege of the enemy army in its camp.

This, as it proved, was decisive for the whole campaign. With their own supply lines secure, Agrippa and Octavian could simply wait Antony out in the knowledge that his supplies would become increasingly difficult to procure. During the next six months, the Antonian forces became hungry, suffered sickness, and began to desert to the enemy, or just desert, in considerable numbers. Several well-known men, Q. Dellius and Cn. Domitius Ahenobarbus among them, are recorded as changing sides,[28] but more serious was the slow weakening of Antony's naval force as sailors deserted, understanding all too clearly that their fleet was hemmed in.[29] They were replaced to some extent by men from the army, and press gangs conscripted Greek sailors where they could find them. (Plutarch recorded that his great-grandfather and the people of Chaeronea in Boiotia were pressed into carrying supplies to Antony's camp.)[30] The fleet was reduced in size, partly by abandoning some ships, which were burned to save them from being taken over by Octavian, but partly by the loss of manpower through disease and desertion. It was also dispiriting for those who remained, who could see that the fleet was blocked up in the Gulf; only a victorious battle could release it. The entrance was so narrow that ships could get out only one at a time, and all their movements could be seen from Octavian's camp on its hill to the north, while Octavian's fleet was camped on the open roadstead to the west of his camp, and was being used to make patrols; a section of men went to take over Leukas.

The anchorage of Octavian's ships in the Bay of Gomaros was adequate for the summer, but would become a dangerous trap when storms began with the change of the seasons. It could therefore be a worthwhile base for the blockade mounted to keep Antony's ships in the Gulf, but only for the moment. It would not take many ships to form a blockade, given the narrow entrance that restricted the passage of ships to one at a time. Considerable building works were done by the Octavianist forces to box in a track from the camp to the shore to deter raiders, and a mole to shelter the ships was built. Most of the ships would be drawn up on the beach, of course, and they would be used in rotation to mount the blockade.

Having achieved their positions on land and by the sea, the two commanders arranged their forces as for the blockade, and brought in any scattered land forces to the main camps. Antony especially had legions spread throughout Greece, and to have a chance of victory on land he had to bring them all to his main camp. The situation was such that Antony's army was superior to

Octavian's, but his navy was inferior (and, of course, trapped). For victory, therefore, Antony would need to win a battle on land, which in turn would allow his fleet to be released from the Gulf. His men fortified their camp, built walls to link it with the shore (just as did Octavian's men) and fortified towers were built on both sides of the strait; if blockade runners could reach the entrance they could get through into the Gulf. If enemy ships chanced it, they could be blocked by a single ship and battered by bombardments from the shore.[31]

The two sides manoeuvred to gain advantage. Agrippa made an attack on the island of Leukas, secured it, and so gained a more sheltered anchorage for his ships; C. Sosius commanded here.[32] This also made Antony's supply ships' task much more difficult. In April, Antony moved part of his army across the strait and gained control of freshwater springs from which Octavian's men had been getting their supplies, but could go no further in the face of the well-fortified camp of the Octavianists on the hill. A cavalry raid aimed at securing the other freshwater supply at the River Louros was defeated after a hard fight, at which King Deiotaros of Paphlagonia changed sides and joined Octavian.[33]

The conflict spread throughout Greece as Octavian sent out detachments to interrupt Antony's overland supply lines; Antony as a result had to send out his own detachments to prevent this, and to carry supplies to his camp. Agrippa at sea chipped away at Antony's posts. He defeated a detachment of Antony's ships that was based at Patras and controlled the Corinthian Gulf; he even captured Corinth briefly, then withdrew, but Antony would now need to garrison the city more strongly.[34] The ruler of Sparta, Eurykles, seeing this Octavianist activity, deserted from Antony (a decision helped by the fact that Antony had captured and executed his father, who had been a pirate).[35]

Eurykles was not the only deserter, but it is noticeable that the desertions tended to be only one way, and no desertions from Octavian's forces are recorded, though the sources are all on his side, and any who left him may not have been remarked. Dellius and Ahenobarbus left, at different times, and other Romans also, but it was Antony's client kings whose political antennae were the most active and sensitive. Apart from the Deiotaros and Eurykles, Rheometalkes of Thrace, Tarkondimotos of the Amanus, and Amyntas of Galatia all left, taking their forces with them; Antony executed Iamblichos of Emesa when it appeared he was about to desert; he also executed Q.

Postumius, a senator, perhaps to show that he was not simply aiming at the client kings.[36] (When he heard of all this, no doubt Herod of Judaea was thankful that he had been sent off to fight the Nabataeans.)

An attempt by Antony to break out of what was increasingly seen as a tightening trap was made in August. Sosius came out to assault the blockade, while Dellius and King Amyntas took the forces into Macedonia, and Antony was ready to march with the full force. But Sosius' initial success at sea was thwarted when Agrippa unexpectedly arrived with his main fleet and drove him back. Antony did not therefore move.[37]

This attempt was mounted because conditions in Antony's camp were becoming so bad as to have become intolerable. Disease and the shortage of food, desertions of rowers and soldiers and kings and senators were undoubtedly depressing for those who remained. The joint Dellius/Amyntas/Sosius/Antony moves had been a serious attempt to break the sea blockade, and to open the way for the army to move elsewhere by land, drawing Octavian's army out of its camp and into a moving campaign that would release the fleet. With the failure of that attempt (Dellius and others deserted as a result), Antony had to resort to concentrating on a single attempt to break the siege, either by land or by sea, not both.

Canidius, Antony's army commander, wanted to take the army and march east across Greece, so breaking the siege that way. On the other hand, Kleopatra, whose presence had continued throughout the siege, advocated moving the fleet, reinforced with plenty of soldiers from the army, and breaking out by sea. Either plan would involve going into battle with a weakened force and tackling a more confident and larger army, and would involve abandoning whichever equipment was not being used. Antony, a land commander perhaps by instinct, inclined to Canidius' choice, and could be fairly confident of defeating Octavian in a straight fight, but he could not abandon the ships, especially not Kleopatra's fleet. This is not necessarily because he was loyal to his wife, but because without a fleet he would in effect be marooned in Greece; Agrippa's fleet would be able to prevent him from leaving Greece, for the only way out would be across the Hellespont, or more likely, across the Bosporos, and in the face of the naval power controlled by Agrippa, this would be impossible. So the next move would be to break out with the fleet, and the army would be able to move only if the Antonian fleet was successful. Antony had been reduced to this, a desperate gamble.[38]

After these months of preparation and manoeuvring, the battle, when it came, was over in a few hours. After waiting for four days for the first storm of autumn to die down, on 2 September Antony's fleet moved out of the Gulf and lined up in order, facing the enemy further out at sea. This move had been signalled before the storm when the surplus ships and other equipment was burnt. Octavian and Agrippa knew what that meant, and the movements of the ships in the Gulf gave them plenty of warning. Antony had about 170 ships in 3 squadrons, with Kleopatra and her 60 ships as a separate force. Agrippa commanded about 400 ships. Each side had a variety of ships ranging from light liburnians up to nines and perhaps tens. He got the whole fleet out of the Gulf without difficulty – Agrippa, in command of Octavian's fleet, had clearly decided that it was time to fight and so did not prevent their exit. No doubt, the advanced season was part of his calculation, since the winter would wreak as much damage to Octavian's forces as to Antony's, and perhaps, since they had to stay at sea to maintain the blockade, more so. As usual, therefore, the battle took place by the consent of both participants.

The weather was the dictator of tactics, and by early September, it was still predictable. After the morning land breeze, which had brought Antony's fleet out of the Gulf, the wind died down for several hours. This would have been the time when a battle would normally be fought, in the calm water between the fleets, but Antony did not want a battle, if he could avoid one; instead, he wanted to escape, as did Kleopatra. His aim was presumably to bring out his ships and then seek naval reinforcements; with the fleets moving away, possibly Canidius could also escape. So the two fleets held their positions, separated by about a mile of open water, until in mid-afternoon the sea breeze developed.[39] It swung slowly around to the north-west, and strengthened sufficiently to allow ships to use their sails and so move away at some speed. But they had to get past Octavian's fleet before this could be done.

It was at that point, therefore, that the fleets got to grips. Whereas it was Antony's aim to escape the trap that had gradually closed around him, it was Octavian's and Agrippa's aim to destroy Antony's fleet, and if possible Kleopatra's squadron as well. Her ships stayed out of the fight, despite the fact that Octavian had deliberately declared war on her rather than Antony; her forces were partly unarmed, or lightly armed, merchant ships, her flagship had the remains of her treasure – Egyptian treasure – on board, and she had much wider responsibilities than fighting a battle in the midst of a Roman civil war.

Antony faced Agrippa's 400 ships with just 170 of his own. (Kleopatra's squadron stood in reserve but had no intention of entering the fight.) He placed his heaviest ships on either wing, with the weaker ships in the centre. (Hannibal's Cannae formation.) He manoeuvred to draw Agrippa's ships to the right (Antony's right), and both fleets' line were stretched out so as to weaken their formation. This was intended to open up to Antony's fleet the way to escape, which was to break through Agrippa's line in order to sail away round Leukas and then south. The fighting was thus concentrated on the two wings, where it looked as though Antony was using his heavy ships to attempt to drive Agrippa's ships away from the centre of their line. In fact, the aim was to weaken the centre of Agrippa's line to permit Kleopatra's ships to sail through and get away. This she accomplished in the later part of the afternoon, and her squadron was accompanied by a number of the Roman ships who also escaped; this rather implies that the various captains in Antony's fleet fully understood the aim of the battle. It was only on Octavian's side that the queen was accused of desertion.

Octavian's fleet may well have been taken by surprise by Kleopatra's manoeuvre, though the disparity of forces should have conveyed a warning that Antony was intending something other than a fight to the death. The escaping ships hoisted their sails as soon as they could, and were able to speed away, while the battle continued behind them. Despite having double the number of ships, the only pursuit made by Octavian's vessels was by the light liburnians, some of whom caught up with the fleeing Egyptian fleet, but were scared off by the larger ships without difficulty; only Eurykles of Sparta in a larger ship managed to attack and disable two of the enemy vessels.[40] At the battle scene, the fighting went on until nightfall, during which time more of Antony's ships got away. Of his fleet, over a third, including Kleopatra's ships, escaped; of the rest, 15 were sunk and 5,000 men killed, but most vessels were captured or surrendered; most of the captured ships were burned, as surplus to Octavian's requirements; their bronze rams were saved for a victory monument in Rome.[41]

Antony had transferred to Kleopatra's flagship when it became clear that the battle was lost, but that Kleopatra and her ships had got away. In fact, he may well have considered that he had won a sort of victory, at least for the queen's sake, since her survival was one of his aims. The fleet called at

Cape Tainaron (where he had left a garrison, which was still in occupation). They waited for several days for any fugitive ships to join, and for those of his friends who wished to leave him and make their peace with the victor to do so. It was at this point, as news slowly arrived of the results of the later fighting, that Antony understood the magnitude of his defeat. He fell into one of his fits of depression, lasting several days.[42]

He still had an army, however, rather reduced by desertion and disease, and bereft of most of the contingents brought over by the client kings. Canidius had started to march it away from the camp when he saw the result of the fighting at sea, according to plan, aiming to cross the Greek mountains and meet up, probably, with Antony at, perhaps, Athens. But he commanded an army largely made up of men with the sometimes bitter experience of civil war going back in some cases for two decades. When Octavian's army, following on, came up to confront them, both forces halted. In Antony's forces, the senior NCOs in the legions, centurions mainly, perhaps with some junior officers, took charge; Canidius and the higher command were shunted aside (and soon made their escape, by night, no doubt with the connivance of their supplanters). The men negotiated with Octavian over their future. Octavian, they knew, had no wish to fight on, or to suffer the casualties that would be expected in a fight between legions. After seven days of discussions and negotiations an agreement was reached: Antony's army would surrender, in formal terms, but only after having negotiated very generous terms; six of their legions, with strong regimental pride, would remain embodied and would be incorporated into Octavian's own army; the other soldiers would be treated to the same benefits and pay as Octavian's men. It was a much more sensible solution than might have been expected from the vindictive Octavian, and implies strongly that, had it been up to the soldiers, the civil war would never have been fought.[43]

Chapter 15

The End of the Ptolemaic Kingdom

Antony, after arranging for his friends to leave in hopes of their evading Octavian's revenge, and after brooding at Tainaron for several days, surveyed his remaining naval and military resources, and so, recovering, he could begin to work out his future strategy. In ships, he could count on Kleopatra's fleet, which had survived the battle undamaged, in addition to those ships she had left on guard at Alexandria and elsewhere. Of his own fleet, most had been sunk or captured, but enough had escaped from the battle and joined him to increase his total naval force at Tainaron to about a hundred ships, some of them merchantman, but mostly warships.[1]

On board the ships was a considerable number of soldiers. Exactly how many is not known, but 100 ships would be carrying anything between 100 and 200 soldiers each. Kleopatra's ships had been necessarily prepared to fight and so would still be fully manned. The Roman ships that escaped the battle will have had a full force on board at the start. Some had probably suffered casualties, but if a ship was damaged it would be unlikely to escape; casualties in naval battles were mainly caused by ships being sunk. Some of the men might have wished to be landed rather than fight on. If so, they would have been well advised to wait until they reached Tainaron or later before voicing their wishes.

On the ships, Antony therefore had up to 20,000 soldiers, although this must be an upper estimate, and it was liable to decrease as the men spotted opportunities to desert. For it was clear to everyone that, even if the battle had not been a complete victory for Octavian, it had certainly been a devastating and destructive defeat for Antony. And the word spread very quickly. Antony had nominal command of perhaps ten legions scattered about the eastern provinces, uninvolved in the fighting at Actium and since. Together with the men on the ships, he could, if all remained loyal to him, field an army of perhaps fifteen legions, plus any men he could recruit in the eastern provinces, and those in Greece of Canidius' command who could not stomach the terms of surrender. It soon became clear, however, that any such calculations were excessively optimistic.

Antony sailed from Tainaron across the sea to Cyrenaica, where he had left four legions under the command of L. Pinarius Scarpus. But Scarpus was Caesar's nephew, and so Octavian's adoptive nephew, if there is such a thing, and his soldiers received the news of Actium as quickly as he did, and before Antony reached them. Both commander and soldiers at once came to the same conclusion; when Antony arrived to claim their allegiance they refused. After he left there arrived Cornelius Gallus, Octavian's appointed governor of Africa, by ship, and to him they surrendered.[2]

And so it went. In Syria, the province came under attack by a group of gladiators who had mutinied at Kyzikos and had broken out of their prison. (Fighting for themselves was preferable to being sacrificed in Octavian's victory games.) They marched through Asia and into Syria, well-armed, superbly fit, highly trained fighters, brutal and determined. It was only in Syria, where Antony's governor, Q. Didius, might have been in their minds as their possible field commander in reviving Antony's fortunes, that they came up against the new politics. Didius and his four or five legions, like Scarpus and the Cyrenaican legions, had deftly changed sides on receiving the news of the battle; the gladiators fighting for Antony were now the enemy. It took those legions to stop them; they were thus sacrificed, after all. They were persuaded to halt at Antioch, taking refuge in the sanctuary at Daphne, and then persuaded to disperse; they were then used up. This was proof to all that Didius and the legions and their commander had adopted Octavian's cause.[3]

Antony and Octavian, believing that their men were loyal to them, were clearly wrong. Antony's forces rapidly deserted him in defeat; if he had won the battle, no doubt Octavian's forces would have themselves deserted to Antony. It seems clear therefore that the soldiers were not fighting for a commander, nor probably for Rome, but for themselves. Those who survived achieved this aim. Octavian could claim the political credit, but it was the men who won, and gained their reward.

Antony presumably knew of Didius' surrender almost as soon as he had failed to claim the loyalty of the Cyrenaican legions. Kleopatra had sailed from Tainaron direct to Egypt, and he joined her there. Octavian meanwhile had serious problems with his swollen army, which, seeing the end, as did all the other forces, wanted to go home, with rewards. It took him all the winter of 31/30, passing to and fro between Asia and Italy more than once, to calm them down and devise ways of dividing them, rewarding some and promising rewards to others.[4] But the new result was still more difficulties, for he now required access to a large amount of money to satisfy the soldiers' demands and requirements; Egypt was the obvious source for this, as it had been for the past half-century of Roman politics. With Antony still in the field, it would be absolutely necessary that Octavian perform his promises; if he welshed on the deal he would be finished. It was the clearest sign that the future of the empire was to be a military monarchy, an alliance between Octavian and his party and the army.

While he made this potentially successful settlement, the Antonian forces successively gave up the fight. In the spring and summer of 30, he could travel through Asia and Syria without too much danger. He dispensed favours to client princes, confirming some, but removing others, particularly those with only small kingdoms. The greater princes – Archelaus of Cappadocia, Polemo of Pontus, and, above all, Herod of Judaea, all having changed sides at the last moment – were confirmed, and, of course, were mulcted of treasure. And so he approached his ultimate goal and his final diplomatic test, the conflict with Kleopatra.

Antony had been brooding silently on the voyage from the battle to Tainaron, but the desertion of the eastern legions pushed him into despair once again. He sailed to Egypt but then sat in his seaside villa, unresponsive. Kleopatra, on the other hand, had a kingdom to govern, and set about organising its defence. She had few forces of her own, and had no time to drum up more, even though the population was largely loyal to her – or perhaps more likely, indifferent; nobody, of course, consulted them. On her arrival, she had swiftly executed a number of her aristocratic subjects who were, or who appeared to be, disloyal – she had never held the loyalty of all that set, the Greco-Macedonian aristocracy – and this quietened any other manifestations of despair or opposition.[5]

While she made plans for survival, Octavian steadily approached. This apparently roused Antony, as his personal enemy came closer. Simultaneously, Cornelius Gallus, with Antony's former Cyrenaican legions, marched from the west. Antony took a squadron of forty ships to Paraitonion, a small port on the border of Egypt with Cyrenaica, which Cornelius Gallus had reached, and from which he was threatening Egypt. But Gallus managed to block his ships in the small harbour, then when Antony attempted oratory on the soldiers in the town (who were probably men who had been in his army until very recently), Gallus ordered the trumpeters to drown out his voice. He probably did not need to bother; the troops knew full well that Antony, and therefore Kleopatra, were already beaten.[6]

Kleopatra could now see it as well. She had attempted to conjure up a defensive force, but Antony, after Cyrenaica, clearly did not share her hopes. In Alexandria she had her two oldest sons, Caesarion and Antyllus, enrolled as ephebes with the rest of the boys of the city, a gesture no doubt meant to emphasise their Hellenicity, and hers. She had ships moved along the Nile canal into the Red Sea, loaded with treasure, and discussed whether to withdraw to the Yemen or to India, but the Nabataean king, her old enemy, who had probably by now recovered the Arabian coast which Antony had taken from him and given to Kleopatra, used his own fleet – 'pirates', of course, to his enemies, even though he was a more legitimate king than Kleopatra was, or queen – to attack and burn her ships.[7] Whether she was serious in this plan is not known, but she did send her son Caesarion south into the Thebaid, with the intention that he might lead a resistance movement when the Romans arrived, or escape even further south into the Merowan kingdom, or – once again – to India.[8] This southern region was where Kleopatra herself had survived at the beginning of her own reign, and where resistance to the reconquest by Ptolemy V had lasted longest; perhaps she thought that he would be able to do the same after she was dead.

Octavian's army took Pelusion from her general Seleukos, who surrendered without fighting; either Antony or Kleopatra had murdered his family, either before or after his surrender, so his desertion is clearly explicable.[9] Then the invaders advanced round the Nile Delta along the traditional invasion route, no doubt seizing Memphis on the way, and approached Alexandria from the south.

There seems no doubt that Kleopatra did not expect to survive the Roman arrival, yet she still struggled to do so. She must have taken some optimism from the survival of the greater client kingdoms in Judaea and Asia Minor, but a single reminder that it was on her that Octavian had declared war would destroy that hope. The approach of Octavian's forces roused Antony, apparently now once more reinvigorated by the prospect of action, and he came out to challenge the threat to the city, driving away a unit of cavalry without difficulty. Again, he tried to persuade the infantry legionaries to change sides, but none moved.[10] His ability to win at this point was now out of the question.

On 1 August – eleven months after the battle of Actium – as the main force of Octavian's army arrived in front of the city, the Ptolemaic fleet sailed from the harbour, while Antony marshalled his land forces to prevent a landing and to repel a land attack. But it was far too late. Egypt needed to be defended at Pelusion, if at all, rather than outside Alexandria. Again, Antony's forces had lost the initiative. The fleet gave in, the rowers raising their oars in surrender; the cavalry deserted; the infantry fought only briefly. This last consisted of whatever Roman forces Antony still commanded, plus no doubt any force that Kleopatra had available; whatever troops they had brought to Egypt seem to have been few, and certainly demoralised; the surrender of the fleet deprived her of many of those soldiers she had left.[11]

There were no defensive forces left. Kleopatra played for more time, having sent Caesarion off to the south. Antony, defeated, and believing Kleopatra was dead, committed suicide, though the attempt was only mortal, not yet lethal. This was the third time he had attempted, or at least threatened, suicide. The earlier attempts had failed because a friend or a servant had intervened; this time he told a servant, Eros, to help him, but Eros killed himself instead. After that, Antony had no choice but to stab himself; even then he only inflected a wound.[12]

Kleopatra shut herself into her mausoleum with the treasure she knew Octavian wanted. For a while, she negotiated with the victor, who had no interest in taking her alive, and certainly encouraged her to suicide. This she finally accepted, Antony having joined her and then died. Eventually, she was tricked into negotiating with Cornelius Gallus at the door while two of Octavian's men climbed in through an open window. She was thus taken prisoner. Octavian made it clear that, unless she killed herself she would be an exhibit in his triumph in Rome. She therefore killed herself, and her two ladies, Iras and Charmian, followed her.[13] Octavian, no doubt to his relief, got her treasure.

Octavian also got the kingdom. Kleopatra's children were tracked down. The two eldest boys were killed, Caesarion, briefly recognised in Upper Egypt as Ptolemy XV, was captured and killed on the way to the Red Sea, probably aiming to continue resistance;[14] Antyllus was dragged from sanctuary and killed.[15] Alexander Helios and the youngest boy, Ptolemy Philadelphus, and Kleopatra Selene, were taken to Rome to walk in Octavian's triumph there,[16] the fate that their mother had avoided. They were taken into the household of Octavia, along with others of Antony's children;[17] the boys disappear from the record after that, quite likely quietly murdered. The removal of the boys blocked any Egyptian succession wars, and the killing of Caesarion blocked any attempt in Rome to recognise him as joint heir with Octavian to Caesar's name and reputation, and wealth.

Octavian had an enjoyable time on his slow journey back to Italy. He was now free of the importunities of the soldiers because he had secured the treasure of the Ptolemies to use to pay them off. Just to be sure, on his way back to Italy, he collected confiscations and fines from all those he could identify as having supported his dead enemy, thus refreshing his own treasury even more. More work was done to organise the empire. Egypt itself became his own possession; he refrained manfully from taking the title of king, though that is in fact what he was in practice. Despite the removal of the treasure and its rapid dispersal, it was still a rich land, and by law, no Roman senator was to be permitted to go there without imperial permission. The governor was to be of a lower social rank than senator. This was supposed to avoid any insurrections based on the wealth of the land; it did that, but the governors all managed to become immensely rich. Just as a reminder to all who might be tempted, a legion or two remained close to Alexandria, in a camp close to the city which was named Nikopolis – 'victory city' – and on the way to Italy Octavian founded another city, at the site of the victory of Actium, and called it also, revealing a certain lack of imagination, 'Nikopolis'

Conclusion

The End of the Dynasty

The Ptolemaic dynasty had been fading away, in the sense of the power it wielded, in the sense of the decline of its members' ambition, and in the sense of its legitimate bloodline, for half a century by the time Kleopatra's death brought the Ptolemaic kingdom to an end. She was an example of the problem, of course: a usurper, the daughter of a king and a non-Ptolemaic woman, and so illegitimate, and the murderer of more than one member of the dynasty, including a brother and a sister. She herself had made a valiant attempt by using her own resources – her attractiveness, her sex, her wealth, her administrative competence – to revive the kingdom she had seized. One of the costs, however, had been a partial demilitarisation – the Ptolemaic army was scarcely visible during her reign. She had also dealt a serious blow to the practice of primogeniture, male or female, by killing or removing four kings or queens – her half-sister Berenike IV, her brothers Ptolemy XIII and XIV, and her sister Arsinoe. And her bloodline was such that she was no more than an eighth Ptolemaic, after her father and her grandfather had both married, or at least had fathered children, out of the family. She did not help that by producing her children by consorting with two Romans – so Ptolemy XV and his siblings were only one-sixteenth Ptolemaic; also Ptolemy XV was out of the reckoning. The other children, by Mark Antony, would have been counted as a different dynasty.

Of the children she produced, only one, Kleopatra Selene, her only daughter, produced a child. She was married to Juba II, King of Mauretania, and they had a son, significantly named Ptolemy rather than a name from one of his male ancestors. He was also, however, through his mother, a grandson of Mark Antony, and this, rather than turning up at the Roman court to outshine the Emperor Caligula in a brighter purple cloak, was the basic reason he was eventually executed. It is worth noting that Juba, Selene and Caligula were all descended from Mark Antony; Caligula probably saw Juba as a dynastic threat.

Beyond Ptolemy of Mauretania, however, we are in the realms of conjecture. Perhaps Ptolemy had a daughter, Drusilla, who may have been the wife of the freedman administrator Antonius Felix, whose children may have married into various Near Eastern royal families in the late first century AD – note the repetition of 'may' in all that. (And if the Emesan family was one of these recipients, and if their family in that century can be linked to later local aristocrats, the Severan emperors might be directed, ever so distantly and conjecturally, from Ptolemy I.) On the other hand, Felix was married three times, each time to a woman of the royal family, and his wife Drusilla was probably descended from a Near Eastern royal family, probably being the daughter of Agrippa II, of the family of Herod the Great. In this case, their children had no relationship to any Ptolemy, and this is a more convincing, if still less than certain, conjecture. But this is scarcely relevant to a discussion of the imperial Ptolemies who ended with Kleopatra VII.

That Ptolemaic dynasty had done well for much of its career. It lasted longer than most Hellenistic dynasties, just under three centuries, even though it was visibly disintegrating during its last fifty years. It had a particularly effective career as an imperial power during the third century BC, and made a good fight to recover after the disasters of the Thebaid revolt between 207 and 185. The treatment of the native Egyptian population was in fact its primary weakness. It extracted wealth in vast quantities from the Egyptian population by a scheme of taxation that was brutal both in its demands and in its collection, but it put little enough back. Only the Egyptian priesthood was favoured with any sort of generous treatment – apart from the Greco-Macedonian immigrant population, of course.

The 20,000 talents Kleopatra VII brought with her to Greece to fund Mark Antony's war in 33–31 is a typical example of the use of Egyptian wealth, for by then she ruled Egypt and a few bits of the Near East, the latter for only a few years, so only Egypt is likely to have been the main source for all those riches, and yet Egypt was rife with discontent, strikes, and sullen enmity, and had survived a series of low Niles, famine and plague in the 40s. There is little indication of these problems in the last years of Kleopatra's reign, though *anachoresis* was not absent, but that can be best explained by the fact that the country had been exhausted by the bad times of the 40s, and was in the process of recovering.

Using that wealth to fund a Roman civil war was, of course, hardly the first time that had happened, but it is a mark of how far the dynasty had fallen that the only way it could survive was by funding Roman warlords to fight each other. And the remains of Kleopatra's wealth, annexed by Octavian, then went to fund the settlement of Roman soldiers on land in other countries. And, having been made part of the Roman Empire because of the country's wealth, the Egyptian peasantry continued to be a major source of Roman imperial finances for the next centuries.

Politically, the dynasty was therefore an oppressive institution for its native Egyptian subjects, which is the antithesis of what a dynasty of rulers ought to be – but there is no indication in previous Egyptian history that any king or dynasty was any less extortionate. (Not that popularity or care for the population was any guarantee of survival – witness the fates of the Antipatrids in Macedon and the Seleukids in the east, both of whom had a better record of governing or taxing their subjects than the Ptolemies, and both of whom died out well before them – but they both were militarily battered by Roman armies, whereas the Ptolemies were merely mulcted of their wealth.) It is virtually certain that the Egyptian population would have been better governed by a native Egyptian dynasty; and the Ptolemaic oppression was continued by Roman oppression. The Emperor Tiberius commented when a governor of Egypt was too zealous in accumulating tax revenues: 'I want my sheep sheared, not skinned', which seems an accurate description of both Ptolemaic and Roman methods of wealth extraction from Egypt.

There were, however, some notable achievements in the dynasty's time of power and wealth, which may count in the balance opposed to its oppression and aggressiveness. These, however, tend not to be specifically Egyptian, in the sense of belonging to, or coming out of, Egyptian culture. Like the intrusive settlement of Europeans in the cleruchic estates, the civilisational achievements of the dynasty were imposed on Egypt, and yet had little effect on the native culture of the country and its people. To a degree, the intrusive Europeans did adopt some elements of the Egyptian pharaonic culture, notably in religion, though Isis and Serapis, for example, were very much adapted to European practices. Serapis was a Ptolemaic invention, but was received as a god by the Greeks, though not seriously adopted by the Egyptians. Upon the major part of the Egyptian religion, with its emphasis on animals and the workings of the great temples, Ptolemaic rule had little effect.

Perhaps the most significant achievement of the Ptolemies was the foundation and development of the city of Alexandria, the greatest city in the Mediterranean region, with the exception of Rome, possibly, for a time. It became a major manufacturing and commercial city, and the host of the greatest cultural achievements of the dynasty, the museum and the library. This was a contribution of profound cultural importance for the Hellenistic period, though less originally creative than in the way of preserving achievements of the past. In literature, it consolidated and produced the accomplishments of 'classical' work, notably that of Athens. In science, it did produce useful original work, some items of which were practical. And yet, we always come back to the description of the city as 'Alexandria-by-Egypt'. It was not an Egyptian city, but a Greek one; Egyptians lived in it, but were never citizens. Like the settlements of Europeans in the country, it was imposed on Egypt, but not really part of it.

The exploration of north-east Africa was a diligent Ptolemaic enterprise, developed in order to conduct elephant hunts for the army, and to gather ivory and gold – a purely exploitative enterprise. This was eventually overtaken by the development of trade with India by way of the Red Sea and the necessary exploration that involved. Like the African ventures, this was directly the result of the initiative of the kings, specifically Ptolemy VIII and Ptolemy XII in the case of India, and was more productive of wealth than the killing of elephants. And like so much else, this was taken up and expanded by the Romans.

The influence of Ptolemaic Egypt (and the Hellenistic world in general) on Rome was crucial, both for the culture of that city and for the developing political system that emerged as an autocratic military empire under the Emperor Augustus. For imperial Rome was essentially a less efficient variant on Hellenistic royal politics and culture. It was, as were the kingdoms it conquered and succeeded, a monarchic dictatorship dependent on the military, and it remained so until the destruction of the empire in the fifteenth century AD. It adopted the administrative practices of the Hellenistic monarchies, established itself in the imperial capitals of the Hellenistic states – Thessaloniki, Antioch and Alexandria – and used their administrative systems and their languages. And yet it was at least two centuries before the Greek-speaking populations accepted the empire, and became seriously involved in governing it. As in Egypt, the native, non-Greek populations, all of them, from Britons to Syrians, were resistant to this Roman political culture, and there is no real sign that the subjected non-Greek population ever did accept it. This was one of the legacies of the Ptolemaic kingdom in Egypt, but one that was universal in the Roman Empire.

Another Ptolemaic legacy was the minimal religious influence on the rest of the Mediterranean that emanated from Egypt. The Egyptian gods that did spread out from their home country remained mysteries and marginal, colourful and cheerful, often involving women, and were unlike the formal, cold, masculin emanating from Roman religion. As such, they opened the way for the spread of, and acceptance of, Christianity, another mystery religion. Here then, though it was hardly a Ptolemaic achievement, was one of the main legacies of Ptolemaic Egypt.

Abbreviations

Austin	M.M. Austin, *The Hellenistic world from Alexander to the Roman Conquest: A selection of historical sources in translation*, second edition (Cambridge, 2006)
C. Ord. Ptol.	M.-Th. Lenger, *Corpus des ordonnances des Ptolemees* (Bruxelles, 1964–1990)
FGrH	F. Jacoby, *Die Fragmente des griechischen Historiker* (Berlin/Leiden, 1923–1958)
Josephos, *AJ*	Josephos, *Antiquities of the Jews*
OGIS	W. Dittenberger, *Orientis Graeci inscriptiones selectae* (Leipzig, 1993)
Pros. Ptol.	*Prosopographia Ptolemaica*
P.	Papyri – denominated by present holding
SEG	*Supplementum epigraphicum Graecum*

Notes

Chapter 1
1. See vol. 2 of this series.
2. *Pros. Ptol.* III and IX 5246; J.D. Ray, 'Observations on the Archive of Hor', *JEA* 64 (1978), pp. 113–120; A. Schubert, 'Une alteration de Ptolemais Eupator regent?', *ZPE* 94 (1999), pp. 119–120.
3. F.M. Walbank, *A Historical Commentary on Polybius*, vol. 3 (Oxford, 1979), p. 738.
4. Polybios 39.7; Josephos, *AJ*, 13.117–118.
5. It is thought that Kleopatra was armed and attempting a coup, but this is going further than the evidence allows; Anssi Lampela, *Rome and the Ptolemies of Egypt* (Helsinki, 1998), pp. 196–197.
6. G. Holbl, *A History of the Ptolemaic Empire* (London, 2001), p. 217, note 63.
7. Justin 32.2.
8. Diodoros 33.6.
9. Justin 38.2.
10. Diodoros 33.6.
11. As, for example, in 33. pp. 12–13.
12. *P. Koln* VIII, p. 350.
13. Polybios 33.12.
14. Polybios 34.14; Menekles of Barka, *FGrH* 270 F 9; P.M. Fraser, *Ptolemaic Alexandria* (Oxford, 1972), vol. 1, pp. 86–87.
15. Athenaios 4.184c.
16. The term is Walbank's, *Commentary*, 3.630.
17. Polybios 33.6a.
18. Diodoros 33.22.
19. Josephos, *AJ*, 13.120.
20. I *Maccabees* 11.22.
21. *Ibid.*, 13.120–125.
22. Josephos, *AJ*, 13.120.
23. Thera: E. van t'Dack, 'Les commandants de place lagides at Thera', *Ancient Society* 4 (1973), pp. 71–90 at pp. 84–89; Itanos: Stylianos Spyradakis, *Ptolemaic Itanos and Hellenistic Crete* (Berkeley and Los Angeles, CA, 1970), pp. 96–97.
24. Josephos, *Contra Apion* 2.50–55.
25. Diodoros 33.13.
26. On the temple at Edfu: S. Cauville and D. Devauchelle, 'Le temple d'Edfou, echappes de la nouvelles donnees historiques', *Revue Egyptienne* 35 (1984), pp. 31–55, at p. 51.
27. W. Clarysse, 'Ptolemies visiting the Egyptian chora', in L. Mooren (ed.), *Politics, Administration, and Society in the Hellenistic and Roman World*, Studia Hellenistica 36 (Louvain, 2007), pp. 29–53, at p. 49.
28. The date of Euphron's death is actually unknown: it was after 143; other than that, it is only by assumption from the absence of any mentions of him.
29. Clarysse, 'Ptolemies visiting', p. 49.

30. Livy, *Periochae* 59; Justin 38.8.5; Holbl, Ptolem*aic Empire*, p. 195 and note 72.
31. Justin 39.5.2; John Whitehorne, *Cleopatras* (London 1994), p. 103.
32. Diodoros 33.20 and 22.
33. Viesse, *Les Revoltes Egyptiennes, Recherches sur les Troubles interieurs en Egypte du regne de Ptoleme II a la conquete romaine*, Studia Hellenistica (Leuven, 2004), pp. 47–48; Lampela, *Rome and the Ptolemies*, pp. 202, 206, note 48.
34. Diodoros 33.22.
35. Ptolemy VIII, *FGrH* 234.
36. Diodoros 33.22.

Chapter 2
1. Josephos, *Contra Apion* 2.50.
2. H. Mavracorti (ed.), *Oratorum Romanorum fragmenti* (Turin, 1953), frags 177–181.
3. Lampela, *Rome and the Ptolemies*, pp. 197–200; the variety of interpretations and speculations on his identity and purpose are noted in footnotes there; add Walbank, *Commentary* 3.630.
4. Polybios 33.11.1–3 and 39.7.6; Diodoros 31.33; A.E. Astin, *Cato the Censor* (Oxford, 1959), p. 111.
5. Ptolemy VIII, *FGrH* 234, F 7; Athenaios 6.229d; this is a quote from Ptolemy's *hieromnemon*, his memoirs.
6. Most historians choose 140–138; but H.B. Mattingly, 'Scipio Aemilinus' Eastern Embassy', *Classical Quarterly* NS 36 (1986), pp. 491, 495, argues strongly for 144–142.
7. Justin 38.9–10.
8. Diodoros 33.28b.1–3.
9. *Ibid*.
10. Dated to 141/140 usually, but no more precisely than that; if the Roman visit was in 140, it had probably taken place before they arrived.
11. Diodoros 32.9; Josephos, *AJ*, 13.118.
12. Livy, *Periochae*, 52; Josephos, *AJ*, 13.116–117.
13. Diodoros 32.9c.
14. Diodoros 33.41; A. Houghton, 'The Revolt of Tryphon and the Accession of Antiochos VI at Apamea', *Schweitzer Numismatische Rundshau*, 71 (1992), pp. 119–141; T. Fischer, 'Zu Tryphon', *Chiron* 2 (1972), pp. 201–213.
15. Appian, *Syriake* 38; Josephos, *AJ*, 13.222–227.
16. Side had contributed ships to the siege of Carthage; Scipio Aemilianus would have been welcome there.
17. Justin 38.2.3; Josephos, *AJ*, 13.185–186.
18. Appian, *Syriake* 68.
19. Josephos, *AJ*, 13.224; I *Maccabees* 15.1–14.
20. *SEG* IX, 7; Austin, 289; see also Erich S. Gruen, *The Hellenistic World and the Coming of Rome* (Berkeley and Los Angeles, CA, 1984), pp. 702–703; M.A. Laronde, *Cyrene et la Libye Hellenistique* (Paris, 1987), pp. 440–442.
21. Strabo 12.2; see Austin 248, introduced by a discussion of the issue, and including a considerable set of references.
22. R.K. Sherk, *Rome and the Greek East to the death of Augustus* (Cambridge, 1984), p. 40; *OGIS* 435.
23. Robert Kallet-Marx, *Hegemony to Empire* (Berkeley and Los Angeles, CA, 1995), pp. 97–122; A.N. Sherwin-White, *Roman Foreign Policy in the East* (Norman, OK, 1983), pp. 80–92.
24. Josephos *AJ*, 13.252; Justin 38.9–10; Athanaios 210d and 540b–c.
25. Josephos, *AJ*, 13.253.

Chapter 3

1. F. Piejko, 'An Act of Amnesty and a Letter of Ptolemy VIII to the Troops in Syria', *Antiquite Classique* 56 (1987), pp. 254–259.
2. C. Ord. Ptol. 43.
3. J-Cl. Grenier, 'Ptolemee Euergete II et Cleopatre II d'apres les textes du temple de Tod', *Alessandia* I (1983), pp. 32–37.
4. Justin 38.8.5; Livy, *Periochae* 59, discussed by Whitehorne, *Cleopatras*, pp. 112–115.
5. Whitehorne, *Cleopatras*, p. 117.
6. *Ibid.*, 117; Holbl, *Ptolemaic Empire*, ignores the issue.
7. Holbl, *Ptolemaic Empire*, p. 197.
8. Justin 38.8.11–15; Livy, *Periochae* 59.
9. Justin 38.8.11.
10. Veisse, 'Revoltes Egyptiennes', pp. 54–55.
11. Holbl, *Ptolemaic Empire*, p. 197.
12. Justin 38.13–14; Diodoros 34.14; Livy, *Periochae* 59.
13. L. Mooren, 'The Governors-General of the Thebaid', *Ancient Society* 4 (1973), p. 127; Veisse, 'Revoltes Egyptiennes', pp. 55–63, discusses the documents.
14. Holbl, *Ptolemaic Empire*, pp. 198–199; Veisse, 'Revoltes Egyptiennes', pp. 48–52; the actual purposes of Harsiese are by no means understood.
15. Holbl, *Ptolemaic Empire*, p. 199, based on dated documents.
16. W. Clarysse and G. van der Velen, *The Eponymous Priests of Ptolemaic Egypt* (Leiden, 1983).
17. Holbl, *Ptolemaic Empire*, p. 199.
18. Justin 38.10.
19. *Ibid.*
20. Justin 38.7–11.
21. Justin 38.10.10.
22. Athenaios 153a (from (Poseidonios).
23. Justin 47.1.4–5; Diodoros 34.18.
24. Justin 39.1.1; Diodoros 34.17.
25. Justin 42.2.1–2.
26. Egnatius was praetor in the mid-130s, Aquillius finished off the war in Asia Minor and held office as proconsul there until 126; the roads, of course, were not actually built, they already existed, and all the Romans were doing was to mark and signpost them with milestones and directions.
27. *OGIS* 396.
28. Strabo 16.2.12.
29. Josephos, *AJ*, 13.245–253.
30. Justin 39.1.1–5; Josephos, *AJ*, 13.267–268.
31. Eusebius, *Chronographia* 1.257.
32. Justin 39.1.1–3.
33. A. Houghton and G. Le Rider, 'Un premier regne d'Antiochos VIII a Antioche en 128', *BCH*, 112, 1988, 401–411.
34. Justin 39.1.4.
35. Eusebios, *Chronographia* 1.257; Appian, *Syriake* 68.
36. Justin 39.1.7; Josephos, *AJ*, 13.268.
37. Justin 39.1.4.
38. Josephos, *AJ*, 13.268; Justin 39.1.7–8.
39. Holbl, *Ptolemaic Empire*, p. 200.
40. Valerius Maximus IX, 2, ext. 5.
41. Justin 39.2.1–6; Josephos, *AJ*, 13.269; Appian, *Syriake* 69.

42. Holbl, *Ptolemaic Empire*, p. 201.
43. Appian, *Syriake* 69; Justin 39.1.9.
44. Appian, *Syriake* 69; Justin 39.2.7–9.
45. *C. Ord. Ptol.* 53; Austin 501 (listing other references as well).
46. M. Chauveau, 'Un ete 145', part 2, *BIFAO* 90 (1990), pp. 135–168, at pp. 154–156.

Chapter 4
1. M. Cary and E.H. Warmington, *The Ancient Explorers*, London 1929, revised edition Harmondsworth 1963, 80–87 and 172–187; on the main subject of this chapter see C. Habicht, 'Eudoxos of Cyzicus and Ptolemaic exploration of the Sea Route to India', in Costas Buraselis *et al.* (eds.), *The Ptolemies, the Sea, and the Nile, Studies in Waterborne Power*, Cambridge 2013, 197–206.
2. Manetho. Loeb (ed.), 101–103.
3. Shereen Ratnagar, *Trading Encounters, from the Euphrates to the Indus in the Bronze Age*, second edition, Oxford, 2004.
4. Arrian, *Indika*, 29.
5. Georges Coedes, *The Indianized States of Southeast Asia*, Honolulu 1968, chapter 3.
6. Arrian, *Anabasis*.
7. Strabo 2.3.4; this is the major source for Eudoxos, and will not be repeated.
8. Clarysse, 'Ptolemies visiting', 49; B. Mond and O. Myers, *The Bucheum*, vol. 2, *The Inscriptions*, Leiden-Zutphen 1983, stela no. 11.
9. Strabo 2.3.5, though most of his scepticism is directed at Eudoxos' later adventures.
10. Herodotos, IV, 42.
11. Habicht, 'Eudoxos', also discusses Hippalos; his work was known to the author of the Periplus of the Erythraean Sea, several decades after Strabo.
12. Pliny, *NH*, 6.101–106.
13. Strabo 17.1.13; elsewhere he says 'a few' (2.5.12).
14. Strabo 2.5.12.
15. Plutarch, *Antony* 71.
16. Strabo 2.3.4.
17. M. Cary and E.H. Warmington, *The Ancient Explorers* (London, 1929), pp. 123–128.
18. Strabo 2.3.4.
19. R.E.M. Wheeler, *My Archaeological Mission to India and Pakistan* (London, 1976), and *Rome Beyond the Imperial Frontiers* (London, 1954).
20. Vimala Begley, 'Arikamedu Reconsidered', *American Journal of Archaeology* 87 (1983), pp. 461–481.
21. Vimala Begley, 'Ceramic Evidence for Pre-*Periplus* Trade on the Indian Coasts', in V. Begley and R.O. de Paor, *Rome and India* (Madison, WI, 1991), pp. 157–197; Berenice Bellini and Ian Glover, 'The Archaeology of Early Contact with India and the Mediterranean World from the Fourth Century BC to the Fourth Century AD', in Ian Glover and P. Bellwood (eds.), *Southeast Asia from Prehistory to History* (Abingdon, 2004), pp. 68–87.
22. Lionel Casson, 'Ancient Naval Technology and the Route to India', in Begley and de Paor, *Rome and India*, pp. 8–11, see also other works by, for example, Lionel Casson, *Ships and Seamanship in the Ancient World* (Princeton, NJ, 1971).
23. Caroline Singer, 'The Incense Kingdoms of Yemen, an Outline History of the South Arabian Incense Trade', in D. Peacock and D. Williams (eds.), *Food for the Gods, New Light on the Arabian Incense Trade* (Oxford, 2007), pp. 4–27.
24. Robert G. Hoyland, *Arabia and the Arabs* (London, 2001); G.W. Bowersock, *Roman Arabia* (Cambridge, MA, 1983), chapters 2 and 5.
25. The later spice trade had the same effect on Mamluk, Egypt, and there was plenty left over to make Venice rich, in the later Middle Ages.

26. *Periplus*, chapters 13–16, with Huntingford's notes on pp. 94–100.
27. *Periplus*, chapter 16; Gervase Mathew, 'The East African Coast until the Coming of the Portuguese', in Roland Oliver and Gervase Mathew (eds.), *History of East Africa*, vol. 1 (Oxford, 1963), pp. 95–97; M.C. Horton, 'Early Maritime Trade and Settlement along the coast of East Africa', in Reade (ed.), *Indian Ocean in Antiquity*, pp. 439–456; Rhapta remains a puzzle; sample discussions are B.A. Datoo, 'Rhapta: the Location and Importance of East Africa's First Port', *Azania* 5 (1970), pp. 65–73, and L.P. Kirwan, 'Rhapta, Metropolis of Azania', *Azania* 21 (1986), pp. 99–104; there are no doubt others, equally inconclusive.
28. G.W.B. Huntingford, 'The Peopling of the Interior of East Africa by the Modern Inhabitants', *History of East Africa*, vol. 1, pp. 58–93.

Chapter 5
1. Holbl, *Ptolemaic Empire*, p. 201.
2. Appian, *Syriake* 69; Justin 39.1.9.
3. Justin 39.2.1–6; Josephos, *AJ*, 13.269; Appian, *Syriake* 69.
4. *C. Ord. Ptol.*, 53; Austin 290.
5. Occupants were listed in Clarysse and van der Veken, 'Eponymous Priests', and also in Wikipedia, 'Ptolemaic Cult of Alexander the Great'.
6. Pausanias 1.9.1.
7. Cauville and Devauchelle, *Le Temple d'Edfou*, pp. 40–45.
8. The date is not known, but evidently, the marriage was concluded when they were children, and when Ptolemy IX was crown prince: Holbl, *Ptolemaic Empire*, pp. 202, 210.
9. Justin 39.2.3.
10. Or so it is assumed, since he was Ptolemy VIII's eldest son (except for Apion).
11. Justin 39.3.1.
12. Strabo 2.3.4; Pausanias 1.2.1–3; Justin 39.3.1–2, and 4.1–5.1; Eusebios, *Chronographia* 1.164–166; the issue is discussed by Dorothy J. Thompson, 'Pausanias and Protocol, the succession to Euergetes II', in *Egitta e storia antica dell'Hellenismo all'eta araba* (Bologna, 1989), pp. 695–701, with plenty of references.
13. Pausanias 1.9.1–3; Justin 39.3.2; Porphyry, *FGrH* 270 F 2.8.
14. P. Rylands dem, 111.20; P.L. Bat 15; P.W. Pestman, *Chronologie Egyptienne d'apres les textes demotiques (332 av J-C–453 ap J-C)* (Leiden, 1967), pp. 64 and 66.
15. Holbl, *Ptolemaic Empire*, p. 205 and note 127.
16. Laronde, *Cyrene*, 445
17. *SEG* XXVIII, 1479, lines 7–9.
18. Holbl, *Ptolemaic Empire*, pp. 285–288, gives the details at some length.
19. T.B. Mitford, 'Seleucus and Theodorus', *Opuscula Atheniensia*, 1 (1953), pp. 130–171, at p. 152.
20. H.A. Ormerod, *Piracy in the Ancient World* (Liverpool, 1924).
21. Sir George Hill, *History of Cyprus*, vol. 1 (Cambridge, 1972), pp. 176–177.
22. Mitford, 'Seleucus and Theodorus', and I. Micaelidou-Nikolaou, *Prosopography of Ptolemaic Cyprus* (Goteborg, 1976); Mitford quotes the inscriptions on which the next paragraphs are based.
23. Hill, *Cyprus*, I.197–199.
24. Justin 39.3.2–3.
25. Justin 39.3.4–11.
26. Justin 39.3.12.
27. Josephos, *AJ*, 13.327.
28. Porphyry *FGrH* 260 F 7.3.
29. Holbl, *Ptolemaic Empire*, p. 205.
30. Mooren, 'Governors-General', pp. 127–130.

31. *OGIS* 135 – Sherk, *Rome and the Greek East*, 47 A.
32. *SEG* XXVIII 1485 and XXX 1750; H. Devijver, 'Le plus ancienne mention d'une tribu romaine en Egypte', *Chronique d'Egypte* 60 (1985), pp. 96–101.
33. *P. Tebt.* I.33 = *Select Papyri*, II, 416 – R. Bagnall and P. Derow, *The Hellenistic Period, Historical Sources in Translation*, second edition (Oxford, 2004), p. 79.
34. It is the evidence of these coins that is the basis of the reconstruction of the history of the Seleukid dynasty and state in these years; the primary account is by A.R. Bellinger, 'The End of the Seleucids', *Transactions of the Connecticut Academy of Arts and Sciences*, 8 (1948), pp. 51–108; this has been modified in details by various articles; the comprehensive catalogue of Seleukid coins is now available: Arthur Houghton, C. Lorber, and O.D. Hoover, *Seleukid Coins, a Comprehensive Catalogue*, vol. 2 (Lancaster, PA, 2006); two important articles are Kay Ehling, 'Seleukidische Geschichte zwischen 130 and 121 v.Ch', *Historia* 47 (1998), pp. 141–151, and Oliver D. Hoover, 'A Revised Chronology for the Late Seleukids at Antioch (121/0–64 BC)', *Historia* 56 (2007), pp. 280–301.
35. C.B. Welles, *Royal Correspondence of the Hellenistic Period* (New Haven, 1935), pp. 71–72 = Austin, p. 173.
36. Justin 39.4.1.

Chapter 6

1. The main accounts are, Holbl, *Ptolemaic Empire*, pp. 207–210; Emil Schurer, *The History of the Jewish People in the Age of Jesus Christ*, vol. 1, (revised edition) (Edinburgh, 1973), pp. 219–221; my own *The Syrian Wars* (Leiden, 2010), pp. 390–402, and *The Fall of the Seleukid Empire* (Barnsley, 2015), pp. 151–168; Whitehorne, *Cleopatras*, pp. 166–167; for Rome, Lampela, *Rome and the Ptolemies*. For the war as a whole as it was conducted see E. van t'Dack *et al.*, *The Judaean-Syrian-Egyptian Conflict of 103–101 BC, a Multilingual Dossier Concerning the 'War of Sceptres'* (Brussels, 1989), which includes a useful collection of papyri and inscriptions; a useful article is by Robert R. Stieglitz, 'Ptolemy IX Soter II Lathyrus on Cyprus and the Coasts of the Levant', in Stuart Swiny *et al.* (eds.), *Res Maritimae Cyprus and the Eastern Mediterranean from Prehistory to Late Antiquity* (Atlanta, GA, 1997), pp. 301–305.
2. Getzel M. Cohen, *The Hellenistic Settlements in Syria, the Red Sea Basin, and North Africa* (Berkeley and Los Angeles, CA, 2006).
3. Josephos, *AJ*, 13.27.
4. Van t'Dack *et al.*, *War of Sceptres*, pp. 20–21; Stieglitz, 'Ptolemy IX Soter'.
5. W. Otto and H. Bengtson, *Zur Geschichte des Nierderganges des Ptolemaerreiches. Ein besting zur Regierungszeit des 8 und des 9 Ptolemaers* (Munich, 1938), pp. 173–176.
6. Josephos, *AJ*, 13.275–283.
7. *Ibid.*, 14.249–250.
8. *Ibid.*, 13.250–251.
9. *Ibid.*, 13.255–258.
10. Cohen, *Hellenistic Settlements in Syria*, pp. 274–277.
11. Justin 39.4.1; Porphyry *FGrH* 260 F 7.8.
12. Pausanias 1.9.2 – though this passage is somewhat confused.
13. Josephos, *AJ*, 13.279.
14. Pausanias 1.9.2.
15. Welles, *Royal Correspondence*, pp. 71, 72.
16. Justin 39.4.2; Diodoros 35/39, 390.
17. Mitford, 'Helenus', p. 129.
18. *Ibid.*
19. Josephos, *AJ*, 13.333.
20. *Ibid.*, 13.324.

21. *Ibid.*, 13.326–329.
22. *Ibid.*, 13.330–331.
23. *Ibid.*, 13.332; Stieglitz, 'Ptolemy IX Soter', doubts the location.
24. *Ibid.*, 13.334.
25. *Ibid.*
26. Cohen, *Hellenistic Settlements in Syria*, pp. 299–302.
27. Josephos, *AJ*, 13.346–347.
28. *Ibid.*, 13.338–344; Josephos' account of the battle is too glorifying of the defeated Maccabee army to be believed, claiming it to be a heroic defeat.
29. Josephos, *AJ*, 13.346–347.
30. *Ibid.*, 13.347.
31. *Ibid.*, 13.343–344.
32. *Ibid.*, 13.349.
33. Justin 39.4.4.
34. Josephos, *AJ*, 13.350.
35. *Ibid.*
36. Cohen, *Hellenistic Settlements in Syria*, pp. 213–221.
37. Josephos, 13.353–355.
38. Clarysse, van der Veken, 'Eponymous Priests'; Wikipedia, 'Ptolemaic Priests of Alexander'.
39. P. dem. BM inv. 69008 + P. dem. Berl. inv. 13381; it is document Papyrus 3 in van t'Dack *et al.*, *War of Sceptres*, pp. 50–61. The translation in Document 3 assumes that 'the town' is Ptolemais, but the sentences following directly are in reference to Damascus, and it would be more natural to assume that is the 'town' meant. The translation of 'company' is also uncertain, but the sense implies a relatively small force; the smallest unit in a Ptolemaic regiment was one of fifty men, commanded by a *pentetontarches*, which could be equated as a 'company': Fischer-Bovet, *Army and Society*, tables 3.3 and 3.4.
40. G. Cohen, 'Damascus at the End of the Second Century', in van t'Dack *et al.*, *War of Sceptres*, pp. 121–124.
41. Quaegebeur, in van t'Dack *et al.*, *War of Sceptres*, pp. 88–108.
42. Josephos, *AJ*, 13. 356.
43. *Ibid.*, 13.351–352.
44. *Ibid.*, 13.353–354.
45. *Ibid.*
46. It was still there in September 102; van t'Dack *et al.*, *War of Sceptres*, Pathyris letter no. 7.
47. Josephos, *AJ*, 13.357–358.
48. Whitehorne, *Cleopatras*, p. 146
49. Justin 39.4.3.

Chapter 7

1. This appears as an independent kingdom in Rome's 'Piracy Law' of 100 BC – see later in the chapter.
2. Justin 39.5.2.
3. Holbl, *Ptolemaic Empire*, p. 203.
4. *C. Ord. Ptol.* 62, 63; P.W. Pestman, *Chronologie egyptienne d'apres les textes demotique (332 av J-C – 453 ap J-C)* (Leiden, 1967), pp. 72, 156.
5. UPZ 106 = *C. Ord. Ptol.* 62, 109; Thompson, *Memphis* (second edition), p. 141, note 208; Clarysse, 'Ptolemies Visiting', p. 51.
6. Livy, *Periochae* 59, 60.
7. Livy, *Periochae* 68; Cicero, *de Oratore* 1.82; Plutarch, *Pompey* 24; A.N. Sherwin-White, *Roman Foreign Policy in the East, 168 BC to AD 1* (Norman, OK, 1983), pp. 97–98; Robert Kallet-Marx,

Hegemony to Empire, the Development of the Roman Empire in the East from 148 to 62 BC (Berkeley and Los Angeles, 1995), pp. 229–231.
8. Ormerod, *Piracy in the Ancient World* (Liverpool, 1920).
9. Theodore K. Rauf, *Merchants, Sailors, and Pirates in the Roman World* (Stroud, 2003), chapter 5.
10. Sherk (ed.), *Rome and the Greek East*, no. 55; there are two inscriptions, each giving parts of the law, and Sherk has both; discussed by Sherwin-White, *Roman Foreign Policy*, pp. 97–100; and Kallet-Marx, *Hegemony to Empire*, pp. 231–238, calling it the *lex de Cilicia Macedoniaque provincia*.
11. Strabo 14.5.2; Plutarch, *Pompey* 28.1; T. Fischer, 'Zu Tryphon', *Chiron* 2 (1972), pp. 201–213.
12. Published originally by M. Hassall, M. Crawford, and J. Reynolds, 'Rome and the Eastern Provinces at the End of the Second Century BC', *JRS* 64 (1974), pp. 195–207.
13. Sherwin-White, *Roman Foreign Policy*, p. 263.
14. Livy, *Periochae* 70; and referred to frequently in later sources; see Lampela, *Rome and the Ptolemies*, pp. 227–229.
15. Justin 39.5.2.
16. Livy, *Periochae* 70; Tacitus, *Annals* 14.18.
17. Which has been suggested to have been part of the royal treasury of the kingdom: Pliny, *NH*, 19.40.
18. Kallet-Marx, *Hegemony to Empire*, appendix J, pp. 364–367.
19. Josephos *AJ*, 13.385; Trogus, *Prologue*, 39; Poseidonios, frag. 36.
20. Appian, *Syriake* 69; Josephos, *AJ*, 13.366.
21. Josephos, *AJ*, 13.368; Appian, *Syriake* 69.
22. Appian, *Syriake* 69.
23. Josephos, *AJ*, 13.371; Bellinger, 'End', 75.
24. Josephos, *AJ*, 13.370.
25. Appian, *Mithradatic Wars* 23.11 and *Civil Wars* 102.
26. Veisse, 'Revoltes Egyptiens', 79; Pausanias 1.9.1–3.
27. *Select Papyri*, I.417.
28. Holbl, *Ptolemaic Empire*, p. 210.
29. Pausanias 1.9.3.
30. These are the documents, papyri and inscriptions, published in van t'Dack *et al.*, 'War of Sceptres', pp. 37–81.
31. Doc. 8.
32. Doc. 1.
33. L. Mooren, 'The Governors-General of the Thebaid in the Second Century BC', *Ancient Society* 4 (1973), pp. 115–132, no. 11.
34. *Select Papyri* I.417.
35. Poseidonios, *FGrH* 87, F 26; Whitehorne, *Cleopatras*, pp. 174–175.
36. *Select Papyri* I.418.
37. Justin 39.
38. Whitehorne, *Cleopatras*, p. 175.
39. Porphyry, *FGrH* 269 F 2.9.
40. Appian, *Mithradatic Wars* 2.13.
41. 'War of Sceptres', pp. 146–149.
42. That Syria was the source of his forces is the usual assumption; it is difficult to see, in the general circumstances, where else he could have got them.
43. Appian, *Mithradatic Wars* 26–27.
44. 'War of Sceptres', p. 132, citing *Pros. Ptol.* VIII 2180a.
45. Cicero, *De Lege Agraria* I, pp. 41–42.
46. Porphyry *FGrH* 260 F 2.8–9; Pausanias 1.9.3; Justin 39.5.1.

47. Pausanias 1.9.3.
48. Clarysse, 'Ptolemies Visiting', p. 51.
49. Fraser, *Ptolemaic Alexandria*, p. 703, note 61.
50. Plutarch, *Lucullus*, 2.4–5.
51. *Ibid.*, 3.1.
52. Lampela, *Rome and the Ptolemies*, p. 226.
53. The will of Ptolemy X is attributed to him, or to his son Ptolemy XI Alexander II, or even to Ptolemy Alexander III; discussion is tangled up with the Roman technical legal terms. Both Ptolemy X Alexander I and Ptolemy XI Alexander II had reasons to seek Roman help in recovering their claimed thrones, but neither had the right to make Rome their heirs, and in neither case was the will executed; see Lampela, *Rome and the Ptolemies*, p. 229 note 158, for discussion and references.
54. Plutarch, *Lucullus*, 3.1.
55. Clarysse and van der Velen, *Eponymous Priests*.

Chapter 8

1. Porphyry, *FGrH* 60, F 2.10–11.
2. Appian, *Civil Wars*, 1.102.
3. Porphyry, *FGrH* 260 F 2.11; Cicero, *de rege Alexandria* 9.
4. Appian, *Civil Wars* 1.102.
5. Lampela, *Rome and the Ptolemies*, 229–230, note 158.
6. Pausanias, 1.9.3; Cicero, *de rege Alexandria* 11.42.
7. Holbl, *Ptolemaic Empire*, p. 223.
8. Ibid.
9. Athenaios 5.206d; Strabo 17.1.11.
10. Holbl, *Ptolemaic Empire*, p. 223, for example.
11. Dorothy J. Thompson, *Memphis under the Ptolemies*, second edition, Princeton, NJ, 2012, 128–136, with a genealogy on 120.
12. Aidan Dobson and Dyan Hilton, *The Complete Royal Families of Ancient Egypt*, London 2004, 247, and in the royal genealogy diagram on 269.
13. Thompson, *Memphis*, 123, note 124; E.A.E. Reymond, *From the Records of a Priestly Family from Memphis*, I, Wiesbaden 1981 reluctance by the officiating priest
14. Plutarch, *Lucullus* 2.4 – five; Sherwin-White, *Roman Foreign Policy*, p. 253.
15. Kallet-Marx, *Hegemony to Empire*, 367.
16. Holbl, *Ptolemaic Empire*, p. 223.
17. *Ibid.*, pp. 257–284 passim; C. Bennett, *Ptolemy XII*, Wikipedia.
18. L. Mooren, 'The Date of SB V 8036 and the Development of the Ptolemaic Maritime Trade with India', *Ancient Society* 3 (1972), pp. 127–133; Steven E. Sidebotham, *Berenike and the Ancient Maritime Spice Route* (Berkeley and Los Angeles, 2011), pp. 34–37.
19. Strabo XI, 118.
20. J. Quaegebaer, 'Une scene historique meconnue au grand temple d'Edfou', in *Egitto e storia antica dell'Ellenismo all'eta araba* (Bologna, 1987), pp. 595–608; Holbl, *Ptolemaic Empire*, p. 222, notes 12 and 13.
21. Holbl, *Ptolemaic Empire*, p. 233; Whitehorne, *Cleopatras*, pp. 182–183, refers to other suggestions that Typhaina died in 69.
22. Josephos, *AJ*, 13.419–420.

Chapter 9

1. Andrew Monson, *From the Ptolemies to the Romans* (Cambridge, 2012), p. 235.
2. Fischer-Bovet, *Army and Society*, pp. 301–323.

3. For historians, one of the prize exhibits is Charles II, King of Spain, 1665–1700, with a hugely exaggerated jaw after several generations of Habsburg interbreeding, difficulty in eating, and who never produce children.
4. The family is discussed by Naphtali Lewis, *Greeks in Ptolemaic Egypt* (Oxford, 1986), pp. 86–102.
5. *P. Tebtunis* 1.35.
6. Note the Greek recluse Ptolemaios, who lived in the Serapion at Memphis for twenty years: Lewis, *Greeks in Ptolemaic Egypt*, pp. 74–87.
7. Colonel Gamel Abdel Nasser was the first ruler of Egyptian descent since the pharaohs who fought the Persians in the fourth century BC.
8. Dorothy J. Crawford, *Kerkeosiris, an Egyptian Village in the Ptolemaic Period* (Cambridge, 1971), p. 25.
9. Holbl, *Ptolemaic Empire*, p. 213.
10. *Ibid.*, 225.
11. Fischer-Bovet, *Army and Society*, p. 110.
12. Ormerod, *Piracy*; McGing, *Mithridates*.
13. Robin Seager, *Pompey, a Political Biography* (Oxford, 1979).
14. Sherwin-White, *Roman Foreign Policy*, p. 187; Seager, *Pompeius*; Kallet-Marx, *Hegemony to Empire*, p. 319.
15. Plutarch, *Pompeius* 25; Dio Cassius 36, 23–24; Appian, *Mithridatic Wars* 94.
16. Plutarch, *Pompeius* 26; Appian, *Mithridatic Wars* 94.
17. Plutarch, *Pompeius* 28; Livy, *Periochae* 99; Dio Cassius 36.37.6; Appian, *Mithridatic Wars* 96.
18. Plutarch, *Pompeius* 29; Appian, *Mithridatic Wars* 95; for Egypt, Florus 1.41.9–10; listed by Kallet-Marx, *Hegemony to Empire*, p. 317.

Chapter 10

1. Appian, *Mithradatic Wars*, 101–102; Cassius Dio 36.50.2; Livy, *Periochae* 120; Orosius 6.5.1–7.
2. Cassius Dio 36.52.1–4; Plutarch, *Pompeius* 33.2–5; Appian, *Mithradatic Wars* 104–105.
3. Sherwin-White, *Roman Foreign Policy*, pp. 209–214.
4. Josephos, *AJ*, 14.29–73.
5. *Ibid.*, 14.48–71.
6. *Ibid.*, 14.80–81.
7. Transpadani: Cicero, *Pro Balbo* 50; Egypt: Plutarch, *Crassus* 13.2.
8. Plutarch, *Crassus* 13.1–2.
9. Suetonius, *Julius* 1.11.
10. Cicero, *de rege Alexandrino*.
11. Appian, *Mithradatic* Wars 114; Josephos, *AJ*, 14.35, quoting Strabo.
12. Josephos, *AJ*, 14.35.
13. Pliny, *NH*, 33.136.
14. Appian, *Mithradatic* Wars 114.
15. *BGH* VIII, 1815; Fischer-Bovet, *Army and Society*, p. 110.
16. The main evidence for the bill is in Cicero, *de lege Agraria*; Erich S. Gruen, *The Last Generation of the Roman Republic* (Berkeley and Los Angeles, 1974), pp. 389–396.
17. Robin Seager, *Pompey, a Political Biography* (Oxford, 1979), pp. 62–63.
18. Appian, *Mithradatic Wars* 116; Plutarch, *Pompeius* 45 lists the booty brought back to Rome.
19. Seager, *Pompey*, chapter VII; Gruen, *Last Generation*, pp. 85–88.
20. Cassius Dio 39.2; Plutarch, *Caesar* 48.8; Holbl, *Ptolemaic Empire*, 224 (unspecific).
21. Holbl, *Ptolemaic Empire*, p. 226.
22. *Ibid.*

23. Other calculations claim it was the entire annual revenue (Seutonius, *Julius*, 52.3; Holbl, *Ptolemaic Empire*, p. 225) or half, if the revenue was 12,500 talents (Strabo 18.1.13; table 3.1 in Fischer-Bovet, *Army and Society*, p. 68, gives a range of 8,000 to 14,800 talents as the annual revenue (omitting the 6,000 figure paid, in theory, by Ptolemy XII). The reduction of the overseas empire under Ptolemy XII will have reduced the actual revenues, whatever they were.
24. Plutarch, *Caesar* 48.8.
25. Seager, *Pompeius*, pp. 80–86, with the ancient sources.
26. Plutarch, *Cato the Younger* 40; Livy, *Periochae* 104; Strabo 14.6.6; Cassius Dio 38.30; Appian, *Civil Wars* 2.23; numerous details in Cicero's speeches and letters; Seager, *Pompey*, pp. 105–107; Hill, *History of Cyprus*, 1.205–208.
27. Cassius Dio 39.12; Plutarch, *Pompeius*, 49.7; Porphyry, *FGrH* 260, 2.14.
28. Plutarch, *Cato the Younger* 33.
29. *Ibid.*, 35; Strabo 17.1.11; Cassius Dio 39.14.2.
30. Holbl, *Ptolemaic Empire*, p. 227
31. Assumed from her absence in the record for 57.
32. Strabo 16.2.8, 18, and 46; Josephus, *AJ*, 14.74–75; A.H.M. Jones, *Cities of the Eastern Roman Provinces*, pp. 257–259; Seager, *Pompeius*, p. 54.
33. Holbl, *Ptolemaic Empire*, p. 227.
34. *Ibid.*; *Ptol. Pros.* VI, 14496.
35. Cassius Dio 39.12.2.
36. Cassius Dio 39.13–14; Strabo 17.1.11; Cicero, *pro Caelio*, 23 and 51.
37. Cassius Dio 39.12.3.
38. Cassius Dio 39.15.1–3; Seager, *Pompey*, pp. 116–117.

Chapter 11
1. Cassius Dio 39.15.1–3.
2. Cassius Dio 39.12; Cicero, *ad Familia* 1.1.3.
3. Cassius Dio 39.55.2–3.
4. Strabo 12.3.34.
5. Cicero, *pro Rabirius Postumus* 20; Sherwin-White, *Roman Foreign Policy*, pp. 277–278.
6. This might be termed the Tenth Syrian War.
7. Josephos, *AJ*, 14.82–97.
8. *Ibid.*, 14.99.
9. Plutarch, *Antony* 3.9.
10. Cassius Dio 39.58.1.
11. Plutarch, *Antony* 3.10; Strabo 12.3.34.
12. Cassius Dio 39.58.3.
13. *Ibid.*
14. Cicero, *pro Rabirius Postumus* 22–28 and 38–45.
15. Holbl, *Ptolemaic Empire*, p. 229.
16. Josephos *AJ*, 14.98–102; Schurer, *Jewish People*, 1.269.
17. Holbl, *Ptolemaic Empire*, p. 229; Gruen, *Last Generation*, pp. 322–331.
18. Caesar, *Civil War*, 3.4.4; Holbl, *Ptolemaic Empire*, pp. 229–230.
19. *OGIS* 741; Holbl, *Ptolemaic Empire*, p. 230, and note 41.
20. Caesar, *Civil War* 3.108; Bellum *Alexandrinum*, 33.1; Cassius Dio 62.35.4.
21. Mond and Myers, *Bucheum*, 2.11–13, no. 13; Thompson, *Memphis*, pp. 116–117.
22. Holbl, *Ptolemaic Empire*, p. 230.
23. *Ibid.*
24. Holbl, *Ptolemaic Empire*, p. 230.

25. Stanley M. Burstein, *The Reign of Cleopatra* (Norman, OK, 2007), pp. 15–16.
26. These three are singled out by Caesar, *Civil War*, 3.108; *Ptol. Pros.* VI.14620; II.2154 and VI.14574; VI.14623.
27. Thompson, *Memphis*, pp. 116–117 and 292–283.
28. Schurer, *Jewish People*, 1.246–247.
29. Caesar, *Civil War* 3.110.
30. Valerius Maximus 4.1.15; referred to by Caesar, *Civil War*, 3.110.
31. *SB* 9065.1.2 and 9764. 16–17, for example.
32. Plutarch, *Antony* 25.4; Lucan, *Pharsalia* 2.636; Caesar, *Civil War* 3.4.4; Appian, *Civil Wars* 2.49.
33. John Malalas 9.279.
34. Plutarch, *Antony* 25.3.
35. Holbl, *Ptolemaic Empire*, p. 232
36. L. Mooren, 'Notes concernant quelques strateges ptolemaiques IV', *Ancient Society* 1 (1970), pp. 17–24.
37. Strabo 17.1.11.
38. Duane W. Roller, *Cleopatra, a Biography* (Oxford, 2010), p. 59, assumes she went to Antioch.
39. A.B. Brett, 'A New Cleopatra Tetradrachm from Ascalon', *AJA* 41 (1937), pp. 452–463; A. Spaer, 'The Royal Male Head and Cleopatra at Ascalon', in M. Amandry *et al.* (eds.), *Travaux de numismatique grecque offerts a Georges le Rider* (London, 1999), pp. 347–350.
40. Caesar, *Civil War*, 3.4 and 3.31.
41. Appian, *Civil Wars* 2.4; Caesar, *Civil War* 3.103.
42. Lucan, *Pharsalia* 5.50–64.
43. Caesar, *Civil War* 3.40; Cassius Dio 42.12.
44. Cassius Dio 42.12.
45. J.F.C. Fuller, *Julius Caesar, Man, Soldier and Tyrant* (London, 1965), chapter 10, with full references.
46. Seager, *Pompey*, pp. 183–184.
47. Caesar, *Civil War*, 1.103–104; Plutarch, *Pompeius*, 77–70; Appian, *Civil Wars* 2.84; Cassius Dio 42.3.3–4.2; Lucan, *Pharsalia* 8.480–486; Seager, *Pompeius*, 183–184.
48. Caesar, *Civil War*, 3.106.4.
49. Caesar, *Civil War*, 3.107.
50. Caesar, *Civil War*, 3.108.
51. Appian, Civil Wars, 2.89; Lucan, *Pharsalia* 10.14–19.
52. Cassius Dio 42.2 4.3–6; Plutarch, *Caesar* 49.1–2; Lucan, *Pharsalia* 10.56–60; Roller, *Cleopatra*, p. 61, suggests the 'bed-sack'.
53. Cassius Dio 42.35.1–5.
54. Caesar, *Civil War* 3.112; *Bellum Alexandria*num 4; Holbl, *Ptolemaic Empire*, 236; *Ptol. Pros.* 11.21564 for Ganymedes.
55. Fuller, *Julius Caesar* 246–253.
56. *Bellum Alexandrinum* 1–32; Cassius Dio 42.43; Josephos *AJ* 14.127–136.
57. Suetonius, *Julius*, 52.1; Appian, *Civil Wars*, 2.90; Cassius Dio 22.45
58. *Bellum Alexandrinum* 33.3–4; Suetonius, *Julius* 76.3.
59. *Bellum Alexandrinum* 33.1–2; Suetonius, *Julius* 35.1; Appian, *Civil Wars* 2.19; Cassius Dio 42.4 4.1–2

Chapter 12

1. Richard Alston, *Soldier and Society in Roman Egypt*, London 1995, 20.
2. Caesar, *Civil War*, 3.106.
3. Roller, *Cleopatra*, pp. 107–108, lists the names of several officials, but no systematic identification can be seen; the offices they held are mainly at a lower level.

4. Strabo 17.1.13.
5. Cassius Dio 42.34.5.
6. Roller, *Cleopatra*, pp. 69–70, on the controversy in Rome over this.
7. Cassius Dio 43.27.3; Cicero, *ad Atticus* 15.15.2; Suetonius, *Julius*, 52.1.
8. A. Abdullatif Aly, 'Cleopatra and Caesar at Alexandria and Rome', in G.P. Carratelli *et al.* (eds.), *Roma e l'Egitto nell'antiquira classica* (Rome, 1992), pp. 47–61; E. van t'Dack, 'La date de C. Ord. Ptol. 80–83 = BCU VI, 1212 et le sojourne de Cleopatre VII a Rome', *Ancient Society* 1 (1970), pp. 53–66; E. Gruen, 'Cleopatra in Rome: Facts and Fantasies', in D.C. Braund and Christopher Gill (eds.), *Myth, History and Culture in Republican Rome* (Exeter, 2003), pp. 257–274.
9. Van t'Dack (previous note).
10. Cassius Dio 44.11.2–3; Appian, *Civil Wars* 2.109.
11. Plutarch, *Caesar* 68; Suetonius, *Julius* 33.
12. *P. Oxy.* 1629.
13. Josephos, *AJ*, 15.89, and *Contra Apion* 2.58; Porphyrius, *FGrH* 260 F 2.16–17.
14. Burstein, *Reign of Cleopatra*, pp. 120–121.
15. Cassius Dio 42.35.5.
16. Appian, *Civil Wars* 3.78, 4.59, and 4.61.
17. *Ptol. Pros.* VI 26595; Cicero, *Ad familiares* 12.13.
18. Pliny, *NH*, 5.8.
19. Seneca, *Natural Questions* 4.2.16.
20. Appian, *Civil Wars* 4.61 and 108.
21. Josephus, *Contra Apion* 60.
22. Appian, *Civil Wars* 5.8.
23. Plutarch, *Antony* 26.
24. Cassius Dio 48.24; Appian, *Civil Wars* 5.8; Plutarch, *Antony* 22–26.
25. Josephos, *AJ*, 15.89; Appian, *Civil Wars* 5.11; Cassius Dio 48.24.2.
26. Cassius Dio 48.40.5
27. Cassius Dio 49.11.2–12.5; Appian, *Civil Wars* 5.122–126; Velleius Paterculus 2.80.
28. Josephus, *AJ*, 14.400–464.
29. Appian, *Civil Wars* 2.24; Cassius Dio 45.3; Suetonius, *Julius* 44; Plutarch, *Caesar* 58; R.M. Sheldon, *Rome's Wars with Parthia* (London, 2010), pp. 56–57.
30. E.M. Smallwood, *The Jews under Roman Rule*, second edition (London, 2001), chapter 3.
31. Josephos, *AJ*, 14.439–447.
32. Josephos, *AJ*, 14.330–333.
33. Cassius Dio 49.20.5 and 22.1.2; Josephus, *AJ*, 14.457; Plutarch, *Antony* 34.4; Sherwin-White, *Roman Foreign Policy*, p. 306.

Chapter 13

1. There is no direct testimony from the queen herself on this matter, and one must derive one's conclusions for her actions; for recent considerations, less wrapped in the consideration of scandal, see Roller, *Cleopatra*, Holbl, *Ptolemaic Empire*, Whitehorne, *Cleopatras*; accounts written from a Roman point of view are inevitably suspect; those adopting a feminist agenda all too easily project modern notions back in time, to a serious distortion of historical process.
2. Eleanor Goltz Huzar, *Mark Antony, a Biography* (Minneapolis, 1978), chapter 10; unlike Kleopatra, Antony has a biography by Plutarch, though he is too dependent on Octavianist sources or propaganda.
3. Michael Grant, *Herod the Great* (New York, 1971), chapter 1; Stewart Perowne, *The Life and Times of Herod the Great* (London, 1956), pp. 49–76; Peter Richardson, *Herod, King of the Jews and Friend of the Romans* (Colombia, SC, 1996), pp. 95–173; these modern accounts vary in emphasis, and must be read with care.

4. Plutarch, *Antony* 35–36; Cassius Dio 48–49; Josephos, *AJ*, 15.91–96; Porphyios, *FGrH* 260, F 2.17; Holbl, *Ptolemaic Empire*, pp. 241–242; R.D. Sullivan, *Near Eastern Royalty and Rome, 100–30 BC* (Toronto, 1990), pp. 171–174.
5. Strabo 16.4.18.
6. E.A. Myers, *The Ituraeans and the Roman Near East* (Cambridge, 2010); A.H.M. Jones, 'The Urbanisation of the Ituraean Principality', *JRS* 21 (1931).
7. M.H. Crawford, *Coinage and Money under the Roman Republic* (London, 1965), p. 253.
8. Plutarch, *Antony* 35.4, 40.5, and 42.3; Cassius Dio 49.24.5 and 50.1.3; Strabo 11.13.4, 11.14.9, and 16.1.28; Huzar, *Mark Antony*, p. 179, and other references there.
9. Plutarch, *Crassus* 33, and *Antony* 37; Justin 42.5.1; Cassius Dio 49.23; none of these can be fully relied on; N.C. Debevoise, *The Political History of Parthia* (New York, 1938), p. 121; Sheldon, *Roman Wars in Parthia*, p. 65.
10. Huzar, *Mark Antony*, pp. 177–178; Sheldon, *Roman Wars in Parthia*, pp. 66–70; Carter, *Battle of Actium*, pp. 158–159.
11. Huzar, Mark Antony, pp. 178–180; Sheldon, *Roman Wars in Parthia*, pp. 69–79; Carter, *Battle of Actium*, pp. 159–160.
12. Plutarch, *Antony* 51.
13. Appian, *Civil Wars* 5.118–121 and 142–144; Cassius Dio 49.8–11.
14. Appian, *Civil Wars* 5.123–126; Cassius Dio 49.11–18; Suetonius, *Augustus* 16.
15. Plutarch, *Antony* 52–53; Cassius Dio 49.33.
16. Plutarch, *Antony* 53.
17. Cassius Dio 49.39–41.3; Plutarch, *Antony* 50 and 55; Josephos, *AJ*, 15.4.2–3; Huzar, *Mark Antony*, pp. 181–182; Sheldon, *Roman Wars in Parthia*, pp. 74–75.
18. Cassius Dio 49.44 and 51.16; Debevoise, *Political History*, p. 135; Sheldon, *Roman Wars in Parthia*, p. 75.
19. Plutarch, *Comparison of Demetrios and Antony* 1.5 and 4.2; Suetonius, *Augustus* 67.3.
20. Cassius Dio 49.46; Plutarch, *Antony* 54.
21. See note 8.

Chapter 14
1. Plutarch, *Antony* 58.5.
2. *Ibid.*, 56.
3. Cassius Dio 49.42–43; Suetonius, *Augustus* 37.
4. Plutarch, *Antony* 56.
5. *Ibid.*; Cassius Dio 49.44.
6. Cassius Dio 50.10; Plutarch, *Antony* 58.
7. Orosius 6.19; Florus 2.21; J.S. Morrison, *Greek and Roman Oared Warships* (Oxford, 1996), pp. 162–165.
8. Josephus, *AJ* 15.5–7.
9. Velleius Paterculus 2.84.2.
10. Suetonius, *Augustus* 17.2; Cassius Dio 50.2–7.
11. Carter, *Battle of Actium*, p. 189.
12. Plutarch, *Antony* 52.2–3.
13. As appears when she was divorced and had to leave Antony's house in Rome: Plutarch, *Antony* 57; Cassius Dio 50.2–3.
14. Plutarch, *Antony* 56.6–57.2.
15. Plutarch, *Antony* 57.
16. A version of this is quoted by A.H.M. Jones, *Augustus* (London, 1970), p. 38.
17. Plutarch, *Antony* 60.
18. Carter, *Battle of Actium*, 196–197 – 'the spontaneity of the oath is a pious fiction'.

19. M. Rostovtzeff, *Social and Economic History of the Hellenistic World* (Oxford, 1941), reprinted 1998, pp. 909–910, and notes 188–190.
20. Plutarch, *Antony* 51; Cassius Dio 49.32.4.
21. Plutarch, *Antony* 56; possibly an Octavianist exaggeration.
22. *Ibid.*, 61.
23. Carter, *Battle of Actium*, p. 200.
24. Cassius Dio 58.16.3.
25. *Ibid.*
26. Plutarch, *Antony* 62.
27. Cassius Dio 50.16.4.
28. Plutarch, *Antony* 59 and 63.
29. Cassius Dio 50.14.4; Plutarch, *Antony* 63.
30. Plutarch, *Antony* 48.4.
31. Carter, *Battle of Actium*, p. 205.
32. Cassius Dio 50.13.5.
33. Carter, *Battle of Actium*, pp. 209–210.
34. Cassius Dio 50.13.5.
35. Plutarch, *Antony* 67, 1–5.
36. Cassius Dio 50.13.7–8.
37. Cassius Dio 50.14.1–2; Carter, *Battle of Actium*, pp. 211–212.
38. Plutarch, *Antony* 63; Carter, *Battle of Actium*, pp. 212–214.
39. Carter, *Battle of Actium*, pp. 218–220.
40. Plutarch, *Antony* 67, 1–5.
41. *Ibid.*, 68.
42. *Ibid.*, 67.
43. Plutarch, *Antony* 68; Cassius Dio 51.1; Carter, *Battle of Actium*, pp. 225–226.

Chapter 15

1. Huzar, *Mark Antony*, p. 220, adding escapees and Egyptians.
2. Cassius Dio 51.5.3–6; Plutarch, *Antony* 63.1–3.
3. Cassius Dio 51.7.2–7.
4. Carter, *Battle of Actium*, pp. 28–230.
5. Plutarch, *Antony* 67.
6. Cassius Dio 51.9.
7. Plutarch, *Antony* 67.
8. Plutarch, *Antony* 81–82; Roller, *Cleopatra*, pp. 149–150.
9. Cassius Dio 51.9.5; Plutarch, *Antony*, 74; the contradiction here is a succinct indication of the confusion that must have existed in Alexandria at the time.
10. Plutarch, *Antony* 74; Cassius Dio 51.10.1–3.
11. Plutarch, *Antony* 76; Cassius Dio 51.10.3–4.
12. Plutarch, *Antony* 76–77; Cassius Dio 51.10.7.
13. The most worthwhile account of their deaths is by Whitehorne, *Cleopatras*, pp. 186–196, who is properly sceptical of the received story, asp and all. It is much more likely that all three women had secured an effective poison to ingest. The asp was unreliable as a suicide weapon, and anyway could they really have imported three asps into the guarded mausoleum?
14. Cassius Dio 51.15.5; alternatively, Plutarch, *Antony* 81.4 claims he was tricked into going to Alexandria and there killed.
15. Plutarch, *Antony* 81.1–3.
16. Cassius Dio 51.15.6–7; Plutarch, *Antony* 87.
17. Cassius Dio 51.15.6–7; Plutarch, *Antony* 87; Suetonius, *Augustus* 17.5.

Bibliography

Alston, Richard, *Soldier and Society in Roman Egypt* (London, 1998).
Aly, A. Abdullatif, 'Cleopatra and Caesar at Alexandria and Rome', in G.P. Carratelli *et al.* (eds.), *Roma e l'Egitto nell'antiquira classica* (Rome, 1992), pp. 47–61.
Astin, A.E., *Cato the Censor* (Oxford, 1959).
Bagnall, R. and Derow, P., *The Hellenistic Period, Historical Sources in Translation*, second edition (Oxford, 2004).
Begley, Vimala, 'Arikamedu Reconsidered', *American Journal of Archaeology*, 87 (1983), pp. 461–481.
Begley, Vimala, 'Ceramic Evidence for Pre-*Periplus* Trade on the Indian Coasts', in V. Begley and R.O. de Paor, *Rome and India* (Madison, WI, 1991), pp. 157–197.
Bellinger, A.R., 'The End of the Seleucids', *Transactions of the Connecticut Academy of Arts and Sciences*, 8 (1948), pp. 51–108.
Bellini, Berenice and Glover, Ian, 'The Archaeology of Early Contact with India and the Mediterranean World from the Fourth Century BC to the Fourth Century AD', in Ian Glover and P. Bellwood (eds.), *Southeast Asia from Prehistory to History* (Abingdon, 2004), pp. 68–87.
Bowersock, G.W., *Roman Arabia* (Cambridge, MA, 1983).
Brett, A.B., 'A New Cleopatra Tetradrachm from Ascalon', *AJA* 41 (1937), pp. 452–463.
Buraselis, Costas, *et al.* (eds.), *The Ptolemies, the Sea, and the Nile, Studies in Waterborne Power* (Cambridge, 2013).
Burstein, Stanley M., *The Reign of Cleopatra* (Norman, OK, 2007).
Carter, John M., *The Battle of Actium; the Rise and Triumph of Augustus Caesar* (London, 1970).
Cary, M. and Warmington, E.H., *The Ancient Explorers* (London, 1929), revised edition (Harmondsworth, 1963).
Casson, Lionel, 'Ancient Naval Technology and the Route to India', in Begley and de Paor, *Rome and India*, pp. 8–11.
Cauville, S. and Devauchelle, D., '*Le temple d'Edfou, echappes de la nouvelles donnees historiques*', *Revue Egyptienne* 35 (1984).
Chauveau, M., 'Un ete 145', part 2, *BIFAO* 90 (1990), pp. 135–168, at pp. 154–156.
Clarysse, W. and van der Velen, G., *The Eponymous Priests of Ptolemaic Egypt* (Leiden, 1983).
Clarysse, W., 'The Ptolemies visiting the Egyptian chora', in L. Mooren (ed.), *Politics, Administration and Society in the Hellenistic and Roman World*, Studia Hellenistica 36 (Leuven, 2000), pp. 29–53.
Coedes, Georges, *The Indianized States of Southeast Asia* (Honolulu, 1968).
Cohen, Getzel M., *The Hellenistic Settlements in Syria, the Red Sea Basin, and North Africa* (Berkeley and Los Angeles, CA, 2006).
Cohen, G., 'Damascus at the End of the Second Century', in van t'Dack *et al.*, *War of Sceptres*, pp. 121–124.
Crawford, Dorothy J., *Kerkeosiris, an Egyptian Village in the Ptolemaic Period* (Cambridge, 1971).
Crawford, M.H., *Coinage and Money under the Roman Republic* (London, 1965).
Datoo, B.A., 'Rhapta: the Location and Importance of East Africa's First Port', *Azania* 5 (1970), pp. 65–73.
Debevoise, N.C., *The Political History of Parthia* (New York, 1938).
Devijver, H., 'Le plus ancienne mention d'une tribu romaine en Egypte', *Chronique d'Egypte* 60 (1985), pp. 96–101.

Dobson, Aidan and Hilton, Dyan, *The Complete Royal Families of Ancient Egypt* (London, 2004).
Ehling, Kay, 'Seleukidische Geschichte zwischen 130 and 121 v.Ch', *Historia* 47 (1998), pp. 141–151.
Fischer, T., 'Zu Tryphon', *Chiron* 2 (1972), pp. 201–213.
Fischer-Bovet, Christelle, *Army and Society in Ptolemaic Egypt* (Cambridge, 2014).
Fraser, P.M., *Ptolemaic Alexandria*, vol. 1 (Oxford, 1972).
Fuller, J.F.C., *Julius Caesar, Man, Soldier and Tyrant* (London, 1965).
Grainger, John, D., *The Syrian Wars* (Leiden, 2010).
Grainger, John D., *The Fall of the Seleukid Empire* (Barnsley, 2015).
Grant, Michael, *Herod the Great* (New York, 1971).
Grenier, J-Cl., 'Ptolemee Euergete II et Cleopatre II d'apres les textes du temple de Tod', *Alessandia* I (1983), pp. 32–37.
Gruen, Erich S., *The Hellenistic World and the Coming of Rome* (Berkeley and Los Angeles, CA, 1984).
Gruen, Erich S., *The Last Generation of the Roman Republic* (Berkeley and Los Angeles, 1974).
Gruen, Erich S., 'Cleopatra in Rome: Facts and Fantasies', in D.C. Braund and Christopher Gill (eds.), *Myth, History and Culture in Republican Rome* (Exeter, 2003), pp. 257–274.
Habicht, C., 'Eudoxos of Cyzicus and Ptolemaic exploration of the Sea Route to India', in Buraselis et al. (eds.), *The Ptolemies, the Sea*, pp. 197–206.
Hassall, M., Crawford, M. and Reynolds, J., 'Rome and the Eastern Provinces at the End of the Second Century BC', *JRS* 64 (1974), pp. 195–207.
Hill, Sir George, *History of Cyprus*, vol. 1 (Cambridge, 1972).
Holbl, Gunther, *A History of the Ptolemaic Empire* (London, 2001).
Hoover, Oliver D., 'A Revised Chronology for the Late Seleukids at Antioch (121/0–64 BC)', *Historia* 56 (2007), pp. 280–301.
Horton, M.C., 'Early Maritime Trade and Settlement along the coast of East Africa', in Reade (ed.), *Indian Ocean in Antiquity*, pp. 439–456,
Houghton, A., 'The Revolt of Tryphon and the Accession of Antiochos VI at Apamea', *Schweitzer Numismatische Rundshau* 71 (1992), pp. 119–141.
Houghton, A. and Le Rider, G., 'Un premier regne d'Antiochos VIII a Antioche en 128', *BCH* 112 (1988), pp. 401–411.
Houghton, Arthur, Lorber, C. and Hoover, O.D., *Seleukid Coins, a Comprehensive Catalogue*, vol. 2 (Lancaster, PA, 2006).
Hoyland, Robert G., *Arabia and the Arabs* (London, 2001).
Huntingford, G.W.B., 'The Peopling of the Interior of East Africa by the Modern Inhabitants', *History of East Africa*, vol. 1, pp. 58–93.
Huzar, Eleanor Goltz, *Mark Antony, a Biography* (Minneapolis, 1978).
Jones, A.H.M., *Cities of the Eastern Roman Provinces*, second edition (Oxford, 1971).
Jones, A.H.M., 'The Urbanisation of the Ituraean Principality', *JRS* 21 (1931).
Jones, A.H.M., *Augustus* (London, 1970).
Kallet-Marx, Robert, *Hegemony to Empire, the Development of the Roman Empire in the East from 148 to 62 BC* (Berkeley and Los Angeles, 1995).
Kirwan, L.P., 'Rhapta, Metropolis of Azania', *Azania*, 21 (1986), pp. 99–104.
Lampela, Anssi, *Rome and the Ptolemies of Egypt* (Helsinki, 1998).
Laronde, M.A., *Cyrene et la Libye Hellenistique* (Paris, 1987).
Lewis, Naphtali, *Greeks in Ptolemaic Egypt* (Oxford, 1986).
Mathew, Gervase, 'The East African Coast until the Coming of the Portuguese', in Roland Oliver and Gervase Mathew (eds.), *History of East Africa*, vol. 1 (Oxford, 1963).
Mattingly, H.B., 'Scipio Aemilinus' Eastern Embassy', *Classical Quarterly* NS 36 (1986).
Mavracorti, H. (ed.), *Oratorum Romanorum fragmenti* (Turin, 1953).

Micaelidou-Nikolaou, I., *Prosopography of Ptolemaic Cyprus* (Goteborg, 1976).
Mitford, T.B., 'Seleucus and Theodorus', *Opuscula Atheniensia* 1 (1953), pp. 130–171.
Mond, B. and Myers, O., *The Bucheum*, vol. 2, *The Inscriptions* (Leiden-Zutphen, 1983).
Monson, Andrew, *From the Ptolemies to the Romans* (Cambridge, 2012).
Mooren, L., 'The Governors-General of the Thebaid in the Second Century BC', *Ancient Society* 4 (1973), pp. 115–132.
Mooren, L., 'The Date of SB V 8036 and the Development of the Ptolemaic Maritime Trade with India', *Ancient Society* 3 (1972), pp. 127–133.
Mooren, L., 'Notes concernant quelques strateges ptolemaiques IV', *Ancient Society* 1 (1970), pp. 17–24.
Morrison, J.S., *Greek and Roman Oared Warships* (Oxford, 1996).
Myers, E.A., *The Ituraeans and the Roman Near East* (Cambridge, 2010).
Ormerod, H.A., *Piracy in the Ancient World* (Liverpool, 1924).
Otto, W. and Bengtson, H., *Zur Geschichte der Niedergang des Ptolemaerreiches. Ein besting zur Regierungszeit des 8 und des 9 Ptolemaer* (Munich, 1938).
Perowne, Stewart, *The Life and Times of Herod the Great* (London, 1956).
Pestman, P.W., *Chronologie Egyptienne d'apres les textes demotiques (332 av J-C – 453 ap J-C)* (Leiden, 1967).
Piejko, F., 'An Act of Amnesty and a Letter of Ptolemy VIII to the Troops in Syria', *Antiquite Classique* 56 (1987), pp. 254–259.
Quaegebaer, J., 'Une scene historique meconnue au grand temple d'Edfou', in *Egitto e storia antica dell'Ellenismo all'eta araba* (Bologna, 1987), pp. 595–608.
Ratnagar, Shereen, *Trading Encounters, from the Euphrates to the Indus in the Bronze Age*, second edition (Oxford, 2004).
Rauf, Theodore K., *Merchants, Sailors, and Pirates in the Roman World* (Stroud, 2003).
Ray, J.D., 'Observations on the Archive of Hor', *JEA* 64 (1978).
Reymond, E.A.E., *From the Records of a Priestly Family from Memphis*, I (Wiesbaden, 1981).
Richardson, Peter, *Herod, King of the Jews and Friend of the Romans* (Colombia, SC, 1996).
Roller, Duane W., *Cleopatra, a Biography* (Oxford, 2010).
Rostovtzeff, M., *Social and Economic History of the Hellenistic World* (Oxford, 1941), reprinted 1998.
Schubert, A., 'Une alteration de Ptolemais Eupator regent?', *ZPE* 94 (1999).
Schurer, Emil, *The History of the Jewish People in the Age of Jesus Christ*, vol. 1, revised edition, (Edinburgh, 1973).
Seager, Robin, *Pompey, a Political Biography* (Oxford, 1979).
Sheldon, R.M., *Rome's Wars with Parthia* (London, 2010).
Sherk, R.K. (ed.), *Rome and the Greek East to the Death of Augustus*, Translated Documents of Greece and Rome (Cambridge, 1994).
Sherwin-White, A.N., *Roman Foreign Policy in the East* (Norman, OK, 1983).
Sidebotham, Steven E., *Berenike and the Ancient Maritime Spice Route* (Berkeley and Los Angeles, 2011).
Singer, Caroline, 'The Incense Kingdoms of Yemen, an Outline History of the South Arabian Incense Trade', in D. Peacock and D. Williams (eds.), *Food for the Gods, New Light on the Arabian Incense Trade* (Oxford, 2007), pp. 4–27.
Smallwood, E.M., *The Jews under Roman Rule*, second edition (London, 2001).
Spaer, A., 'The Royal Male Head and Cleopatra at Ascalon', in M. Amandry *et al.* (eds.), *Travaux de numismatique grecque offerts a Georges le Rider* (London, 1999), pp. 347–350.
Spyadakis, Stylianos, *Ptolemaic Itanos and Hellenistic Crete* (Berkeley and Los Angeles, CA, 1970).
Stieglitz, Robert R., 'Ptolemy IX Soter II Lathyrus on Cyprus and the Coasts of the Levant', in Stuart Swiny *et al.* (eds.), *Res Maritimae Cyprus and the Eastern Mediterranean from Prehistory to Late Antiquity* (Atlanta, GA, 1997), pp. 301–305.

Sullivan, R.D., *Near Eastern Royalty and Rome, 100–30 BC* (Toronto, 1990).
t'Dack, E. van, 'Les commandants de place lagides at Thera', *Ancient Society* 4, (1973).
t'Dack, E. van et al., *The Judaean-Syrian-Egyptian Conflict of 103–101 BC, A Multilingual Dossier Concerning the 'War of Sceptres'* (Brussels, 1989).
t'Dack, E. van, 'La date de C. Ord. Ptol. 80–83 = BCU VI, 1212 et le sojourne de Cleopatre VII a Rome', *Ancient Society* 1 (1970), pp. 53–66.
Thompson, Dorothy J., 'Pausanias and Protocol, the succession to Euergetes II', in *Egitta e storia antica dell'Hellenismo all'eta araba* (Bologna, 1989), pp. 695–701.
Thompson, Dorothy J., *Memphis under the Ptolemies*, second edition (Princeton, NJ, 2012).
Veisse, A.-E., *Les "Revoltes Egyptiennes": recherches sur les troubles interieur en Egypte du regne de Ptolrmee III Evergete a la conquete romaine*, Studia Hellenistica 421 (Leuven, 2004).
Walbank, F.M., *A Historical Commentary on Polybius*, vol. 3 (Oxford, 1979).
Welles, C.B., *Royal Correspondence of the Hellenistic Period* (New Haven, 1935).
Wheeler, R.E.M., *My Archaeological Mission to India and Pakistan* (London, 1976).
Wheeler, R.E.M., *Rome Beyond the Imperial Frontiers* (London, 1954).
Whitehorne, John, *Cleopatras* (London, 1994).
Wikipedia, 'Ptolemaic Cult of Alexander the Great'.

Index

Achaian League, 17, 19
Achillas, 151, 156–60
Actium, x, 120, 188, 190–5, 198, 201–202
Adriatic Sea, 27, 36, 155, 167, 169, 185, 188
Adulis, viii, 46
Aegean Sea, 185
   bases abandoned, 7–8, 14, 18, 21
   Roman control, 37, 66
Aemilius Lepidus, M., *triumvir*, 168–9, 178
Aemilius Scaurus, M., 133
Africa, 45, 49–50, 113, 130, 156, 168–9, 178, 198
Agathokles, 107–108
Agrippa II, 204
Alexander the Great, xi, 35, 42, 75, 98, 110–11, 138, 158, 181
Alexander I Balas, Seleukid king, 1, 23, 39, 119
Alexander Helios, son of Kleopatra VII, 182, 201
Alexander Iannai, Jewish king, 77–85, 87
Alexander II Zabeinas, Seleukid king/pretender, 39–41, 58, 62–3, 67
Alexandria, ix, 1–3, 6, 12, 16–22, 24, 28–34, 37, 40–1, 49–50, 58–61, 63–6, 70, 72–3, 76–7, 81, 86, 88, 91, 98–103, 106, 108–10, 114, 126, 128, 144–5, 149–55, 157–9, 162, 164–8, 175, 179, 183–4, 187, 197, 200, 202, 206
Amathos, Palestine, 80
Ambrakia, Gulf of, x, 188, 190–2, 194
Ammonios/Pakorbis, 125
Amyntas, Galatian king, 192–3
Ananias, Ptolemaic general, 86
Andriskos ('Philip VI'), pretender, 17, 19
Antigonos, Jewish king, 170
Antigonos III, Macedonian king, 108
Antioch, 23, 39, 68, 78, 117, 119, 120, 173, 176, 198
Antiochos IV, Seleukid king, 4, 18, 34, 65
Antiochos VII, Seleukid king, 19–20, 24, 26–7, 34–5, 38–9, 75, 119
Antiochos VIII Grypos, Seleukid king, 40, 42, 58–9, 67–8, 78, 81, 83–4, 95
   married to Tryphaina, 62–3

Antiochos IX Kyzikenos, Seleukid king, 40, 67–9, 73–6, 78, 81, 86, 95
Antiochos X Eusebes, Seleukid king, 95, 112, 117
Antiochos XIII, Seleukid king, 144
Antiochos, son of Selene, 117
Antonius, C., 137
Antonius, M., 91–2
Antonius Felix, 204
Antony, Mark, 120, 123, 148, 162, 164
   and Kleopatra, 167–9, 171, 184
   and Parthia, 170, 171–81
   war with Octavian, 182–96
   army of, 185
   will, 188
   after Actium, 197–8
   return to Egypt, 199
   suicide, 201
Antyllus, son of Kleopatra VII, 200, 201
Apamea, Syria, 39
Apollonia/Senmonthis, wife of Dryton, 126
Arabia, 43, 53, 174, 186
Arabian Sea, 52–4
Arados, 37, 71
Archelaus, married to Berenike IV, 145, 148–9, 182
Archelaus, Cappadocian king, 199
Arikamedu, India, 51
Aristarchos, librarian, 4–5, 15, 57, 66
Aristobulus, Judaean prince, 148
Aristonikos ('Eumenes III'), 26–7
Armenia, 132, 159, 176–85
Aromaton Emporia, Somalia, 51
Arsinoe II, 4, 111–12, 121
Arsinoe III, 121
Arsinoe, daughter of Ptolemy XII, 155, 159, 164, 166, 168, 203
Artabanus II, Parthian king, 36
Artavasdes, Armenian king, 176, 180–1
Ashkelon, 76, 78, 155
Asia Minor, 18, 25–7, 32, 36–8, 42, 65, 71, 96, 99–100, 103, 129–30, 141, 162, 168–70, 173, 175, 178, 185–6, 200
Asia, south-east, 43
Asophon, Palestine, 80

Athamania, 12
Athens, 40, 92, 102, 178–9, 188, 196, 206
Attalid kingdom, 17, 19, 26
Attalos II, 19, 22, 25–6
Attalos III, will of, 25–6, 93
Augustus, xi, 48, 56, 161, 206
　see also Octavian
Auletes (Zeila), Somalia, 51
Aulus Gellius, 48

Bab el-Mandeb, viii, 43, 46, 53
Babylonia, 24, 34–5, 37–8, 43–4, 53
Baktria, 36
Bantu peoples, 55
Barygaza, India, viii, 47
Bekaa valley, 174
Berenike III, wife of Ptolemy X, 101
　sole ruler, 104, 105, 108, 122, 161
　murdered, 106
Berenike IV, 122, 161, 203
　ruling queen, 144, 145
　married to Seleukos, 144–5
　married to Archelaus, 145, 148–9, 151, 182
Berenike, daughter of Ptolemy IX, 62
Berenike, mother of Pedubast, 112, 117–19, 128
Berenike, Egypt, 46, 48–9
Beroia, Macedon, 95
Bogud, Mauritanian king, 190
Bosporos, 193
Brundisium, 169, 190
Byblos, 174
Byzantion, 141

Caecilius Metellus, L., 19
Caecilius Metellus Nasica, governor of Syria, 155
Caesarion (Ptolemy Caesar), 40, 159, 163, 164, 172, 180, 184, 200–201
　murdered, 201–202
Caligula, emperor, 203
Calpurnius Bibulus, M., 152
　sons murdered, 153
Cambay, Gulf of, India, 47, 52
Canidius Crassus, 176, 185, 193–4, 196, 197
Cappadocia, 175
Carthage, 17, 19–20
Cassius Longinus, C., 152, 166–7
Central Asia, 42
Chaeronea, Greece, 191
Chalkis, kingdom, 174
Charmian, maid to Kleopatra, 201
Chelkias, general, 86
Cicero, M. Tullius, 137
Cimmerian Bosporos, kingdom, 131–2

Cisalpine Gaul, 134, 153
Clodius Pulcher, P., 141–2
Comorin, Cape, India, 47–8
Corcyra, Greece, 188, 190
Corinth, 17, 19–20, 192
Corinth, Gulf of, 192
Cornelius Dolabella, P., 166
Cornelius Gallus, 198, 199–200
Cornelius Lentulus Marcellinus, P., 114
Cornelius Lentulus Spinther, 145–7
Cornelius Scipio Aemilianus, L., 19, 27, 69
Cornelius Sulla, L., 102–109
Coromandel, India, 48, 51
Crete, 7, 18, 66, 92, 102, 114, 125, 130, 175, 190
Cyprus, 18–19, 22, 24, 32, 33, 49, 61–7, 69, 72–4, 76–7, 84, 87, 90, 98, 100–101, 103, 108, 113, 118, 174, 176
　Roman annexation, 141–2, 144
　returned to Kleopatra VII, 166, 168, 174
Cyrenaica, xi, 17, 25, 31, 38, 62–4, 72–3, 77, 84, 89–90, 92–6, 98–9, 102, 111–14, 120, 130, 137, 143, 163, 167, 175–6, 190, 198–200
Cyrene, 6, 11, 31–3, 102, 175, 182

Damascus, 40, 54, 83–4, 95, 135
Daphne, Syria, 68, 198
Deiotaros, Paphlagonian king, 192
Dellius, Q., 168, 191–3
Delos, 70–1
Delphi, 92
Demetrios I, Seleukid king, 65
Demetrios II, Seleukid king, 5–6, 20, 23–4, 26–7, 35–41, 71, 119
　death, 40
Demetrios III, Seleukid king, 95
Demetrios, freedman, 168
Diodotos of Kasiana, Seleukid pretender ('Tryphon'), 23
Dion, philosopher, murdered, 145
Dionysios/Plenis, 125
Djibouti, 51
Domitius Ahenobarbus, C., 186–7, 191–2
Dor, Palestine, 78–9
Dositheos, Ptolemaic official, 8
Drusilla, 204
Dryton, Ptolemaic officer, 124–8
Dyrrhachium, 155

East Africa, 52–6
Edfu, temple, 8–9, 115
Egypt, 189
　civil war, 28–34, 45
　discontent, 204

and Rome, 52, 148–50, 159, 161–2
trade, 52–3
Eirene, concubine of Ptolemy VIII, 11, 61, 90, 111
Elephantine Island, Egypt, 65
elephants, 5, 42–4, 51, 55–7, 206
Eleutheros River, Syria, 172
Epeiros, 12, 190
Ephesos, 146, 160, 185, 187
Eros, servant, 201
Esthladas, 125
Ethiopia, 55
Eudaimon Arabia (Aden), viii, 43, 46
Eudoxos, 44–52, 55, 57, 59, 69, 115
Euhemeria, Egypt, 115
Euphrates River, 147, 169, 176–7
Eurykles, ruler of Sparta, 192, 195

Fayum, 9, 70, 115, 127, 129
Fulvia, wife of Antony, 187

Gabiniani, Roman army detachment, 149, 152–4, 159
Gabinius, Aulus, 130, 144, 147–9, 152, 154
Gadara, Palestine, 85
Gades, Spain, 50, 183
Galaistes, plotter, 12–14, 19–26
Galatia, 141, 175, 192
Ganymedes, eunuch, 159
Gaul, 139, 141, 164, 169, 176
Gaza, Palestine, ix, 24, 44, 54, 76–86, 89, 174
Gerizim, Mount, 75
Gladiator mutiny, 198
Gomaros, Bay of, 191
Greece, x, 99, 185, 188, 193, 197
Roman conquest, 7, 17, 19
Guardafui, Cape, viii, 49, 51, 55

Haifa, Bay of, 78
Harsiese, attempted usurper, 33, 125
Hatshepsut, Egyptian pharaoh, 43
Helenos, *strategos*, 61, 69
Heliodoros, 13
Hellespont, 36–7, 193
Herakleon, Seleukid commander and usurper, 95
Herakleopolis, Egypt, 129, 136
Hermias, 70
Hermonthis, Egypt, 9, 34, 45, 97, 104, 128, 150, 152
Herod, Jewish king, 170, 172–6, 185–6, 193, 199, 204
el-Hibeh, Egypt, 33
Hierax, Ptolemaic officer, 13–14, 28
Hierax, Ptolemaic commander, 98–9, 101, 104, 126

Himyar, Yemen, 54
Hippalos, 47–8, 50–2, 55, 118
Hyrkanos II, Jewish high priest, 148
Hyrkanos, John, Jewish leader, 73–5, 86

Iamblichos, Emesan king, 192
India, viii, 15, 40, 43, 48–9, 200
voyages to, 52, 56–7, 59, 116, 132, 174
Indian captain, shipwrecked, 45–7, 57
Indian Ocean, 42–3, 47, 53, 115–16, 166
Indus River, 42–3, 47, 52
Ionian Islands, 190
Iran, 24, 27, 34–5, 37, 43–5, 75
Iras, 201
Italy, xi, 26, 37, 91, 94, 103, 114, 130, 132, 134, 136–8, 149, 153, 165, 167, 169, 179, 185, 188, 190, 199, 202
Itanos, Crete, 7, 18, 175
Iunius Brutus, M., 143

Jerusalem, 6, 75, 133, 136, 173
Jews, in Egypt, 8, 98
Jonathan, Maccabee, 6
Joppa, Palestine, 74–6, 78
Jordan River and Valley, 75, 80, 84–5
Juba II, Mauritanian king, 203
Judaea, Jewish kingdom, ix, 37, 74–5, 78–80, 85–6, 132–3, 136, 147–8, 170, 173, 175, 185, 193, 199–200
Julius Caesar, C., 123, 133–5, 137, 139–41, 183
invasion of Italy, 153
victory, 155–6
in Egypt, 157–61, 163–4
murder, 184–5

Kallimachos, *strategos*, 56, 154, 166–7
Karrhai, battle, 152, 170
Kerala, India, 47
Kerkeosiris, Egypt, 129
Kilikia, 66–7, 78, 117, 143, 145, 147, 168–9, 174, 176
Roman anti-piracy campaign, 91, 130
Kleopatra I Syra, 121–2, 161
Kleopatra II, 1–2, 8, 10–12, 24–5, 28–33, 70, 121, 161
usurpation, 33–4, 37–8, 40, 45, 58
expulsion and return 58–9
peace with Ptolemy VIII, 63
sole ruler, 64, 66–7
death, 64, 67
Kleopatra III, 10–11, 13–14, 21, 24, 28–9, 31–2, 40–1, 58, 61, 64–5, 69, 73–4, 76, 80, 82, 86–7
death, 87–90, 95, 151
sole ruler, 48–9, 52, 59, 66, 70–2

Kleopatra IV, 62, 67–9, 71, 81, 119, 122
  murdered, 68–9
Kleopatra VI Tryphaina:
  married to Ptolemy XII, 105, 109
  divorced, 116–17
  ruling queen, 144
  death, 144, 146
Kleopatra VII, xi, 48, 56
  birth, 116, 118–19
  expulsion, 120, 123, 150
  sole ruler, 150–1, 161–71
  excluded from power, 151–4
  leaves Egypt, 154–5
  and Caesar, 157–60, 163
  visit to Rome, 163–4
  and Antony, 161–83
  territories acquired, 172, 174–5
  war with Rome, 182, 185
  naval force, 185, 197, 201
  at Actium, 194–6
  returned to Egypt, 198
  suicide, 201–202
  end of dynasty, 204
Kleopatra Berenike III, 89–90
  see also Berenike III
Kleopatra Selene, 181, 201, 203
  see also Selene
Kleopatra Thea, 23–4, 26, 34, 38, 39–40
  death, 41
Knidos, 92–3
Koele Syria, 5, 84
Kommagene, 37, 170
Koptos, Egypt, ix, 49
Kos, 81, 90, 95, 99, 102, 105
Krokodilopolis, Egypt, 97
Krokos, *strategos* of Cyprus, 66
Kyzikos, 40–1, 44, 50, 67, 198

Laodike, Seleukid princess, 35–6
Laodike, Seleukid queen, 13
Laodikeia-ad-Mare, 166
Leukas, x, 191–2, 195
Libya, 18, 182
Licinius Crassus, M., 133–5, 149, 152, 170
Licinius Lucullus, L., 102–103, 113, 129, 130, 139
Lochos, son of Kallimedes, 70
Louros River, 192
Lutatius Catulus, M., 134
Lykia, 93, 101

Macedon, 36, 42, 44, 92, 108, 166, 185, 188, 193, 205
  Roman conquest, 7, 17
Madagascar, 55
Madain Saleh, Arabia, 54

Malao (Berbera), Somalia, 51
Massinissa, King, 18, 57
Mauritania, 164
Mecca, 44
Media Atropatene, 176–8, 181–2
Medina, 44
Mediterranean Sea, 53
Memphis, Egypt, 4, 9, 19, 21, 31, 34, 90, 98, 101, 110–12, 114, 117–18, 123–4, 128, 152, 200
Mendes, Egypt, 85
Merowan kingdom, 200
Methana, Greece, 7, 17
Methoni Cape, Greece, x, 188, 190
Mesopotamia, 38, 95, 147, 170, 176, 181
Minucius Thermus, L., 16, 20
Minucius Thermus, Q., 16
Mithradates VI, Pontic king, 95–6, 145
  war with Rome, 99–103, 105, 109, 114–15, 129–30, 132
Mithradates, Parthian king, 24
Mithradates of Pergamon, 159
Monaeses, 176
Mopsuestia, 95
Mummius, Sp., 19
Munatius Plancus, L., 188
Mussollum, Somalia, 51
Muza (Mocha), Arabia, 43, 46
Muziris, India, 48
Myos Hormos, Egypt, 55, 155
Myra, Lykia, 101

Nabataeans, 44, 54, 132–3, 147, 172, 174–5, 185–6, 193, 200
Nearchos, 43, 47
Nikomedes, Bithynian King, 99
Nikopolis, 162, 202
Nile River, 9, 21, 45, 49, 96, 151, 159, 161–3, 166–7, 173, 189, 200, 204
Nile–Red Sea Canal, 49–50, 200
Numisius, Roman envoy, 16

Octavia, 169, 171, 177–81, 184, 187–8, 202
Octavian, 120, 164, 167, 169, 174, 178–80, 183–4
  army of, 185
  war with Antony, 185–96
  post-war problems, 198–9, 201–202
  see also Augustus
Onias, Ptolemaic officer, 8
Oricum, 190

Palestine, 5–7, 44, 53, 71, 73–4, 76–84, 86–7, 89, 155, 169–70, 173–4, 176
Pamphilos, 125
Pamphylia, 24, 37, 101

Panaetios, 19
Panobchounis, son of Phmois, 53
Panormus, 190
Paos, *strategos*, 33–4
Paphlagonia, 175, 192
Paphos, Cyprus, 66
Paraitonion, 199
Parthian kingdom, 24, 26–7, 34, 38, 75, 95, 101, 117, 120, 147, 164, 168–9, 173, 176
  Antony's war, 176–8, 180, 182, 185
Pasherenptah II, Memphite priest, 111–12, 118–19
Pasherenptah III, 112, 114
Patala, India, 47, 52
Patala, Lydia, 100
Pates, 97
Pathyris, 83–5, 96–7, 104, 118, 125–8
Patras, Greece, x, 190, 192
Pedubast II, Memphite priest, 110–12, 114
Peloponnesos, x, 7, 188, 190
Pelusion, 39, 72, 76, 81, 84–6, 96–7, 118, 126, 155–6, 159, 162, 200–201
Pergamon, 22, 25, 74, 159, 184
Persian Gulf, 43
Petesis, 70
Petra, Arabia, 133
Pharsalos, battle, 155
Philae, Egypt, 70
Philammon, 96–7
Philip II, Seleukid king, 144
Philip V, Macedonian king, 17
Philippi, Macedon, battle, 166–7
Philostephanos, tactician, 80
Philoteria, Palestine, 121
Phoenicia, 37, 81, 85, 116, 183
Phraaspa, Media, 177
Phraates II, Parthian king, 35–6
Phraates IV, Parthian king, 176, 280
Pinarius Scarpus, L., 198
Piracy, 90–2
Plato, *strategos*, 97
Polemo, Pontic king, 199
Polybios, 3, 19
Pompeius, Cn., 153–4, 169
Pompeius Magnus, Cn., 130
  piracy campaign, 130–2, 134, 137–9
  and Egypt, 135, 145, 147
  Senate commander against Caesar, 153–5
  defeat, 155
  death, 156–7
Pompeius, Sex, 174, 176, 178, 188
Pontos, 95, 100, 109, 132, 164
Porcius Cato, M., 139, 142–3, 146, 156
Postumius, Q., 192–3
Potheinos, eunuch, 151, 158–9

Promachos, *see* Alexander II Zabeinas
Ptolemaic army, 8
Ptolemaic dynasty, end of, 204–207
Ptolemaic royal customs, 2–3, 11–12, 14, 23, 119–21, 123–4, 132
Ptolemais, Egypt, 124–5, 127, 166
Ptolemais-Ake, Palestine, 6, 27, 40, 77, 78–80, 82, 85–7, 95, 115, 117, 169, 174
Ptolemy I, 7, 62, 108, 181
Ptolemy II, 14, 43, 55, 62, 112, 121, 176
Ptolemy III, 109, 115
Ptolemy IV, 121
Ptolemy V, 14, 200
Ptolemy VI, xi, 1, 5, 7, 8, 25, 38, 66, 121
Ptolemy VII Neos Philomator, 1–2, 8
  death, 3–4, 6, 10
Ptolemy VIII, xi, 1–3, 20, 54, 62, 93, 111, 113, 121
  and India, 45–7, 51–2, 57, 206
  and Rome, 16–22
  death, 48–9, 63, 64–7
  deposition, 33
  early measures, 4–15
  return to Egypt, 34, 40, 58–9
  war with Kleopatra II, 28–32, 45, 58, 63
  amnesty decree, 59–60
  and Kleopatra III, 61, 66
Ptolemy IX Soter, accession, 43, 48, 61, 107, 124, 126
  as *strategos* in Cyprus, 61, 63, 71, 89, 95, 118
  king, 64–5, 72–3, 76–88, 96, 99–100, 103–104
  death, 104–105
Ptolemy X Alexander, 34, 61–2, 64, 67, 72, 76, 80–7, 89–90, 93, 96–8, 101
  governed Cyprus, 64–5, 69, 99–101, 105, 118, 122
  death, 101
  will, 103, 133, 150
Ptolemy XI Alexander II, 103, 105, 108, 131
  accession and murder, 106–107
Ptolemy XII Theos Philadelphos (Auletes), 55, 162, 206
  accession, 109
  and Rome, 110, 133, 135, 138–40, 143
  coronation, 111
  and Cyrenaica, 113
  marriage, 116, 118–19, 123, 128, 132
  finances, 129, 136
  expulsion from Egypt, 143
  return to Egypt, 145–8, 150
  death, 150–1
  will, 157–9
Ptolemy XIII, 150–1, 153

king, 155–7
  defeat and death, 159, 161, 166, 203
Ptolemy XIV, 150, 159–61, 164–5, 203
  killed, 165
Ptolemy Apion, 11, 30, 61, 64, 89, 93–4, 96, 105, 113, 118
Ptolemy of Cyprus, 141–4
Ptolemy Eupator, 12, 29, 30
Ptolemy Keraunos, 4, 62
Ptolemy Memphites, 4, 8–11, 25, 30–1, 63, 65
  murder, 33, 41, 50, 91, 121
Ptolemy Philadelphos, 176, 181–2, 201
Ptolemy, son of Kleopatra Selene, 203
Punt, 43, 51
Puteoli, 145

Qana, Arabia, 54

Rabirius Postumus, C., 149, 151
Ras Hafun, viii, 49–50
Red Sea, 42–5, 48–50, 55, 155, 174, 200–201
  strategos of, 56, 115, 154, 166
Rhapta, East Africa, 55
Rheometalkes, Thracian king, 192
Rhodes, 18–19, 22, 66, 92, 100, 143
Rhodogune, 24, 38
Rome:
  and Attalid bequest, 25–6
  and Ptolemy VIII, 19–22
  conquest of Greece and Asia Minor, 36, 130
  and Egypt, 19, 30, 67, 69, 90–1, 107, 109, 128, 134–5, 138–40
  and Syria, 120
  and Ptolemies, 120
  and India, 56
  and Jewish kingdom, 74
  piracy law, effects of, 91, 93
  bequest to, 93–4, 103, 113
  civil wars, 102, 165, 184–96
  war with Mithradates, 99–103, 105, 114–15

Saka, nomads, 35–6
Salamis, Cyprus, 66
Samaria, Palestine, 73–5, 86
Samos, 188
Samosata, 170–1
Selene, daughter of Ptolemy VIII, 62, 67, 72, 76, 81, 83, 89, 95, 100, 105, 107, 112, 114–15, 117, 119–20, 122, 128
Seleukeia-in-Pieria, 24, 71, 76, 78, 120
Seleukaia-Zeugma, 177, 183
Seleukid dynasty, 205

Seleukos IV, king, 13
Seleukos V, murdered, 41
Seleukos VI, king, 95
Seleukos, son of Selene, 112
Seleukos, brief husband of Berenike IV, murdered, 194–5
Seleukos of Rhodes, *strategos* of Cyprus, 66–7
Seleukos, Ptolemaic commander, 200
Sephoris, Palestine, 80
Septimius, L., murderer of Pompeius, 156–7
Serapias, wife of Dryton, 129
Serapion, governor of Cyprus, 166–8
Sicily, 169, 178, 180
Side, 24
Sidon, 71, 77, 82
Sigaros, India, 47, 52
Sinai, 38, 84, 86, 148
Skythopolis, Palestine, 82–4
Somalia, 49–51
Sosibios, 108
Sosius, C., 170, 173, 186–7, 192, 193
Spain, 159, 176, 184
Sparta, 192, 195
Strato's Tower, 76–81
Surat, India, 47
Sykaminos, Palestine, 78
Syria, 5, 7, 12, 14, 19, 21–2, 34, 37–8, 40, 117, 143, 199
  Roman annexation, 144, 173
  and Parthia, 170
  civil warfare, 69–71
Syrian wars:
  sixth, 4
  seventh, 38

Tainaron, Cape, Sparta, 188, 190, 196–9
Tarkondimotos, king, 192
Taurus Mountains, 24, 38
Termessos, 100
Theadelphia, Egypt, 115
Thebaid, Egypt, 33, 54, 70, 84, 96, 98, 100–101, 118, 155, 167, 200
Thebes, Egypt, 9, 28, 45, 96, 100–101, 104, 126, 128
Theodoros, lord of Amathos, 80, 85
Theodotos of Chios, 152, 157
Thera, 7, 18
Thermos, Roman envoy, 16–19
  see also Minucius
Theron, 125
Thessalonike, 4
Thessaly, 12, 155
Thrace, 16–17, 192
Tiberius, Emperor, 128, 205
Tigranes, Armenian king, 115, 117, 129–32

Titius, M., 178, 188
Transpadana, 134–5, 137
Tripolis, 71, 74
Tryphaina, daughter of Ptolemy VIII, 62–3, 68, 119, 122–3
    murdered, 68
Tryphon, Seleukid usurper, 20, 23–4, 27
Tyre, ix, 40, 71, 82, 107, 168

Ventidius, P., 169–70, 173
Via Aquillia, 36, 42
Via Egnatia, 36, 42
Vipsanius Agrippa, M., 184, 188–96

West Africa, migration from, 55

Yemen, 43–4, 53, 200

Zabdiel, Arab chief, 23
Zakynthos, x, 188, 190
Zanzibar, 52, 55
Zeila, 51, 56
    see also Auletes
Zela, battle, 129
Zoilos, lord of Strato's Tower, 77–9, 83

Dear Reader,

We hope you have enjoyed this book, but why not share your views on social media? You can also follow our pages to see more about our other products: facebook.com/penandswordbooks or follow us on X @penswordbooks

You can also view our products at www.pen-and-sword.co.uk (UK and ROW) or www.penandswordbooks.com (North America).

To keep up to date with our latest releases and online catalogues, please sign up to our newsletter at: www.pen-and-sword.co.uk/newsletter

If you would like a printed catalogue with our latest books, then please email: enquiries@pen-and-sword.co.uk or telephone: 01226 734555 (UK and ROW) or email: uspen-and-sword@casematepublishers.com or telephone: (610) 853-9131 (North America).

We respect your privacy and we will only use personal information to send you information about our products.

Thank you!